SCHIZOPHRENIA: TREATMENT OF ACUTE PSYCHOTIC EPISODES

SCHIZOPHRENIA: TREATMENT OF ACUTE PSYCHOTIC EPISODES

Edited by

Steven T. Levy, M.D.
Philip T. Ninan, M.D.

American Psychiatric Press, Inc.

1400 K Street, N.W.
Washington, D.C. 20005

Note: The authors have worked to ensure that all information in this book concerning drug dosages, schedules, and routes of administration is accurate as of the time of publication and consistent with standards set by the U.S. Food and Drug Administration and the general medical community. As medical research and practice advance, however, therapeutic standards may change. For this reason and because human and mechanical errors sometimes occur, we recommend that readers follow the advice of a physician who is directly involved in their care or the care of a member of their family.

Books published by the American Psychiatric Press, Inc., represent the views and opinions of the individual authors and do not necessarily represent the policies and opinions of the Press or the American Psychiatric Association.

The paper used in this publication meets the minimum requirements of the American National Standard for Information Sciences—Permanence of Paper for Printed Library Materials, ANSI Z39.48-1984. ♾

Manufactured in the United States of America
First Edition

93 92 91 90 4 3 2 1

Library of Congress Cataloging-in-Publication Data

Schizophrenia: treatment of acute psychotic episodes/edited by Steven T. Levy, Philip T. Ninan.—1st ed.
p. cm.
Includes bibliographical references.
ISBN 0-88048-164-1
1. Schizophrenia—Treatment. I. Levy, Steven T. II. Ninan, Philip T.
[DNLM: 1. Schizophrenia—therapy. WM 203 S3394]
RC514.S336484 1989
616.89'8206—dc20
DNLM/DLC
for Library of Congress 89-17556
CIP

CONTENTS

CONTRIBUTORS

Gail Anderson, M.D.
Private Practice, Atlanta, Georgia

Ross J. Baldessarini, M.D.
Professor of Psychiatry, Harvard Medical School;
Mailman Research Center, McLean Hospital

Bruce M. Cohen, M.D., Ph.D.
Associate Professor of Psychiatry, Harvard Medical School;
Associate Director, Mental Health Clinical Research Center;
Chief, Clinical Pharmacology Laboratory, Mailman Research
Center, McLean Hospital

Christopher C. Colenda III, M.D., M.P.H.
Assistant Professor of Psychiatry, Medical College of Virginia

Jeffrey L. Houpt, M.D.
Professor and Chairman, Department of Psychiatry,
Dean, Emory University School of Medicine

Lawrence B. Inderbitzin, M.D.
Associate Professor of Psychiatry, Director of Clinical Services,
Emory University School of Medicine at Grady Memorial
Hospital; Training and Supervising Analyst, Emory University
Center for Psychoanalytic Training and Research

Salley S. Jessee, M.D.
Assistant Professor of Psychiatry, Director of Emergency
Services, Emory University School of Medicine at Grady
Memorial Hospital

Steven T. Levy, M.D.
Professor of Psychiatry, Chief of Psychiatry, Emory University
School of Medicine at Grady Memorial Hospital; Clinical
Professor of Psychiatry and Psychoanalysis, Morehouse School
of Medicine

Richard R. J. Lewine, Ph.D.
Associate Professor of Psychiatry (Psychology), Chief Research Psychologist, Emory University School of Medicine at Grady Memorial Hospital

Rosalind Mance, M.B.B.S.
Assistant Professor of Psychiatry, Director of Family Studies, Co-Principal Investigator, Schizophrenia Treatment Program, Emory University School of Medicine at Grady Memorial Hospital

Philip T. Ninan, M.D.
Associate Professor of Psychiatry, Principal Investigator, Schizophrenia Treatment Program, Emory University School of Medicine at Grady Memorial Hospital

Elias Shaya, M.D.
Resident in Psychiatry, Emory University School of Medicine at Grady Memorial Hospital

Martin H. Teicher, M.D., Ph.D.
Assistant Psychiatrist, Laboratory for Psychiatric Research, Director, Psychopharmacological Services, Outpatient Clinic—Adult, Mailman Research Center, McLean Hospital

Bandupriya P. Vidanagama, M.D.
Assistant Professor of Psychiatry, Director of Ambulatory Psychiatry, Emory University School of Medicine at Grady Memorial Hospital

Hugo J. Zee, M.D., F.A.P.A.
Assistant Professor of Psychiatry, Emory University School of Medicine; Training and Supervising Analyst, Emory University Center for Psychoanalytic Training and Research

FOREWORD

GRADY MEMORIAL HOSPITAL opened its doors to the indigent of Atlanta in 1892. Psychiatric patients were spread throughout the hospital, and more unfortunately, housed in the jail within Grady. Not until 1958 did Bernard Holland, M.D., the newly appointed Chairman of Emory University's Department of Psychiatry, and Joseph S. Skobba, M.D., Emory faculty member and staff psychiatrist at Grady, initiate a formal psychiatry service. Today that service has grown into a comprehensive community mental health center, with 8,760 inpatient days, and 66,066 visits per year. At any one time, 8,025 patients with chronic psychotic illnesses are receiving care.

This book taps the expertise of the dedicated staff who treat these people. In addition, Ross Baldessarini, M.D., has lent his considerable talent to the chapter on psychotropic drug management. This book grew out of the Seventh Joseph S. Skobba Symposium, a conference dedicated to the psychiatrist who worked 30 years at Grady and who was "the doctor" to Atlanta's indigent psychotic population.

Jeffrey L. Houpt, M.D.
Professor and Chairman, Department of Psychiatry,
Dean, Emory University School of Medicine

PREFACE

THE INPATIENT CLINICAL and teaching service of the Department of Psychiatry at Grady Memorial Hospital has evolved over many years in ways reflecting the development of new information about how best to treat acutely psychotic patients. This service has served as a model to a generation of psychiatrists in our region for the optimal treatment of such patients on a short-term inpatient unit. The ideas presented throughout the text are reflections of clinical practices at Grady Memorial Hospital. The staff of the unit, the faculty who have taught there, and the many psychiatric residents and other trainees who have received part of their clinical education on the unit have all contributed to refining therapeutic techniques for best caring for acutely psychotic patients. The unit and all individuals associated with it have maintained an enthusiastic, inquisitive, and compassionate attitude toward the very difficult work of helping individuals in the throes of psychosis to reorganize their mental processes in order to resume their lives with as little deficit as possible. Each can take some pride in having contributed to the ideas and experiences documented in the text.

Several individuals deserve thanks for their help in the preparation of this manuscript. First and foremost is Mrs. Bettie Reynolds, secretary to the Chief of Service and administrative coordinator of the Department of Psychiatry at Grady Memorial Hospital. She has been involved in all aspects of preparing the manuscript, including coordinating the work of the contributing authors, editing and processing the innumerable drafts of the individual chapters, developing the format for the text, and most importantly, keeping the entire operation running in a harmonious manner despite the sometimes erratic and irritable behavior of the editors. Credit should also be given to Jeffrey L. Houpt, M.D., Professor and Chairman of the Department of Psychiatry at Emory University, for his support and encouragement.

Steven T. Levy, M.D.

INTRODUCTION

PATIENTS WITH SCHIZOPHRENIA present diagnostic and treatment dilemmas for the psychiatric clinician that severely test him or her as a scientist and as a compassionate and well-integrated human being. No other mental illnesses wreak emotional devastation as regularly and relentlessly as those conditions grouped together as schizophrenia. This book addresses the treatment of the schizophrenic patient during the acute psychotic phase of illness. In the face of clinical data, as well as social and economic pressures that favor shortened hospitalization, community-based treatment, and pharmacological management of mental disorders, an ever increasing percentage of psychiatric hospital beds are taken up by acutely psychotic schizophrenic patients receiving short-term inpatient treatment. While there are a few settings in which longer-term inpatient care or innovatively designed outpatient or partial hospitalization approaches are available, most acutely psychotic individuals receive treatment on inpatient units where a 2- to 6-week hospitalization period is the rule. Such units may be located in psychiatric hospitals or on psychiatric wards in general hospitals.

The treatment rendered to acutely psychotic schizophrenic patients will be examined from many different perspectives and with emphasis on current clinical practices and ongoing controversies. The aim is to provide the clinician with ready access to information that will help in developing an optimal treatment plan for managing such patients.

There are many unanswered questions about the diagnostic and treatment strategies applicable to the care of schizophrenic patients. Such questions have been central preoccupations of organized psychiatry and related mental health professions throughout their history. Different emphases, methods of investigation, and theoretical perspectives have led to an enormous amount of information that presents the clinician with a very difficult task in integrating what is known in the service of rendering optimal care. Such information may or may not remain useful as it is applied in a brief treatment setting that differs radically from the research or long-term setting from which it originates. In particular, many psychosocial approaches have evolved in highly varied and specialized settings and may not "transfer" well from one treatment unit to another.

Promising pharmacological treatments rapidly become widely followed before adequate research data are available to support or refute their appropriateness. Integrating pharmacological and psychosocial approaches often presents serious challenges to value and belief systems cherished by many clinicians. Because the treatment of acutely psychotic patients is extremely difficult and because so much depends upon it, it seems logical for an inpatient treatment team to attempt to distill what is best from all the areas of expertise developed by workers claiming success in treating such patients. Whether the many different approaches are really compatible and synergistic has received little systematic research attention. Yet most treatment units other than those specifically advocating or studying a particular treatment model adopt a multimodal approach that includes individual, group, family, milieu, and pharmacological interventions of various sorts. Expertise is drawn from different team members, usually under the leadership of the physician responsible for the overall care of the patient. It is this physician's responsibility to monitor and coordinate treatment efforts, usually involving many individuals, in the best interest of the patient. Doing so requires flexibility, honesty, compassion, and commitment.

The focus of this text is on brief inpatient treatment. This is not because there is conclusive evidence that brief inpatient stays (here defined as 2–6 weeks of hospitalization) are optimal for all acutely psychotic patients or even for certain particular types of acutely psychotic patients. This mode of treatment has become the most common one in the United States and in Western Europe. Various scientific, economic, and social arguments can be marshalled to support or at least explain why this is so. Frequently heard complaints among clinicians of various persuasions about the pressure to treat all patients during relatively brief hospitalizations indicate that the issue is hardly a closed one. For purposes of this text, we will proceed under the assumption that the evolution of brief hospital treatment of acutely psychotic schizophrenic patients as the clinical norm reflects a consensus of accumulated expertise as well as economic and social forces that should not invariably be vilified as unwanted intrusions into the clinical domain. It is in such settings that clinicians currently provide care. It is necessary for them to fashion a treatment program in such settings that is best for the patient.

Throughout the text, component parts of the diagnostic and

treatment approaches important in the care of acutely psychotic schizophrenic patients will be described separately. While the particular areas of expertise and biases of the contributing authors may be reflected in what is emphasized in the various chapters, the text aims at presenting a unified and comprehensive approach to a particular mode of clinical care of an important class or group of psychiatric patients. Rather than being competing points of view, the chapters describe complementary diagnostic and treatment approaches, all of which should play a role in the optimal care of the patient. No area described can be disregarded and the care provided still be considered adequate. Nevertheless, each treatment unit must determine its strengths and weaknesses in personnel, physical plant, patient population, and other resources in arriving at the final mix that maximizes its potential. This determination of strengths and weaknesses requires effective leadership and a nondoctrinaire attitude if the treatment team is to carry out its many functions most effectively. Each component of the patient's care is important and should be carefully monitored for deficiencies.

Acutely psychotic patients, by virtue of their dramatic, bizarre, and often frightening symptomatology, severely tax the resources of those involved in their care. Treatment intervention can easily deteriorate from providing humane care to very troubled people into mechanically managing severe cases of illness. Personal detachment, routinization of procedures, avoidance of extra effort, and a general pessimism and therapeutic nihilism are the constant enemies of units that deliver care to significant numbers of acutely psychotic patients. When such units function well, they deliver an invaluable and essential service to desperately ill people and can be exciting and rewarding places to work.

Steven T. Levy, M.D.

Chapter 1

DIAGNOSTIC ISSUES

Philip T. Ninan, M.D.

> It is first of all necessary to rectify names. . . . A superior man shows a cautious reserve in regard to what he does not know. If names be not correct, language is not in accordance with the truth of things. If language be not in accordance with the truth of things, affairs cannot be carried on successfully.
>
> Confucius 488 B.C.

THE DIAGNOSIS OF AN ILLNESS in medicine is the basis for grouping patients who share characteristic clinical signs and symptoms, laboratory abnormalities, course of illness, and response to treatment. Such a diagnosis is then the basis for treatment planning, clinical care, communication among clinicians, and research endeavors to advance knowledge about the illness. Diagnostic classifications in psychiatry do not have the same level of significance as those in other areas of medicine because of the limitations of our knowledge of pathological processes that occur in the mind and brain. This is particularly true in the area of schizophrenia.

Schizophrenia is an illness that is present in all cultures; descriptions suggestive of schizophrenia go back over 5,000 years. Yet the nature of schizophrenia continues to be debated. Though

This work was supported in part by NIMH Grant Nos. MH-40597 and MH-42298 (PTN). The epigraph to this chapter is from Douglas 1919.

it can be described as a disorder of the brain that results in abnormalities in thinking, emotions, and behavior, the personal mental experience of the illness is often remarkably different from its appearance to an observer. Furthermore, there is tremendous variation in the presenting symptomatology, course of illness, and response to treatment.

Because mental intrapsychic experiences are so variable and diagnostically unreliable, diagnosis based on phenomenology has come into vogue to provide diagnostic labels that are more reliable (American Psychiatric Association 1987). This diagnostic approach has facilitated meaningful communication among researchers and clinicians. Such increased reliability in diagnosis has also allowed epidemiological, genetic, familial, psychological, and biological studies to be undertaken at a far more sophisticated level. For example, a recent epidemiological study reported that the 6-month prevalence of schizophreniform and schizophrenic disorders varied between 0.6 and 1.3% in the general population (Myers et al. 1984), whereas the lifetime prevalence of schizophrenia was between 1.0 and 1.6% (Robins et al. 1984).

Three major areas in the diagnosis of schizophrenia need to be addressed: the symptoms and signs that constitute the illness; the boundaries of schizophrenia that separate it from other illnesses; and the division of schizophrenia into relevant subgroups. Before these areas are examined in greater detail, the limitations of the discussion need to be explored.

VALIDITY AND RELIABILITY

The diagnosis of many medical illnesses is supported by known etiological agents, morphological abnormalities, and measurable biochemical or physiological anomalies. Because our capacity to obtain each of these components in schizophrenia is lacking, and because there is no diagnostic test for schizophrenia, construct validation (i.e., the objective confirmation of the phenomenological diagnosis) is not possible. What is labeled schizophrenia is a set of symptoms that cluster together but often have a variable course. Predictive validity has become the next best alternative; similar outcomes or responses to treatment are evidence used to confirm the diagnosis. However, when the course of illness itself is part of the diagnostic criteria (i.e., symptoms present for at least 6 months in the DSM-III-R criteria), such arguments become inherently circular in nature and are of limited value. Reliability, on the other hand, measures consistency over time and among raters (i.e., test-retest and inter-rater reliability). Reliability does not assure validity, but validity cannot be established without reliability.

Reliability in the diagnosis of schizophrenia can be compromised by many sources (Spitzer et al. 1975):

1. **Within patient differences**. The patient might have two different (yet connected) conditions within the same episode of illness, as is seen in the development of postpsychotic depression in a patient with schizophrenia. Between episodes, the characteristics of the illness might change. Thus some patients might have predominantly positive symptoms during their early episodes but predominantly negative symptoms later on in the course of the illness.
2. **Between patient differences**. The tremendous heterogeneity in the presentation of schizophrenia in different individuals is generally believed to be the result of schizophrenia actually being a group of illnesses subsumed under a unitary label. Another explanation is that an illness like schizophrenia that affects the highest functions of humans should be expected to reflect the inherent variability among individuals. Thus the same illness expresses itself differently in individual patients because of variations in biological expression, developmental and life experiences, sociocultural factors, and the effects of the immediate environment.
3. **Criterion differences**. If definitions of the illness differ (i.e., what to include or exclude), poor diagnostic reliability can result. This has prompted the development of specific and objective criteria that are phenomenologically based and operationally defined to characterize critical aspects of the illness that are necessary and sufficient for the diagnosis.
4. **Informational differences**. The diagnosis made by a clinician might vary with the amount of information available. The assumption is that the more information available, the better the reliability of the diagnosis. Because in clinical situations the amount of information gathered varies, structured and semistructured interviews have been developed. Such interviews ask specifically worded questions and cover specified areas, with the aim of having available the same amount of information across patients (presuming equal communication) to make the diagnosis more reliable.
5. **Observational differences**. Disagreements among clinicians viewing the same observable data may result regarding the presence or absence of a symptom. This is particularly prob-

lematic with specific symptoms such as emotional blunting. Uniform training can help with this problem.

Patients with schizophrenia are often unable to communicate significant aspects of their illness, thus limiting the information domain available for making a reliable diagnosis. Critical information that is not observable or elicitable is thus excluded from diagnostic consideration (e.g., formal thought disorder in a mute patient). Furthermore, information that cannot be reliably obtained is also not taken into consideration. This is particularly true of psychodynamic and interpersonal processes, which are undoubtedly occurring but cannot be operationally defined or reliably reproduced. Thus the search for diagnostic reliability results in a definition of the illness that is inherently constricted.

BIOLOGICAL CLASSIFICATION OF SCHIZOPHRENIA

Over the last two decades numerous attempts have been made to classify schizophrenia using biological variables in order to develop homogenous subgroups in schizophrenia. Platelet monoamine oxidase (MAO) activity, brain atrophy as detected by use of CT scans, and the levels of different neurotransmitters and their metabolites and peptides in various body fluids are just some of the variables studied. The results so far have been confusing and disappointing, partly because of tremendous methodological limitations.

An illness like schizophrenia that affects the functioning of the brain might not have a specific structural abnormality but could be the result of purely abnormal function. To observe such functional abnormalities requires the ability to study dynamic physiological and biochemical processes as they occur. Such functional measures (e.g., regional blood flow studies) are still relatively primitive or not available at all. One must await advances in the basic sciences and biomedical technologies in order to have the tools to ask the sophisticated questions needed to point research in the relevant directions. The aim ultimately is to develop a classification system for schizophrenia that is based on etiology and pathophysiology.

DEVELOPMENT OF DIAGNOSTIC SYSTEMS FOR SCHIZOPHRENIA

The modern concept of schizophrenia began to be crystallized when Kraepelin (1907) combined Morel's "demence precoce," Kahlbaum's katatonia, and Hecker's hebephrenia under the label of dementia praecox, differentiating it from manic-depressive illness. The concept of dementia praecox, or the precocious development of intellectual impairment, was based on the acute symptomatology course and prognosis (see Appendix 1). Inherent in the definition was an early onset of symptoms and deterioration over a period of time, resulting in an end stage of intellectual impairment. The issue of what to label patients who had the acute symptoms but not the deteriorating course was never adequately resolved by Kraepelin.

Bleuler (1911) introduced the name schizophrenia to describe a group of illnesses. He shifted the focus from outcome to symptomatology by taking a cross-sectional approach to the diagnosis of the illness. Bleuler described problems with association, affect, autism, and ambivalence as "fundamental" and hallmarks of the illness, and excluded a deteriorating course as part of the definition. Delusions and hallucinations were considered to be secondary and derived from the fundamental symptoms. When the fundamental symptoms were present without the secondary manifestations, the diagnosis of simple schizophrenia was made. Bleuler also thought that there was a basic organic cerebral or metabolic defect that was etiologically related to schizophrenia and that this defect could exist without expressing itself in the fundamental symptoms (i.e., latent schizophrenia).

The lack of concrete operational definitions for the fundamental symptoms resulted in problems with the reliable recognition of these symptoms by clinicians. This was complicated by the lack of a systematically defined threshold of how prominent a symptom had to be to allow the diagnosis to be made. Nonpsychotic individuals with mild fundamental symptoms (analogous to the current concept of schizotypal personality disorder) would be diagnosed as having schizophrenia. The boundary between patients with schizophrenia and individuals without the illness was blurred by the concepts of latent and simple schizophrenia. Thus, loosely defined criteria were used to diagnose an individual as having simple schizophrenia. Furthermore, an individual could be labeled a latent schizophrenic person even in the absence of the fundamental symptoms. Bleuler's ideas about schizophrenia took root in the United States, whereas the Kraepelinian ideas about schizophrenia were more appealing to European psychiatrists.

Langfeldt (1956) tried to refine the Kraepelinian criteria for schizophrenia by labeling patients with psychotic symptoms who did not have a downhill course as schizophreniform (see Appendix

1). Schneider (1959) rejected outcome as a defining criterion for schizophrenia and came up with a list of symptoms that he felt were, in the absence of organic pathology, pathognomonic for the illness (i.e., these symptoms were necessary and sufficient for the diagnosis of schizophrenia) (see Appendix 1). The choice of which symptoms should be considered first-rank symptoms was based on his clinical perceptions rather than the appropriate statistical methods. Because the Schneiderian symptoms are ones that are experiential to the patient, one has to obtain the cooperation of the patient to be able to elicit them. Further, Schneiderian first-rank symptoms have been shown to be present, even if transiently, in the manic phase of bipolar disorder and other psychotic states, and to be present only in 50% of patients clinically diagnosed as having schizophrenia (Fenton et al. 1981). Thus the Schneiderian criteria for schizophrenia are very narrow and exclude a significant group of patients who would otherwise be given such a diagnostic label. In addition, with the heterogeneity of the illness, cross-sectional approaches to the diagnosis of schizophrenia have not been found to be good predictors of outcome.

Carpenter et al. (1973) developed the "flexible system," another cross-sectional approach, for the diagnosis of schizophrenia. This system was based on the World Health Organization study of schizophrenia involving nine countries and 1,121 patients. The assumption was that because schizophrenia was present in every culture, distilling the features of this illness across cultures would clarify its basic elements. Carpenter et al. empirically arrived at 12 signs and symptoms that were most commonly found in patients diagnosed as schizophrenic (see Appendix 1). Based on the degree of sensitivity and specificity required in the diagnosis, one could vary the cut-off number of symptoms and signs required for the diagnosis. Thus the diagnosis of schizophrenia could be made with a sensitivity of 91% (i.e., 91 out of 100 patients with schizophrenia would be diagnosed by this system), but with a specificity of 38% (i.e., 38 out of 100 nonschizophrenic subjects would also be given the diagnosis) when four criteria were considered adequate to make the diagnosis. The sensitivity decreased to 63%, while the specificity decreased to 6% when six criteria were required to make the diagnosis. A number of the criteria pertained to the absence of depressive symptoms. The flexible system had good inter-rater reliability, but only restricted affect was significantly associated with outcome.

More recent longitudinal diagnostic systems (see Appendix 1) have taken the best of the cross-sectional approach and included a time frame for the symptoms. This not only provides good reliability but also better prediction for outcome, because the past is a good indicator of future events. Feighner (1972) required a 6-month duration of symptoms, an absence of affective symptoms, and an age of onset before 40. However, use of these criteria resulted in 20–30% of clinically diagnosed schizophrenic patients falling into the undiagnosed category.

The Research Diagnostic Criteria (RDC) (1978) elaborated on Feighner's criteria and relied on Schneiderian first-rank symptoms (Spitzer et al. 1978). This system required a 2-week period of symptoms and an absence of affective symptoms.

The DSM-III (American Psychiatric Association 1980), essentially a modification of the RDC, also defined schizophrenia narrowly (see Appendix 2). It required a 6-month period of active symptoms, thus taking both the course of illness and the prognosis into consideration in the diagnosis. The DSM-III also delineated a separate category, called schizophreniform disorder, for patients with the symptomatology of schizophrenia but without the symptoms lasting for 6 months.

The DSM-III-R (American Psychiatric Association 1987) essentially lifted the age limitation of 45 years for the onset of the symptoms of schizophrenia that was a requirement in the DSM-III. The DSM-III-R also recognized the possibility that early treatment response could modify the symptom picture in individual patients (see Appendix 3).

The DSM-III and DSM-III-R approaches to diagnostic classification are based on providing a reliable diagnosis as a necessary preliminary step toward achieving validity. These approaches have limited the phenomena used in diagnostic criteria to observable and descriptive ones, thus improving reliability considerably. However, a purely descriptive approach has limitations, because not all psychic phenomena can be adequately described in a reliable manner. Thus symptoms that might be relevant in making the diagnosis of schizophrenia, but cannot be described reliably, are not included.

The DSM-III and DSM-III-R approaches to diagnosis are atheoretical, because definitions of an illness should not be confused with etiological theories that are still debated. It has been argued that cross-sectional and longitudinal aspects of schizophrenia are independent and therefore should not be confounded in the same axis, as is done in the DSM-III and DSM-III-R. The multiaxial system of psychiatric diagnosis instituted by DSM-III is based on the premise that the totality of a patient's situation cannot be reduced to one dimension without leaving out significant information.

Making a diagnosis using a system such as the DSM-III-R is only a first step in the complex process of evaluating a patient. Just as in other branches of medicine in which illnesses are diagnosed but patients are treated, more information than the diagnosis of the illness is required for treatment planning purposes.

THE BOUNDARIES OF SCHIZOPHRENIA

Schizophreniform Disorder

The DSM-III-R has delineated schizophreniform disorder as a separate condition from schizophrenia, the differentiating factor being the length of time the symptomatology is present (between 2 weeks and 6 months). The DSM-III-R attempts to differentiate schizophreniform patients into those with and without good prognostic features. There are some suggestions that schizophreniform disorder (as against schizophrenia) is more often characterized by sudden onset, emotional turmoil, confusion, and vivid hallucinations, but these differences are not concise enough for diagnostic purposes. Thus there are no major cross-sectional differences between schizophreniform disorder and schizophrenia, the difference being longitudinal. The rationale behind this differentiation is the inability to predict outcome during an episode of illness presenting with symptoms of schizophrenia. Waiting for a period of time (which includes the prodrome, acute symptomatology, and residual symptoms) allows the separating out of patients who are going to improve, at least in the short-term. Whether this will signify a better prognosis in the long run is as yet uncertain (Coryell and Tsuang 1986).

Outcome studies, family studies, and biological studies of schizophreniform disorder suggest that it is a heterogenous group of disorders subsuming conditions that are on a spectrum between schizophrenia and affective disorders. Thus patients who are currently diagnosed as schizophreniform include those who were earlier labeled "good prognosis" schizophrenic persons and those with atypical forms of affective disorder. There will be two categories of patients diagnosed as having schizophreniform disorder: one group of truly schizophreniform patients and the other, patients thought to be schizophrenic who are waiting for 6 months to pass after the appearance of symptoms so that they can be diagnosed as having schizophrenia. Differentiating schizophreniform disorder from schizophrenia does not automatically mean there is no connection between the two illnesses, or that they are not related in terms of psychobiological factors. Based on outcome and other studies, it is likely that at least some of the schizophreniform patients have more of an affective illness, even though affective symptoms are not prominent.

Affective Disorder

The boundary between schizophrenia and affective disorder has been confusing because of the complex issues involved. Phenomenological, familial, prognostic, and treatment response studies have been divided on whether schizoaffective disorder is a separate condition, or whether patients with this disorder behave more like patients in the affective or schizophrenic group of disorders. Again, the differences in the cross-sectional approach versus the longitudinal approach have a major impact on defining the schizoaffective disorder population. Although affective disorders are a group of disorders with a central abnormality in mood, one cannot say that there is such a universal abnormality in the schizophrenic group of disorders. The DSM-III had, in a way, attempted to purify the diagnosis of both affective and schizophrenic disorders by having a schizoaffective disorder group that was not well defined.

The DSM-III definition of schizoaffective disorder consisted of affective disorder patients who continue to have mood-incongruent psychotic features or bizarre behavior when affective symptoms are no longer prominent, or patients with otherwise schizophrenic features who develop a major affective disorder prior to the onset of schizophrenic symptoms. The differential diagnosis for schizoaffective disorder should include schizophreniform disorder, major depression or bipolar disorder with mood congruent or incongruent psychotic features, and schizophrenia with a superimposed atypical affective disorder.

The DSM-III-R defines schizoaffective disorder as a condition that has both schizophrenic and mood disorder symptoms, but that at one time presented with delusions and hallucinations for 2 weeks without any prominent mood symptoms.

Age of Onset

The DSM-III required that the initial episode of schizophrenia occur before the age of 45. This raises questions about the paraphrenias, i.e., those patients who have late-onset (fifth and sixth decade) delusions of paranoia with hallucinatory experiences. The presence of hallucinations excluded the paraphrenic patients from the DSM-III diagnosis of paranoid disorders; hence, the clinician was forced to diagnose these patients as having atypical psychosis. The DSM-III-R lifts the age restriction for onset of schizophrenia.

Schizophrenia Spectrum

Another boundary issue for schizophrenia is the schizotypal personality disorder diagnosis. Kety et al. (1971) have suggested a "schizophrenia spectrum" of disorders, with the milder versions presenting as personality disorders. The terms borderline, paranoid, and schizoid personality disorders came into existence because these patients were thought to have conditions that were close to schizophrenia. However, long-term studies have found these patients not to be at high risk for the development of schizophrenia. Schizotypal personality disorder, a term introduced by the DSM-III, is characterized by criteria that have numerous similarities to the symptoms seen in the prodromal phase of schizophrenia. Though some patients with schizotypal personality disorder do develop schizophrenia, the vast majority do not. There are preliminary reports of an increased incidence of schizotypal personality disorders in the families of schizophrenic patients. Thus the relationship between schizophrenia and schizotypal personality disorder needs to be clarified further. Because of the issue of tardive dyskinesia, the use of neuroleptics in the management of schizotypal personality disorder, if attempted, should be judicious and targeted.

THE TYPOLOGY OF SCHIZOPHRENIA

Moving from the question of what is different between schizophrenia and other conditions, the question arises whether one can subclassify the presenting symptoms in schizophrenia, and whether such a subclassification has any inherent value. The symptoms of schizophrenia can be divided into positive and negative symptoms. Positive symptoms are ones that are added onto the premorbid state. These include abnormal behaviors, thought disorders, delusions, and hallucinations. Negative symptoms consist of the absence of faculties that were present or would be expected to be present before the onset of the illness. There is great difficulty in differentiating negative symptoms from the "defect state," which is considered the end state in chronic schizophrenia. Differentiation is also difficult between negative symptoms and depression, including postpsychotic depression and pharmacologically induced bradykinesia or other medication-induced states. Gibbons et al. (1985) have written about the problems differentiating the various etiologies of negative symptoms; they recommend that these symptoms be seen as multidimensional rather than unidimensional ones.

Andreasen and Olsen (1982) have described negative symptoms along the following lines:

1. Affective flattening or blunting, which presents as unchanging facial expression, decreased spontaneous movements, paucity of expressive gestures, poor eye contact, affective nonresponsivity, lack of vocal inflection, and emotional emptiness.
2. Alogia, which presents as poverty of speech and speech content, as well as blocking and increased latency of speech.
3. Avolition, which presents as lack of energy, drive, and interest.
4. Anhedonia, which presents as difficulty experiencing interest or pleasure in areas of recreation, sex, and intimacy.
5. Attentional problems, which are reflected in social inattentiveness and inattention during testing.

The concept of negative and positive symptoms is important in the delineation of two hypothetical syndromes in schizophrenia (Crow 1985). Type I form of schizophrenia is characterized by the predominance of positive symptoms, reversible outcome, good response to neuroleptics, and the absence of intellectual impairment. Type II form of schizophrenia is characterized by predominantly negative symptoms, possibly irreversible outcome, poor response to neuroleptics, and intellectual impairment. The postulated abnormality in Type I schizophrenia is related to an increase in dopamine receptors, whereas the abnormality in Type II schizophrenia is related to cellular loss and structural changes in the brain. Crow noted that these two syndromes could overlap, and that over time, some of the patients with the Type I syndrome could develop the Type II variety of schizophrenia. Though such a division is theoretically enticing, attempts to support such distinctions have not been uniformly successful.

Stages of Schizophrenia

Just as a patient with diabetes mellitus goes through a series of stages prior to reaching diabetic coma, so also the schizophrenic patient often goes through various stages of the illness prior to reaching frank psychosis. Such stages of schizophrenia have been conceptualized as "the sequential appearance of hierarchically ordered, distinguishable, and recognizable psychological states" (Docherty et al. 1978). Though not clearly differentiated in each patient, such staging is helpful in conceptualizing the illness and might be important for diagnosis and treatment.

Stage 0: Equilibrium. The relationship between the external world and the internal processes of the patient is a harmonious one. There is good adaptation to the current environmental situation, with a minimal amount of anxiety.

Stage 1: Overextension. Because of external pressures or unrelenting internal conflict, arousal becomes intense and continuous, leading to an overwhelming sense of loss of control. The person has to run faster and faster to keep up and can appear anxious, distractible, and overstimulated, with an associated functional decrement.

Stage 2: Restricted consciousness. The response to the sense of being overwhelmed is an attempt to regain control of one's environment by withdrawal and constriction of the range of thought, emotion, and action. Social withdrawal, somatization, and feelings of hopelessness and loneliness can appear and grow pronounced.

Stage 3: Disinhibition. As the overstimulation continues and the initial steps taken to regain control are unsuccessful, the psychotic process takes over. Mood, thinking, and behavior are released from their usual controls, resulting in a transient state not dissimilar to hypomania. Mood elevation and rage attacks, sexual promiscuity, and uncharacteristic risk taking can occur. Ideas of reference and primitive thought content are observable.

Stage 4: Psychotic disorganization. There is a terrifying loss of internal control accompanied by a shattering of the sense of self and the perception of external reality. This loss of control results in a tumultuous state of psychotic symptoms that are fluctuating and disorganized.

Stage 5: Psychotic resolution. A new level of organization is achieved in an attempt to make sense of the experiences as the overstimulation settles down. In a way, this stage can be seen as a complication of the psychotic break, just as agoraphobia is a complication of panic attacks, or myocardial infarction is a complication of vascular insufficiency. The factors that determine the permanence of the new state of equilibrium are not known but could be quite different from the factors that began the psychotic break.

Significance of Stages to Diagnosis and Treatment

Understanding schizophrenia along these sequential lines may be useful in improving diagnostic reliability. More importantly, if reliable measures of the early stages of the illness were available, they would open areas of study that would have an impact on understanding critical etiological issues in the development of the psychotic break. The treatment could then focus on the specific issues relevant to the stage of the illness, and attempts at preventing the evolution of the psychotic episode would be possible. An example of such an approach is the concept of early warning signs that indicate an impending relapse. These early warning signs can be used as signals to aggressively treat an evolving exacerbation and prevent an episode of illness. Such specific and targeted treatments are a generation removed from the unitary treatment approaches that are provided to the majority of patients today.

Conclusions

At a fairly basic level, a diagnostic system should serve a number of functions: to prevent confusion in communication about patients with the same constellation of symptoms within the framework of individual variations; to help define a homogenous group of patients for clinical and research studies; to classify a group of patients for the definition of treatment issues in a clinical setting; and to have some predictive capacity.

The evolution of the various diagnostic systems for schizophrenia has been based on the data available. The DSM-III-R is probably the most clinically useful diagnostic system at present, despite its limitations. For research studies, the information necessary for diagnosis based on multiple diagnostic systems should be collected so that the population of patients being studied is well characterized. Further, as diagnostic systems continue to evolve, the data will have been collected to rediagnose patients already studied. In this way, valuable information will not be lost. In short, schizophrenia as a label should be used judiciously.

REFERENCES

American Psychiatric Association: Diagnostic and Statistical Manual of Mental Disorders, Third Edition. Washington, DC, American Psychiatric Association, 1980

American Psychiatric Association: Diagnostic and Statistical Manual of Mental Disorders, Third Edition—Revised. Washington, DC, American Psychiatric Association, 1987

Andreasen NC, Olsen S: Negative *v* positive schizophrenia. Arch Gen Psychiatry 39:789–794, 1982

Bleuler E: Dementia Praecox or the Group of Schizophrenias. Translated by Zinkin J. New York, International Universities Press, 1960 (original German edition 1911)

Carpenter WT, Strauss JS, Bartko JJ: Flexible system for the diagnosis of schizophrenia: report from the WHO international pilot study of schizophrenia. Science 182:1275–1278, 1973

Coryell W, Tsuang MT: Outcome after 40 years in DSM III schizophreniform disorder. Arch Gen Psychiatry 43:324–328, 1986

Crow TJ: The two-syndrome concept: origins and current status. Schizophr Bull 11:471–485, 1985

Docherty JP, van Kammen DP, Siris SG, et al: Stages of onset of schizophrenic psychosis. Am J Psychiatry 135:420–426, 1978

Douglas RK: Rise of Confucius, the Chinese sage, in The Great Events by Famous Historians, Vol 1. Edited by Johnson R. The National Alumni, 1919, p 293

Feighner JP, Robins E, Guze SB, et al: Diagnostic criteria for use in psychiatric research. Arch Gen Psychiatry 26:57–63, 1972

Fenton WS, Mosher LR, Matthews SM: Diagnosis of schizophrenia: a critical review of current diagnostic systems. Schizophr Bull 7:452–476, 1981

Gibbons R, Lewine R, Davis J, et al: An empirical test of a Kraepelinian vs. a Bleulerian view of negative symptoms. Schizophr Bull 11:390–396, 1985

Kety SS, Rosenthal D, Wender P, et al: Mental illness in the biologic and adoptive families of adopted schizophrenics. Am J Psychiatry 128:302–306, 1971

Kraepelin E: Textbook of Psychiatry. Translated by Diefendorf AR. London, Macmillan, 1907

Langfeldt G: The prognosis in schizophrenia. Acta Psychiatr Neurol Scand 110:7–66, 1956

Myers JK, Weissman MM, Tischler GL, et al: Six month prevalence of psychiatric disorders in three communities, 1980–1982. Arch Gen Psychiatry 41:959–967, 1984

Rieder RO: The origins of our confusion about schizophrenia. Psychiatry 37:197–208, 1974
Robins LN, Helzer JE, Weissman MM, et al: Life-time prevalence of specific psychiatric disorders in three sites. Arch Gen Psychiatry 41:949–958, 1984
Schneider K: Clinical Psychopathology. Translated by Hamilton MW. New York, Grune & Stratton, 1959
Spitzer RL, Endicott J, Robins E: Clinical criteria for psychiatric diagnosis and DSM III. Am J Psychiatry 132:1187–1192, 1975
Spitzer RL, Endicott J, Robins E: Research diagnostic criteria: rationale and reliability. Arch Gen Psychiatry 35:773–782, 1978

APPENDIX 1

DIAGNOSTIC CRITERIA FOR VARIOUS DEFINITIONS OF SCHIZOPHRENIA

Emil Kraepelin—Dementia Praecox (1907) (Abstracted from Rieder 1974)

1. Clinical symptoms: hallucinations, delusions, and poor judgment; withdrawn and impulsive behavior; constant shifting of interests and attention; dissociation between thought content and affect.
2. Usually begins early in life and tends to lead to a similar end stage of dementia.
3. Probable common etiology involving a disease process that affects the cortical neurons.

Eugen Bleuler—Schizophrenia (1911)

Fundamental symptoms:

Altered associations
Altered affectivity
Ambivalence
Autism

Gabriel Langfeldt (1956) (Abstracted from Rieder 1974)

Symptoms that define schizophrenia:

Depersonalization and derealization described as a special type of disturbance of volition and sense of self.
A break in the development of personality (emotional blunting and bizarre behavior).
Catatonic stupor or excitement.
Primary delusions as seen in paranoid cases.

Process schizophrenia: Patients with a deteriorating course.

Schizophreniform: Patients who have precipitating factors and who improve.

Kurt Schneider (1959)

Any one of the following symptoms:

1. Certain types of auditory hallucinations, including hearing audible thoughts, hearing voices arguing, and hearing voices commenting on one's actions.
2. The experiences of influences playing on the body (tactile hallucinations).
3. Certain types of disturbances of thought, including thought withdrawal or other interferences of thought, and diffusion of thought (the experience of others knowing one's thoughts).
4. A delusional perception (an abnormal significance, usually some message to or about the self, attached to a genuine perception when there is no comprehensible rationale or emotional justification).
5. The experience of one's feelings, impulses, and acts as the work or influence of others.

Outcome rejected as criterion for defining the illness.

Flexible System—Carpenter, Strauss, and Bartko (1973)

Restricted affect
Poor insight
Thoughts aloud
Poor rapport
Widespread delusions
Incoherent speech
Unreliable information
Bizarre delusions
Nihilistic delusions
Absence of early awakening (1–3 hours)
Absence of depressed facies
Absence of elation

Feighner Criteria (1972)

A through C necessary:

A. Both of the following are necessary:

A chronic illness with at least 6 months of symptoms before the index evaluation without return to premorbid level of psychosocial adjustment.

Absence of a period of depressive or manic symptoms sufficient to qualify for affective disorder or probable affective disorder.

B. At least one of the following:

Delusions or hallucinations without significant perplexity or disorientation associated with them.

Verbal production that makes communication difficult because of a lack of logical or understandable organization. (In the presence of muteness, the diagnosis must be deferred.)

C. At least three of the following for definite, two for probable:

Single (never married).
Poor premorbid social adjustment or work history.
Family history of schizophrenia.
Absence of alcoholism or drug abuse within one year of onset of psychosis.
Onset of the illness before the age of 40.

Research Diagnostic Criteria—Spitzer, Endicott, and Robins (1978)

A through C are required for the period of illness being considered:

A. At least two of the following are required for definite and one for probable (if the symptoms occur only during a period of alcohol or drug abuse or withdrawal from either, do not score here):

1. Thought broadcasting, insertion, or withdrawal.
2. Delusions of being controlled (or influenced), other bizarre delusions, or multiple delusions.
3. Delusions other than persecutory or jealousy, lasting at least 1 week.
4. Delusions of any type if accompanied by hallucinations of any type for at least 1 week.

5. Auditory hallucinations in which either a voice keeps up a running commentary on the subject's behaviors or thoughts as they occur, or two or more voices converse with each other.
6. Nonaffective verbal hallucinations spoken to the subject.
7. Hallucinations of any type throughout the day for several days or intermittently for at least 1 month.
8. Definite instances of marked formal thought disorder accompanied by either blunted or inappropriate affect, delusions or hallucinations of any type, or grossly disorganized behavior.

B. Either 1 or 2:

1. The current period of illness has lasted at least 2 weeks from the onset of a noticeable change in the subject's usual condition.
2. The subject has had a previous period of illness lasting at least 2 weeks in which he or she met the criteria and residual signs of the illness have remained, e.g., extreme social withdrawal, blunted or inappropriate affect, formal thought disorder, or unusual thoughts or perceptual experiences.

C. At no time during the active period of illness being considered did the subject meet the criteria for probable or definite manic or depressive syndrome to such a degree that manic or depressive symptoms were a prominent part of the illness.

Subtyping of the illness is done by course (acute, subacute, subchronic, and chronic) and clinical phenomenology (paranoid, disorganized, confusional, catatonic, undifferentiated, or mixed).

APPENDIX 2

DIAGNOSTIC AND STATISTICAL MANUAL—THIRD EDITION (DSM-III)

Schizophrenia

A. At least one of the following during a phase of the illness:

1. Bizarre delusions (content is patently absurd and has *no* possible basis in fact), such as delusions of being controlled, thought broadcasting, thought insertion, or thought withdrawal.
2. Somatic, grandiose, religious, nihilistic, or other delusions without persecutory or jealous content.
3. Delusions with persecutory or jealous content if accompanied by hallucinations of any type.
4. Auditory hallucinations in which either a voice keeps up a running commentary on the individual's behavior or thoughts, or two or more voices converse with each other.
5. Auditory hallucinations on several occasions with content of more than one or two words having no apparent relation to depression or elation.
6. Incoherence, marked loosening of associations, markedly illogical thinking, or marked poverty of content of speech if associated with at least one of the following: (a) blunted, flat, or inappropriate affect; (b) delusions or hallucinations; (c) catatonic or other grossly disorganized behavior.

B. Deterioration from a previous level of functioning in such areas as work, social relations, and self-care.

C. Duration: Continuous signs of the illness for at least 6 months at some time during the person's life, with some signs of the illness at present. The 6-month period must include an active phase during which there were symptoms from A, with or without a prodromal or residual phase, as defined.

D. The full depressive or manic syndrome, if present, developed after any psychotic symptoms, or was brief in duration relative to the duration of the psychotic symptoms in A.

E. Onset of the prodromal or active phase of the illness before age 45.

F. Not due to any Organic Mental Disorder or Mental Retardation.

Types: Disorganized, catatonic, paranoid, undifferentiated, and residual.

Course: Subchronic, chronic, subchronic with acute exacerbation, chronic with acute exacerbation, in remission.

Schizophreniform Disorder

A. Meets all the criteria for Schizophrenia, except for duration.

B. The illness (including prodromal, active, and residual phases) lasts more than 2 weeks but less than 6 months.

Schizoaffective Disorder

This category was retained without specified diagnostic criteria in the DSM-III.

Schizotypal Personality Disorder

The following are characteristic of the individual's current and long-term functioning, are not limited to episodes of illness, and cause either significant impairment in social or occupational functioning or subjective distress.

A. At least four of the following:

1. Magical thinking, e.g., superstitiousness, clairvoyance, telepathy, "6th sense," "others can feel my feelings" (in children and adolescents, bizarre fantasies and preoccupations).
2. Ideas of reference.
3. Social isolation, e.g., no close friends or confidants; social contacts limited to essential everyday tasks.
4. Recurrent illusions, sensing the presence of a force or person not actually present (e.g., "I felt as if my dead mother were in the room with me"), depersonalization, or derealization not associated with panic attacks.
5. Odd speech (without loosening of associations or incoherence), e.g., speech that is digressive, vague, overelaborate, circumstantial, metaphorical.

6. Inadequate rapport in face-to-face interaction due to constricted or inappropriate affect, e.g., aloof, cold.
7. Suspicious or paranoid ideation.
8. Undue social anxiety or hypersensitivity to real or imagined criticism.

B. Does not meet criteria for Schizophrenia.

APPENDIX 3

DIAGNOSTIC AND STATISTICAL MANUAL—THIRD EDITION—REVISED (DSM-III-R)

Schizophrenia

A. Presence of characteristic psychotic symptoms in the active phase: either (1), (2), or (3) for at least 1 week (unless the symptoms are successfully treated):

1. Two of the following:
   (a) Delusions.
   (b) Prominent hallucinations (throughout the day for several days or several times a week, each hallucinatory experience not being limited to a few brief moments).
   (c) Incoherence or marked loosening of associations.
   (d) Catatonic behavior.
   (e) Flat or grossly inappropriate affect.
2. Bizarre delusions (i.e., involving a phenomenon that the person's culture would regard as totally implausible, e.g., thought broadcasting, being controlled by a dead person).
3. Prominent hallucinations (as defined in [1b] above) of a voice with content having no apparent relation to depression or elation, or a voice keeping up a running commentary on the person's behavior or thoughts, or two or more voices conversing with each other.

B. During the course of the disturbance, functioning in such areas as work, social relations, and self-care is markedly below the highest level achieved before onset of the disturbance (or, when the onset is in childhood or adolescence, failure to achieve expected level of social development).

C. Schizoaffective Disorder and Mood Disorder with Psychotic Features have been ruled out, i.e., if a Major Depressive or Manic Syndrome has ever been present during an active phase of the disturbance, the total duration of all episodes of a mood syndrome has been brief relative to the total duration of the active and residual phases of the disturbance.

D. Continuous signs of the disturbance for at least 6 months. The 6-month period must include an active phase (of at least 1 week, or less if symptoms have been successfully treated) during which there were psychotic symptoms characteristic of Schizophrenia (symptoms in A).

E. It cannot be established that an organic factor initiated and maintained the disturbance.

F. If there is a history of Autistic Disorder, the additional diagnosis of Schizophrenia is made only if prominent delusions or hallucinations are also present.

Schizophreniform Disorder

A. Meets criteria A and C of Schizophrenia.

B. An episode of the disturbance (including prodromal, active, and residual phases) lasts less than 6 months. (When the diagnosis must be made without waiting for recovery, it should be qualified as "provisional.")

C. Does not meet the criteria for Brief Reactive Psychosis, and it cannot be established that an organic factor initiated and maintained the disturbance.

Schizoaffective Disorder

A. A disturbance during which, at some time, there is either a Major Depressive or a Manic Syndrome concurrent with symptoms that meet the A criterion of Schizophrenia.

B. During an episode of the disturbance, there have been delusions or hallucinations for at least 2 weeks, but no prominent mood symptoms.

C. Schizophrenia has been ruled out, i.e., the duration of all episodes of a mood syndrome has not been brief relative to the total duration of the psychotic disturbance.

D. It cannot be established that an organic factor initiated and maintained the disturbance.

Schizotypal Personality Disorder

A. A pervasive pattern of deficits in interpersonal relatedness and peculiarities of ideation, appearance, and behavior, beginning by early adulthood and present in a variety of contexts, as indicated by at least *five* of the following:

1. Ideas of reference (excluding delusions of reference).
2. Excessive social anxiety, e.g., extreme discomfort in social situations involving unfamiliar people.
3. Odd beliefs or magical thinking, influencing behavior and inconsistent with subcultural norms, e.g., superstitiousness, belief in clairvoyance, telepathy, or "sixth sense," "others can feel my feelings" (in children and adolescents, bizarre fantasies or preoccupations).
4. Unusual perceptual experiences, e.g., illusions, sensing the presence of a force or person not actually present (e.g., "I felt as if my dead mother were in the room with me").
5. Odd or eccentric behavior or appearance, e.g., unkempt, unusual mannerisms, talks to self.
6. No close friends or confidants (or only one) other than first-degree relatives.
7. Odd speech (without loosening of associations or incoherence), e.g., speech that is impoverished, digressive, vague, or inappropriately abstract.
8. Inappropriate or constricted affect, e.g., silly, aloof, rarely reciprocates gestures or facial expressions, such as smiles or nods.
9. Suspiciousness or paranoid ideation.

B. Occurrence not exclusively during the course of Schizophrenia or a Pervasive Developmental Disorder.

Chapter 2

EMERGENCY SERVICES

Salley S. Jessee, M.D.
Gail Anderson, M.D.

PSYCHIATRIC EMERGENCY SERVICES play an increasingly important role in the treatment of schizophrenic patients. Deinstitutionalization, emphasis on short-term hospitalization, and inadequate community resources have resulted in a greater utilization of psychiatric emergency services by schizophrenic patients. For some patients, the emergency services are their primary source of psychiatric care and even total health care (Bachrach 1981). For many others, they are a valuable resource in times of crises.

Schizophrenia is believed to be a group of illnesses that have multiple etiologies. Certainly, the clinical presentation, the course of illness, and the response to treatment vary considerably. The clinical presentation of schizophrenia typically includes disturbances in thinking, emotion, and behavior. Schizophrenic patients may come to an emergency room floridly psychotic with extreme agitation or violent behavior. The chronically ill patient may come requesting help with a psychosocial problem. Subjectively, both patients perceive their problem as emergent, and both require intervention.

ASSESSMENT

Triage

A psychiatric emergency service that deals with large numbers of patients needs a system of triage to ensure immediate intervention for emergent and potentially volatile patients. An experienced clinician should be selected to fulfill the role of triage officer. The triage officer's responsibility is to be aware of all the patients presenting to the emergency service and to assign patients based on the apparent urgency of the problem. The urgency of the problem is determined by direct behavioral observation in addition to consideration of the patient's or others' stated reasons for the visit. Nonemergent patients are interviewed briefly and, depending on the results of the interview, either asked to wait for a more thorough assessment or referred to an appropriate outpatient facility or community resource.

Among the acutely psychotic patients who present to emergency rooms, the schizophrenic patient who is agitated, out of control, or violent receives first priority. Immediate intervention in the form of medication or physical restraint is often necessary before a complete assessment can occur (Perry 1976). Patients who are out of control, showing signs of increasing agitation such as restlessness, pacing, clenching of fists or jaws, loud or threatening verbalizations, or emotional lability, should be interviewed immediately to avoid further emotional and physical escalation. Other frequently encountered clinical presentations of schizophrenic patients that constitute psychiatric emergencies include acute dystonic reactions, gross confusion and disorganization, and catatonia. Catatonic states, whether a manifestation of schizophrenia or of another mental illness, are an emergency because of the potential for uncontrolled excitement.

By definition, an emergency service should provide rapid assessment and treatment of acute problems first, but should not neglect patients with chronic or less acute problems. Appropriate intervention for the latter patients may prevent further misuse of the emergency service as well as future decompensation or worsening of illness.

EMERGENCY INTERVIEW

General Principles

The emergency psychiatric interview is ideally both diagnostic and therapeutic. For the schizophrenic patient, the interview should be conducted in an environment in which both the patient and the interviewer feel as comfortable as possible. In most instances, the interview is conducted in a well-lit room that allows adequate space and privacy. The room should be arranged so that both the patient and the interviewer have ready access to the door. Ideally, the room should be equipped with a silent alarm system that can be activated if assistance is needed.

If the patient indicates acute discomfort about being seen alone in a private room, or if the interviewer is fearful of the patient, the interview arrangement can be modified in various ways (Perry 1976). The patient may wish a family member or friend to be included in the interview. Usually, as the patient's anxiety decreases, the other person may be excused. Other modifications of the interview arrangement include leaving the door open, having another staff member present, or conducting the interview in an open space. As previously mentioned, extremely agitated patients often require medication or physical restraint before a full interview can be conducted.

The interviewer should always maintain an appropriate physical distance from the patient. He or she should address the patient by last name and introduce himself or herself by last name and professional identity. Keeping an appropriate distance from the patient and defining the professional nature of the relationship emphasizes ego boundaries that are often tenuous or disrupted in the schizophrenic patient. However, this does not imply that the interviewer should not try to make emotional contact with the patient to clarify problems and understand overwhelming feelings. Because of the schizophrenic patient's characteristic disturbances in thought, affect, and behavior, as well as his or her ambivalence about relationships, making emotional contact can be quite difficult. In general, the interviewer is more active in the interview than he or she would be with less disturbed patients; the interviewer's own emotional responses to the patient are utilized in order to try to understand the patient's feelings and underlying thought processes (Perry 1976).

The traditional concept of confidentiality may be modified in psychiatric emergencies (Shwed 1980). With any patient who is psychotic, it is imperative that additional history be gathered from all available sources. Contact with physicians or other mental health professionals may provide significant history regarding the patient's risk of dangerousness to himself or others. Similarly, relatives and friends often provide information that is vital to assessment and treatment. Because of anxiety, confusion, or paranoia, the schizophrenic patient often cannot clearly define a chief complaint or identify precipitating factors for his or her decompensation. Family or friends can provide recent and past psychiatric history and identify precipitants for the current illness such as noncompliance with medication, drug or alcohol abuse, or significant psychological stressors. Some interviewers prefer to interview the family with the patient present, whereas others interview the family separately. The experienced interviewer is flexible and weighs the advantages and disadvantages of both approaches depending on the particular patient and circumstances.

Finally, the length of the emergency interview will vary depending on the patient and the complexity of the situation. If it is clear that the patient requires inpatient admission, the emergency interview may be brief, since further exploration of the patient's problems will be accomplished during hospitalization. However, it is still necessary to explain to both the patient and the family why hospitalization is indicated and to elicit their support for the treatment.

Specific Techniques

For the most acutely disturbed schizophrenic patients, it is impossible to conduct an open-ended interview in the same way that one would with less disturbed or nonpsychotic patients. Conducting an interview with a severely disturbed schizophrenic patient requires considerable skill and patience (MacKinnon and Michels 1971).

Often schizophrenic patients do not come to the emergency service by choice. They may be brought by family, friends, police, or sent by a court order. In order to establish any rapport with these patients, the interviewer should acknowledge the patient's understandable anger. The interviewer may then inquire about the patient's reactions regarding the family's or others' concerns about him. Frequently, this will lead to some description of the acute event even if the patient minimizes the need for concern by others. Inquiry about previous contacts with psychiatrists or previous hospitalizations can be followed by questions regarding the patient's circumstances and overt symptoms at previous times. Obtaining this information is a useful preface to questions regarding current symptoms (MacKinnon and Michels 1971).

Paranoid patients are particularly difficult to interview because of their basic mistrust of others, their extensive use of projection and denial, and their anger. The interviewer is often met with either hostile silence or overt anger. By acknowledging the patient's anger, the interviewer can often convert the hostile, silent patient to an angry but communicative patient. However, with a patient who remains resistant and silent, it is necessary to let him or her know that the interviewer must make a decision regarding the patient and will be gathering information from others, but would likc to hear what the patient has to say. The interviewer allows the patient to ventilate anger and to tell his or her story, but does not allow the patient to completely control the interview.

At some point, the interviewer has to intervene by explaining to the patient that other issues must be discussed before the interviewer can figure out how best to help the patient. Inquiry about unusual experiences leads some paranoid patients into a discussion of hallucinations or delusional material. Others must be questioned directly regarding hallucinations, ideas of influence, ideas of reference, and persecutory or grandiose ideation. The interviewer investigates how the patient responds to these experiences or ideas in order to assess dangerousness or likelihood of bizarre behavior. Delusional ideation is not challenged, but neither should the interviewer imply that he or she agrees with the delusion. Nor should the interviewer give in to unreasonable demands, including promising not to hospitalize the patient. The interviewer attempts to convey his or her understanding of the patient's current difficulties and to enlist the patient's active participation in whatever treatment is indicated, i.e., medication, hospitalization, etc. (MacKinnon and Michels 1971). If this cannot be accomplished, and the patient must be involuntarily hospitalized, the reason for this action should be carefully explained to the patient. Although patients will likely respond immediately with anger, they are less likely to feel betrayed if the reasons for hospitalization are carefully delineated.

The extremely disorganized and agitated patient presents different difficulties for the interviewer. It is particularly difficult for these patients to identify a chief complaint or precipitating stress. Once it is clear that the patient is disorganized and confused, the interviewer should actively provide structure. Allowing a patient with loose associations to ramble aimlessly and endlessly only increases anxiety and ego fragmentation. The interviewer can intervene with a comment that he or she is not following the patient and ask a question that brings the patient back to a relevant point (Robbins and Stern 1976). If a patient continues to return to a particular topic, this should be noted and inquired about (MacKinnon and Michels 1971). The interviewer listens and observes carefully for clues to the patient's underlying feelings and attempts to make some affectual contact. For instance, the patient may at times appear to be responding to auditory hallucinations with a startled, frightened facial expression. The interviewer can verbalize this observation and inquire about the frightening content of the hallucinations. If, however, no clear feeling can be identified, the experienced interviewer may use his or her own emotional responses as a guide in identifying the patient's feelings. Emotional contact diminishes the patient's agitation and helps organize his or her thoughts. However, at times it may be necessary to abbreviate the initial interview, provide the patient with medication, and then reinterview the patient.

Emotional withdrawal, including complete silence, is another common presentation of schizophrenic decompensation. The withdrawal may have begun insidiously and gradually increased over time. Complete silence may have existed for several days prior to the patient's arrival at the emergency service and may be the primary reason the family brings the patient for evaluation. Assessing the silent patient requires gathering information from accompanying persons, carefully observing the patient's nonverbal behavior, and the interviewer monitoring his or her own emotional responses to the patient. Initially, the interviewer may have few clues about the severity of the decompensation or precipitating stressors. Often the family will report that the patient's withdrawal from interpersonal contact has included autistic, seclusive behavior. As the patient sits in the interview room, the interviewer carefully notes the silent patient's nonverbal behavior and facial expression. The patient may appear frightened, withdrawn, and preoccupied, or he or she may stare intently at the interviewer. These patients often elicit either protective feelings or a sense of detachment within the interviewer. If the interviewer feels protective toward a silent patient, he can state that he feels the patient is frightened and that he would like to understand what the patient is experiencing that is frightening. If he feels detached, the interviewer can state that it is difficult to know what the patient is experiencing or he can make a comment that the patient must feel a strong need to keep his thoughts and feelings to himself.

The catatonic patient may present with mutism, immobility, muscle rigidity, and waxy flexibility. This patient should be approached with the assumption that he or she is aware of the surroundings. The interviewer should acknowledge the patient by name and should identify himself or herself. The interviewer must rely on nonverbal cues in attempting to establish communication with the patient. Some responses may be elicited by asking the patient to follow simple commands and to nod answers to simple questions, or by closely observing the patient as he or she is physically examined (Robbins and Stern 1976). The patient should be allowed ample time to answer questions and should never be bombarded with them. Catatonia is best thought of as a syndrome with multiple etiologies, among which are neurological diseases, idiosyncratic responses to neuroleptics, and various psychiatric illnesses, including schizophrenia and affective disorders.

The Amytal interview. An Amytal sodium (amobarbital sodium) interview may be helpful in differentiating functional from organic catatonic conditions. A 10% solution of Amytal is given slowly at an approximate rate of 1 ml per minute. This is continued until the patient shows obvious effects of the Amytal, including nystagmus, slurred speech, and drowsiness. Most patients respond to between 0.1 g and 0.5 g. The maximum dose is 1 g given over a long period of time. Once the patient shows the effects of the Amytal, questioning may begin and proceeds much like any other clinical interview. Medical contraindications to the use of an Amytal interview include CNS depression, porphyria, and barbiturate addiction or allergy. Caution should be used in patients with impaired renal or liver function and in patients with congestive heart failure. Emergency resuscitation equipment should be readily available (Naples and Hackett 1978).

Theoretically, patients with organic disorders will have lower sedation thresholds than normal control subjects, i.e., will require less Amytal (mg/kg) to induce slurred speech, nystagmus, and drowsiness. Additionally, organic patients will characteristically show increased disorientation, confabulation, and denial of illness under the influence of the drug (Weinstein et al. 1953). On the other hand, in acute or chronic schizophrenic patients, the sedation threshold approaches that of healthy controls or is elevated. Characteristically, catatonic schizophrenic patients under the influence of Amytal become mobilized and frequently communicate psychotic material, including symptoms such as delusions and hallucinations. Patients with affective disorders may relate increased depressive material (Kramer 1983).

There are reports in the literature of cases in which the Amytal interview has aided in the differential diagnosis of both organic and functional disorders. However, there are also reports of false positives and negatives as well as reports of patients who have been found to have coexisting organic and functional impairments (Roy-Byrne and Edelstein 1982). Consequently, the Amytal interview should only be used as one tool in the diagnostic armamentarium and should never replace a complete medical evaluation (Stoudemire 1982). However, an Amytal interview at times can be helpful in differentiating functional from organically induced catatonia. Finally, rapid tranquilization with neuroleptics over several hours can result in some functionally catatonic patients becoming verbally responsive. The vast majority of these patients require hospitalization.

The chronic schizophrenic patient. Unique problems are encountered in the assessment of the chronic schizophrenic patient who presents to the emergency service. These patients are often perceived by emergency staff as unchallenging and unrewarding and may be given short shrift. Chronic schizophrenic patients often use the emergency service for psychosocial support, and the interviewer must realize that the emergency service can be a lifeline for them. Medications and supportive care may be extremely helpful in preventing the development of a complete psychotic relapse. The interviewer also needs to keep in mind that chronic schizophrenic patients can develop other acute psychiatric or medical problems and that they may be at risk for suicidal or violent behavior. Thus a thorough assessment with emphasis on recent psychosocial stressors, change in mental status, and evaluation of the potential for suicidal or violent behavior toward others is critical in chronic schizophrenic patients.

EVALUATION OF SUICIDAL AND HOMICIDAL RISK

Suicide

Assessing the danger of suicide in schizophrenic patients is a crucial part of the emergency room interview. Epidemiological studies suggest that approximately 1 in 10 schizophrenic patients successfully commits suicide (Roy 1982). On the psychiatric emergency service, an acutely psychotic patient with command auditory hallucinations or compelling or persecutory delusions is at particular risk because of the powerful influence of the psychosis. Schizophrenic patients who are undergoing a postpsychotic depression or who recently experienced a significant personal loss are also at risk for suicide.

Direct questions about self-destructive thoughts and impulses are critical in the evaluation. However, the patient may be so psychotically preoccupied that he or she is unable to respond reliably to direct questions. Bizarre or incoherent responses to questions about the patient's intent to hurt himself or herself, especially if accompanied by an inappropriate affect, should be taken seriously. Self-injuries and occasional deaths are not necessarily premeditated. A patient may commit suicide in response to relentless auditory hallucinations commanding him or her to die or to escape from persecution, while another may be so grandiosely delusional that he or she attempts to fly from a building (Torrey 1983).

In a less psychotic patient, exploring thoughts and fantasies of death may reveal frustration at the impact of the illness on the patient's life and ambitions. Such discouragement can lead to suicidal behavior (Waltzer 1984). Similarly, a schizophrenic patient's emotional response to an interpersonal loss can be suicidal in nature. The loss might be a recent divorce or death, geographic relocation of family members, a serious medical illness, job loss, public loss of self-esteem, or the loss of a therapist.

Homicide

Specific data regarding homicide by schizophrenic patients are lacking. Case reports of homicidal schizophrenic patients give the impression that homicide committed by schizophrenics is often in "self-defense," stemming from persecutory delusions (Campion 1985). In the emergency assessment, the interviewer must pay particular attention when a paranoid patient talks of needing protection or of retaliation. Open threats, homicidal fantasies, and previous homicidal behavior during a psychotic episode are reasons for hospitalization.

Crisis Intervention

The treatment approach of a psychiatric emergency service is oriented toward crisis resolution. Conventional crisis intervention techniques, along with medication, may be used with the schizophrenic patient who does not require immediate hospitalization and who still maintains some grasp on reality and awareness of his or her illness. The focus of crisis intervention is on the immediate identifiable problem that has led to the patient's decompensation and disruption of usual coping skills.

Crisis intervention begins with an assessment of the patient's strengths and weaknesses, i.e., degree of insight, history of compliance with treatment, and ability to control impulses. Available environmental resources and support systems must be thoroughly assessed (Hoff 1984). Even for patients who have no defect in reality testing, a crisis often causes so much tension that the immediate stressor is not perceived or defined in an integrated way. This is particularly true of the schizophrenic patient because of his or her disordered thinking. One of the primary goals of crisis intervention is to help the schizophrenic patient define the immediate problem. At times this may be sufficient to resolve the acute problem or at least to define further steps needed in crisis resolution.

Mobilization of available resources is a crucial step in crisis resolution. Psychosocial problems are frequently the cause of schizophrenic decompensation or regression. Some psychosocial problems have no good solutions because community resources have not been adequately developed to meet the needs of the large number of mentally ill persons. However, often the patient is simply unaware of available resources or too overwhelmed by his or her illness to discern options. Emergency service clinicians should be knowledgeable about the availability and range of community resources.

Whenever possible the patient's family or other persons who are the primary social support for the patient should be involved in the crisis intervention. Involvement of family or significant others increases the likelihood of their support for the patient. As mentioned previously, family can often identify precipitating stresses for the patient's illness. Family can also assist in helping the patient comply with medication and appointments. They can help the therapist determine when the patient has returned to his or her previous level of functioning. Education of the family about the patient's illness can result in future recognition of the early signs of decompensation, allowing for prompt intervention before the development of a full-blown psychosis (see Chapter 8 of the present volume).

Crisis intervention is by definition a time-limited therapy. After the crisis is ameliorated or resolved and the patient is relatively stable, he or she should be referred for ongoing outpatient treatment.

Observation Unit

An observation or holding unit where a patient can be observed, medicated, and periodically reassessed for up to 24 hours is a valuable adjunct to an emergency service (Kritzer and Pittman 1968; Ianzito et al. 1978). Ideally, the observation unit should be located in a separate but adjacent area to the emergency service. Ample space for patients to sit, eat meals, or sleep is needed. Space should also be available for patients who require restraints. The unit must be adequately staffed at all times in order to closely observe patients and attend to their needs. Any patient admitted to the observation unit should be thoroughly searched to ensure the safety of other patients and staff. A record of medication, vital signs, and behavioral observations should be kept on each patient. Any physical restraints authorized by the physician must be checked every 15 minutes and documented.

The observation unit can be used to contain and often resolve acute problems, thereby averting hospitalization. Schizophrenic patients who were initially thought to be too dangerous, agitated, or psychotic to be released may stabilize within 24 hours and can be referred for outpatient treatment. Use of the observation unit allows staff time to gather further pertinent history, to medicate the patient while observing mental status changes, and to plan an appropriate disposition. Aside from providing a safe place for rapid tranquilization of acutely agitated psychotic patients, the observation unit offers a place where the chronic schizophrenic patient can recompensate when his or her fragile sense of balance in the community is disturbed. The unit offers a form of respite care where the chronic schizophrenic patient can talk to a staff member, eat a meal, or even sleep overnight.

Medication

The first question is whether or not one should use medications in the emergency room. There are situations in which further evaluation over time without medications is indicated. For example, a patient suspected of having neuroleptic-induced catatonia should not be given more neuroleptics. Confusional and delirious states are best observed and medically evaluated without medications unless behavioral control is essential. On the other hand, drug side effects such as acute dystonic reactions and akathisia might need immediate action.

Consensus on "rapid tranquilization" or "rapid neuroleptilization" is still lacking. Some authors use these terms interchangeably, while others use rapid tranquilization to mean the use of sedative-hypnotic medication with neuroleptics. Because various routes of administration of neuroleptics as well as the use of medications other than neuroleptics to control unmanageable psychotic behavior will be discussed, the term rapid tranquilization will be used in this chapter.

The idea of using multiple doses of neuroleptics administered over several hours to treat acute psychosis is based on the premise that more neuroleptic medication should be better than standard amounts. However, controlled studies have indicated that moderate or even low doses of neuroleptics are as effective in the treatment of acute psychotic symptoms as high doses in most patients (Cole 1982). Baldessarini et al. have analyzed these studies (see Chapter 4 in the present volume) and have concluded that doses of neuroleptics of more than the approximate equivalent of 500–600 mg of chlorpromazine (i.e., 10–12 mg haloperidol) within the first 24 hours do not appear to provide additional clinical benefit in the treatment of acute psychosis.

In some patients, the initiation of neuroleptic treatment results in, within hours, an immediate decrease in the intensity of specific symptoms such as excitement and belligerence, disorganization of thought, suspiciousness, hallucinations, and delusions (Anderson and Kuehnle 1981). Whether this is a true "antipsychotic" effect or a sedative effect is unclear. The use of combination neuroleptic treatment and benzodiazepine treatment in the short-term has advantages because more conservative doses of neuroleptics can be used (Guz et al. 1972). Because intramuscular administration of neuroleptics results in a more rapid rise in blood levels, it is preferred over oral administration for acutely agitated or belligerent patients (Schaffer et al. 1982). Information on intramuscular doses of various neuroleptics is provided in Table 1. When acute agitation recedes, oral medication may be substituted.

Regardless of the specific agents, routes, or methods used, all patients receiving medication in an emergency service must be closely supervised for potentially dangerous adverse effects. Specific target symptoms and vital signs should be monitored prior to each dose of medication. For the schizophrenic patient who is not acutely disturbed, maintenance medication is often initiated or adjusted at the time of the emergency service. The choice of neuroleptic and dose should be based on the patient's medication

Table 1. Neuroleptics: Estimated equivalent doses, usual intramuscular doses, and available injection forms

Generic name	Estimated equivalent dose (mg)	Intramuscular dose (mg)	Available injection form (mg/ml)
Haloperidol	2	2–10	5
Fluphenazine	2	2.5–5	2.5
Thiothixene	5	5–10	2 and 5
Trifluoperazine	5	4–6	2
Chlorpromazine	100	25–50	25
Loxapine	10	12.5–50	50

history, physical condition, and careful consideration of the desired effects versus the potential side effects. If there is a history of extrapyramidal side effects, a low-potency neuroleptic may be chosen or an antiparkinsonism agent prescribed. Titration of the dose for each individual is the only way to determine the maintenance dose (Mason and Granacher 1980). Extremely high doses of medication should not be prescribed initially at the time of the emergency service, and preferably only one neuroleptic should be prescribed.

SECLUSION

Physical Restraint

Seclusion or physical restraints can be used when a patient's behavior is out of control or when the patient is assessed to be on the verge of losing control. They may also be used to prevent the elopement of an acutely psychotic patient or to control the behavior of a grossly disorganized patient who disrupts other patients and the operation of the service.

The minimum of physical restraints necessary should be used. Most patients require only a posey belt and one or two wrist restraints. However, extremely agitated or violent patients are initially placed face down on a bed with four-point restraints that completely immobilize the patient.

When seclusion or restraints are required, the reason should be clearly stated to the patient. However, intervention must be swift and non-negotiable. For this to occur, an adequate number of staff and, if necessary, security personnel should be on hand. The patient will frequently become cooperative when there is an adequate show of force. If the patient does not cooperate, then staff must act in a coordinated manner under the direction of a designated and experienced leader. In applying physical restraints, one person is typically assigned to each limb and one person to support the head. The patient is carried to the bed. Restraints are secured to the bedframe and not to siderails. The patient must be thoroughly searched and any weapons and lighters or matches removed. Once in place, restraints must be checked every 15 minutes. This not only protects the patient's physical safety, but provides human contact (Soreff 1984). Restraints should be removed as quickly as possible by bringing the patient's behavior under control with medication.

Disposition

The emergency service is often pivotal in the treatment of schizophrenic patients because of its round-the-clock availability. The crucial question that arises in disposition planning is whether the patient requires hospitalization. This decision involves weighing the severity of manifest psychopathology, current family and situational factors, and the availability of appropriate treatment and community resources. Unnecessary hospitalizations can often be averted by directly linking patients with outpatient treatment facilities or with available community resource agencies. Available modes of outpatient treatment should include crisis intervention, supportive psychotherapy, medication maintenance, partial hospitalization, and transitional living programs. The patient should also understand that he or she may return to the emergency service in the future if the need arises. In addition to linking the patient up with treatment programs, the emergency service clinician should be able to direct the patient to other appropriate resources for assistance, i.e., shelters, welfare offices, Social Security offices, and vocational rehabilitation centers.

Whenever feasible, emergency service clinicians should work in concert with the patient's mental health center or other treatment source to devise and follow a treatment plan for that particular patient. Under some state laws, copies of records of emergency room visits may be forwarded to mental health centers and are extremely helpful in follow-up treatment contacts. Likewise, it is advantageous for regional hospitals to communicate patients' discharge plans to the emergency service so that a unified treatment plan can be followed. This is particularly true in the case of chronic patients who may use the emergency service as their primary treatment source. In especially difficult cases, treatment planning sessions involving emergency services staff, mental health center staff, and regional hospital staff can be extremely helpful in providing optimal treatment, including guidelines for hospitalization for a particular patient.

The following criteria are offered as general guidelines for hospitalization of schizophrenic patients: (1) The patient is experiencing a first psychotic break and is willing to be hospitalized voluntarily. (2) The patient is dangerous to himself or others because of specific psychotic symptoms or because of suicidal or homicidal ideation (Glick et al. 1984). (3) The patient is so psychotically confused and disorganized that he is unable to avoid potentially dangerous situations. (4) The patient, having been in sustained remission, is beginning to decompensate because of acute stress and requests admission. (5) The patient is not improving or is worsening in outpatient treatment and is in need of treatment that is best initiated in the hospital, i.e., high dosage medication and/or ECT. (6) The patient's support system, often the family but sometimes others, is so overwhelmed by the patient's symptoms and behavior that some relief must be offered (Arieti 1974).

Hospitalization is usually not indicated when the following circumstances apply: (1) The patient has been functioning outside the hospital with symptoms that are chronic and unlikely to be modified by hospitalization (Glick et al. 1984). (2) The patient has an adequate support system and is motivated to engage in outpatient treatment. (3) There is a reasonable chance that crisis intervention and outpatient medication will decrease the patient's overt symptoms. (4) The patient shows a good response to rapid tranquilization. (5) Hospitalization would interfere with the level of functioning that the patient has been able to maintain in the community and would likely promote regression (Arieti 1974). These guidelines are not inflexible and cannot substitute for sound clinical judgment regarding individual patients. The risks and benefits of hospitalization must be carefully weighed in each case. In general, the more treatment options and community resources available for the schizophrenic patient, the less likely that hospitalization will be required.

Research

Studies of psychiatric emergency services are difficult for a variety of reasons. Profiles of the population served vary widely. Data collected at one site may not be representative of all emergency services. Additionally, the staffing of each emergency service is unique with respect to qualifications and professional disciplines of team members. Studies on patterns of use of emergency services, diagnostic variations among patients served, patterns of referral to other agencies, and factors influencing hospital admission are necessary. Follow-up of particular subgroups of patients, such as those with first psychotic episodes or those with combined psychiatric illness and drug-related diagnoses, is also possible. Data obtained from urban and rural emergency services can be compared.

Research questions posed that require a prospective study design are difficult to address in psychiatric emergency services. Many acutely psychotic patients will have difficulty giving informed consent. Interviews and interventions are subject to limitations when the patient is mute, withdrawn, disorganized, or paranoid. Often family members do not accompany the patient to the emergency service, and sometimes they cannot be contacted by telephone. Therefore, important social or historical data cannot be obtained. Staff are much more accustomed to making clinical decisions than to recording detailed demographic or objective observational data. Variations in professional training may influence diagnostic acumen and interview technique. Additionally, the values and reactions of the providers of crisis treatment can strongly influence the data obtained. For these reasons, outside investigators observing activities within a psychiatric emergency service may gather the most complete and consistent data.

Despite the inherent difficulties, research conducted over the past two decades has begun to provide an information base for establishing and evaluating the activities of psychiatric emergency services. Such services play an ever more important role in providing health care for a large segment of the population of mentally ill patients, particularly those with acute psychoses.

REFERENCES

Anderson WH, Kuehnle JC: Diagnosis and early management of acute psychosis. N Engl J Med 304:1128–1130, 1981

Arieti S: Interpretation of Schizophrenia. New York, Basic Books, 1974

Bachrach LL: The effects of deinstitutionalization on general hospital psychiatry. Hosp Community Psychiatry 32:786–790, 1981

Campion J: A study of 15 matricidal men. Am J Psychiatry 142:312–317, 1985

Cole JO: Psychopharmacology update—antipsychotic drugs: is more better? McLean Hosp J 7:61–87, 1982

Glick ID, Klar HM, Braff DL: Guidelines for hospitalization of chronic psychiatric patients. Hosp Community Psychiatry 35:934–936, 1984

Guz I, Moraes R, Sartoretto JN: The therapeutic effects of lorazepam in psychotic patients treated with haloperidol: A double-blind study. Curr Ther Res 14:767–774, 1972

Hoff LA: People in Crisis: Understanding and Helping. Menlo Park, CA, Addison-Wesley Publishing Company, 1984

Ianzito BM, Fine J, Sprague B, et al: Overnight admission for psychiatric emergencies. Hosp Community Psychiatry 29:728–730, 1978

Kramer MS: Use of the amobarbital sleep threshold in a withdrawn catatonic. Psychosomatics 24:593–595, 1983

Kritzer H, Pittman FS III: Overnight psychiatric care in a general hospital emergency room. Am J Psychiatry 19:303–306, 1968

MacKinnon R, Michels R: The Psychiatric Interview in Clinical Practice. Philadelphia, PA, WB Saunders, 1971

Mason AS, Granacher RP: Clinical Handbook of Antipsychotic Drug Therapy. New York, Brunner/Mazel, 1980

Naples M, Hackett TP: The Amytal interview: history and current uses. Psychosomatics 19:98–105, 1978

Perry S: Acute psychotic states, in Psychiatric Emergencies. Edited by Glick RA, Myerson AT, Robbins E, et al. New York, Grune & Stratton, 1976, pp 51–88

Robbins E, Stern M: Assessment of psychiatric emergencies, in Psychiatric Emergencies. Edited by Glick RA, Myerson AT, Robbins E, et al. New York, Grune & Stratton, 1976, pp 9–48

Roy A: Suicide in chronic schizophrenia. Br J Psychiatry 141:171–177, 1982

Roy-Byrne P, Edelstein C: Identifying organic brain disease by amobarbital sodium interview: diagnostic pitfalls. Psychosomatics 23:1069–1075, 1982

Schaffer CB, Shahid A, Javaid JI, et al: Bioavailability of oral versus intramuscular haloperidol in schizophrenic patients. J Clin Psychopharmacol 2:274–277, 1982

Shwed H: Teaching emergency room psychiatry. Hosp Community Psychiatry 31:558–562, 1980

Soreff SM: Violence in the emergency room, in Phenomenology and Treatment of Psychiatric Emergencies. Edited by Comstock BS, Fann WE, Pokorny AD, et al. New York, SP Medical and Scientific Books, 1984, pp 39–53

Stoudemire A: The differential diagnosis of catatonic states. Psychosomatics 23:245–252, 1982

Torrey EF: Surviving Schizophrenia. New York, Harper and Row, 1983

Waltzer H: Suicide risk in young schizophrenics. Gen Hosp Psychiatry 6:219–225, 1984

Weinstein EA, Kahn RL, Sugarman LA, et al: The diagnostic use of amobarbital sodium (amytal sodium) in brain disease. Am J Psychiatry 109:889–894, 1953

Chapter 3

PSYCHOLOGICAL EVALUATION

Richard R. J. Lewine, Ph.D.

THE INTENT OF THIS CHAPTER is to provide the clinician with a conceptual framework for deciding, in conjunction with a qualified testing psychologist, when and what type of testing would be useful in evaluating the acutely psychotic schizophrenic patient. We hope to alert the clinician to the general strengths and weaknesses of psychological testing and to the questions to which testing is appropriately addressed, thereby allowing the optimal integration of testing into everyday clinical practice. Detailed reviews of the literally hundreds of available tests are available elsewhere (Buros 1978; Goldstein and Hersen 1984; Korchin 1976; Lezak 1976; Matarazzo 1972; Newmark 1985).

The appropriate use of psychological testing should be determined by the nature of the patient population, the duration of patient contact available to the clinician, and the purposes for which the testing data are needed. Assessment and treatment of the acutely psychotic schizophrenic patient is especially problematic because the length of inpatient stays is generally limited and careful posthospital follow-up is very difficult at best (Caton 1984). The assumption in this chapter is that the clinician's contact with acutely ill schizophrenic patients is in an inpatient setting, because the vast majority of these individuals ultimately are hospitalized (Gottesman and Shields 1982; Keith et al. 1976). It must be recognized that the need for rapid intervention and disposition in

Preparation of this chapter was supported, in part, by NIMH grant MH-37898 and by the help of Bettie Reynolds, Christine Rowell, Alison Sommers, and Brent In.

psychiatric emergencies often constrains the amount of time available for formal testing. Nevertheless, psychological evaluation can serve as a valuable adjunct to psychiatric care.

THE NATURE OF PSYCHOLOGICAL TESTING

Psychological testing has its roots in the assessment of intellectual functioning, achievement, and personality (Dubois 1970). Traced by some to the "civil service" system of China around 2000 B.C., and molded into its modern form by the demands of World War II, contemporary psychological assessment has, as observed by Newmark (1985, p. 186), ". . . evolved into a complex range of tasks . . . [including] interviewing, observing behavior in structured and unstructured settings, constructing tests, interpreting their results, and analyzing their utilization." We can expect, therefore, that the strength of psychological testing will be in the evaluation of the psychobehavioral mechanisms underlying these broad domains.

Evaluation of Psychological Mechanisms

D. Klein (1978) suggested the development of an extensive roster of psychological functions, such as memory, deductive thinking, and anticipation, on which individual patients could be evaluated. With sufficient normative data, such an assessment could yield a profile of functioning that could reveal the particular weaknesses and strengths of the schizophrenic patient. Ideally, different psychiatric disorders would yield distinctive profiles. There is in fact considerable research being conducted on learning ability and strategies, memory storage, attentional deployment, perception, and sensorimotor responding (Lipton et al. 1983; Nuechterlein and Dawson 1984). This research serves as part of the empirical basis for what has come to be termed neuropsychological assessment. (See Appendix for summary of tests cited in this chapter.)

Although there is as yet no universally adopted battery of neuropsychological tests, the following functions are usually considered to be relevant (Lezak 1976): intellectual ability tests (e.g., Wechsler Adult Intelligence Scale [WAIS]), verbal functions (aphasia, fluency), perceptual functions (e.g., color, recognition, organization, scanning, dichotic listening), visuopractic and manual dexterity, memory (e.g., visual recognition of digits and letters, storage vs. retrieval), cognition (concept formation, ordering, planning, reasoning), orientation, self-regulation, and attention. Because these tests were originally validated on various samples of patients with known neuropathology, it is generally expected that the results of neuropsychological testing can help in localizing existing dysfunctions. However, even in the absence of localizing ability, this type of testing provides an extensive examination of individual systems, information about which can be important, independent of psychiatric diagnosis or determination of brain pathology.

A thorough analysis of a schizophrenic patient's psychological functions can be used to tailor an environment for maximum therapeutic efficacy. For example, a schizophrenic patient who suffers from a memory disturbance (as revealed by testing but not sufficiently gross as to be found upon interviewing) may have difficulty in keeping to his or her medication schedule for reasons other than the impact of motivational factors. Such a patient would benefit from the implementation of systematic memory aids in medication use. Once a clinician begins thinking in this manner, dozens of interventions become possible to begin to compensate for the disrupted functioning found in schizophrenia.

Social Skills Assessment

The primary assessment questions during an acute episode of schizophrenic psychosis are necessarily focused on the more florid, active, positive symptoms. When these symptoms and signs begin to lessen, the schizophrenic patient often exhibits a wide range of characteristics that impede the individual's negotiation with the social environment. For example, inappropriate affect, posturing, bizarre gestures, and nonresponsiveness interfere with the establishment of rapport and social networks.

The application of social skills assessment techniques is particularly useful in addressing these areas of the patient's life (Bellack 1983; Liberman 1982). Relying heavily on behavioral observation and functional assessment, it is possible to obtain a detailed picture of the patient's reinforcers and social interaction skills, including verbal and nonverbal behavior, perception of social cues, problem-solving ability, and capacity for obtaining social and emotional gratification.

Once deficit areas have been determined, targeted social skills training programs can be implemented (Argyle 1981; Holmes et al. 1984; Liberman 1982). These programs are typically embedded in a combination of therapy and education that draws on multiple levels of intervention. Social skills assessment and training are most usefully implemented after the patient has either returned to a prepsychotic level of functioning or established a new level of optimal functioning (see also Chapter 7 of the present volume).

Style and Motivation

Sometimes, especially with respect to treatment disposition, the schizophrenic patient's motivation and premorbid personality are of paramount importance, rather than the absolute level of functioning of a particular psychological system. For example, Matarazzo (1972) points out that a high IQ score on the WAIS does not necessarily indicate a successful adaptation to the environment, because "extra intellective factors," such as emotional immaturity or interpersonal abrasiveness, can seriously interfere with the application of the person's intellectual tools to everyday life. Similarly, mental retardation not only is a matter of formal IQ, but also encompasses interpersonal effectiveness and behavioral success in coping with the physical environment. Exclusive concentration on narrow mechanisms in such cases would result in the serious omission of clinically relevant material. Therefore, a complete assessment of the patient must also include a careful analysis of these sorts of processes.

There are four types of information, not necessarily independent, that a clinician can expect to obtain from a thorough evaluation that takes into account the above processes: (1) cognitive and emotional styles, (2) defense mechanisms, (3) dynamic themes, and (4) developmental level. Projective tests such as the Rorschach and the Thematic Apperception Test (TAT) are used for these purposes. These tests are characterized by sufficient ambiguity of stimulus content, i.e., responses are more influenced by idiosyncratic processes than is the case with, for example, a WAIS question that has a universally correct response.

How the individual approaches testing, including any affect that is stimulated, is a useful clue to cognitive style (e.g., Shapiro 1954). Defense mechanisms are often inferred from the formal characteristics of Rorschach and TAT responses, while content analysis of TAT stories yields insight into dynamic themes. The nature of the defense mechanisms and the adequacy and stability of reality testing reflect developmental level.

PSYCHOLOGICAL TESTING AND THE DIAGNOSIS OF SCHIZOPHRENIA

In general, psychological testing will be of limited usefulness for the purpose of making formal DSM-III-R diagnoses. First, referral questions are most frequently addressed to differential diagnosis (e.g., schizophrenia vs. organic disorder and bipolar illness vs. schizophrenia). Despite reasonable success in differentiating schizophrenic patients from nonpsychiatric, neurological controls and "neurotic" patients on numerous tests, our ability to distinguish among schizophrenia, psychotic affective disorders, and neurological disorders is modest at best, especially when testing patients with a high school-level education or less (e.g., Graca et al. 1984; Hellkamp and Hogan 1985; Holland et al. 1981; Malec 1978; Moses et al. 1983; Roy 1984; Trifiletti 1982; Watson 1984; Watson et al. 1968, 1981). All such patient groups tend to do poorly, and irrespective of the quality of the testing data gathered, there are no critical tests for distinguishing among these different forms of severe psychopathology.

Furthermore, because virtually all psychological tests with pretensions to diagnostic utility are validated against standard clinical diagnoses made by psychiatric staff using traditional interview techniques, and because none reach 100% "accuracy" (i.e., concordance with clinical diagnoses), all must fall short to varying degrees. As long as psychological testing is validated against standard interview-based psychiatric diagnoses, use of the interview for diagnosis will continue to be the most appropriate strategy. Attempts to develop a psychologically based diagnostic system have been largely unsuccessful (McClemore and Benjamin 1979). Finally, even those instruments such as the Minnesota Multiphasic Personality Inventory (MMPI) that have demonstrated acceptable utility in the past have only been validated against DSM-II criteria and now require revalidation against DSM-III-R criteria (Johnson et al. 1980).

Consider one of the most likely circumstances in which the clinician requests psychological testing for an acutely psychotic patient: when there is insufficient information for making a diagnosis on the basis of the clinical interviews. Failure to obtain the necessary information may be due to factors such as hostility, mutism, incoherence, tangentiality, and severe attentional problems. Such factors also interfere with psychological testing. Psychological testing cannot compensate for the serious problems in communication that accompany acute schizophrenia. In most instances, when the patient is well enough to test, he is also well enough to interview. The decision to subject a patient to extensive psychological testing during an acute psychotic episode should be weighted by the quality of the test results, which are affected by the disorder itself, and by the costs in professional time and patient discomfort.

The various perceptual and cognitive aspects of the psychopathology of schizophrenia that interfere with cooperation make suspect the individual's ability to serve as an accurate reporter of his or her own internal state or to engage in performance tasks not seriously distorted by extraneous factors. It is for this very reason that clinical inference is often necessary, both in interviewing and in testing. The clinician must constantly decide about the accuracy, truthfulness, and completeness of the patient's report; the patient's responses often require interpretation as to personal significance. This means that the referring clinician must ultimately have confidence in the individual interpreting the test results, because the tests by themselves are often constrained by the quality of the patient's participation in testing. For example, consider a patient who fails to correctly solve block designs, a perceptuomotor task, on the WAIS. The patient could be distracted by voices, attach some idiosyncratic meaning to the blocks, experience high levels of anxiety, have a perceptuomotor problem, be unmotivated, be hostile, or suffer medication side effects. The test interpreter's task is to use as much information as possible to select the best hypothesis to account for the performance; the hypothesis does not necessarily inhere in the test itself.

Even psychological testing that attempts to circumvent the need for clinical inference by using empirical relationships between questionnaire responses and a priori groups (actuarial tests) is vulnerable to these same sorts of obstacles because it relies on the patient's response being valid. The more disturbed the patient, the more likely it is that such testing (e.g., the MMPI) will yield invalid profiles.

There are occasions when testing may be less threatening to a patient than interviewing and therefore indicated even if interviewing is possible. Lewine (1978) has reviewed evidence suggesting that paranoid schizophrenic patients' experimental test behavior is adversely affected when another person is physically present. He interpreted this finding as consistent with the paranoid's social guardedness. Extending this hypothesis to test-taking in general, the clinician might want to consider a self-report measure of psychopathology (such as the MMPI) to assess this sort of individual, because a somewhat more honest picture may emerge than in a face-to-face interview. Psychological testing might, in this type of situation, yield more information more quickly than standard interviewing.

Systematic Behavioral Observations

When testing and interviewing of psychotic patients are difficult, it can be helpful to engage in systematic behavioral observation with instruments such as the Nurses' Observational Scale for Inpatient Evaluation (NOSIE) (Honigfeld et al. 1966), and the Psychotic Reaction Profile (PRP) (Lorr et al. 1961). These rating scales formalize and quantify common clinical observations. For example, the NOSIE has 30 items (such as "shows interest in activities around him," "keeps clothes neat," "starts a conversation with others," and "has difficulty completing tasks on his own") reflecting everyday behavior, most of which are easily observable during the course of a typical day in an inpatient unit. Combining the items into six major areas—social competence, social interest, personal neatness, irritability, manifest psychosis, and retardation—the clinician can systematically track the behavioral profiles generated by the NOSIE on a weekly basis to fine-tune treatment.

The Referral Question

It is not uncommon for a clinician to request psychological testing to "rule out Organic Disorder," "rule out Psychosis," or "rule out Affective Disorder" when assessing the acutely ill schizophrenic patient, despite differential diagnosis not being the forte of psychological testing. Another set of questions the clinician is likely to ask centers around aggression and suicide. While psychological test data may provide some insight into a person's style (e.g., impulsive vs. overly controlled), characteristic defenses (e.g., denial, projection, intellectualization), presence or absence of psychosis, and general capability, the actual prediction of rare events such as suicide and homicide is based most reliably on previous behavior (Meehl and Rosen 1955). That is, if the clinician wants to know what the patient is likely to do in the future, that patient's past behavior, especially as interpreted within appropriate sociodemographic referent groups, is still the best predictor. For example, to estimate a depressed patient's chances of suicide, evidence of previous attempts weighted by age, sex, and degree and type of stress will be as predictive as or more predictive than psychological test findings.

The two conditions under which psychological assessment will prove most useful involve those patients who require systematic, standardized behavioral observation and those who require systematic assessment of specific functions and the motivational variables that affect these functions. In either case, the referral should ask specific, substantive questions: Is the patient's memory sufficiently intact to entrust him or her with keeping his or her medication schedule? If not, what memory aids would be appropriate? What are likely to be the primary interpersonal conflicts preventing the patient's accepting therapy? How long and under what conditions can we expect the patient to function at his or her maximum intellectual level? What psychosocial factors can we expect will exacerbate the patient's thought disorder, and what can be instituted to counteract them? What milieu conditions minimize anxiety?

While these sorts of questions cannot always be answered with certainty, the careful analysis of circumscribed functioning will provide a useful map by which to guide intervention as suggested above. It is in this context that a baseline (ideally premorbid) assessment would prove most useful in working with a patient over time; specifically, what is needed is a profile of the patient's optimal level of functioning. Systematic appraisal of the patient's status might then reveal subtle, yet meaningful changes in functioning that could lead to the prevention of more serious clinical disturbance. It has been emphasized that even subtle change may be a powerful predictor of psychopathology (Lewine 1984; Ricks 1980). Psychological testing provides the tools to monitor rigorously such changes in order better to implement treatment, monitor progress, and ultimately understand schizophrenia.

REFERENCES

Argyle M: The contribution of social interaction research to social skills training, in Social Competence. Edited by Wine JD, Smye MO. New York, Guilford, 1981, pp 261–286

Bellack A: Recurrent problems in the behavioral assessment of social skill. Behav Res Ther 21:29–42, 1983

Buros O: The Eighth Mental Measurements Yearbook. Highland Park, NJ, Gryphon Press, 1978

Caton C: Management of Chronic Schizophrenia. New York, Oxford University Press, 1984

Dubois P: A History of Psychological Testing. Boston, MA, Allyn and Bacon, Inc, 1970

Exner J: The Rorschach. A Comprehensive System. New York, Wiley and Sons, 1974

Exner J: The Rorschach. A Comprehensive System, Vol 2, Current Research and Advanced Interpretations. New York, Wiley and Sons, 1978

Goldstein G, Hersen N: Handbook of Psychological Assessment. New York, Pergamon Press, 1984

Gottesman I, Shields J: Schizophrenia. The Epigenetic Puzzle. Cambridge, UK, Cambridge University Press, 1982

Graca J, Hutzell R, Gaffney J, et al: A comparison of the effectiveness of MMPI indices in the discrimination of brain-damaged and schizophrenic patients. J Clin Psychol 40:422–431, 1984

Hellkamp D, Hogan M: Differentiation of organics from functional psychiatric patients across various IQ ranges using the Bender-Gestalt and Hutt Scoring System. J Clin Psychol 41:259–264, 1985

Holland T, Levi M, Watson C: MMPI basic scales vs two-point codes in the discrimination of psychopathological groups. J Clin Psychol 27:394–396, 1981

Holmes M, Hansen D, Lawrence J: Conversational skills training with aftercare patients in the community: social validity and generalization. Behav Ther 15:84–100, 1984

Honigfeld G, Gillis R, Klett J: NOSIE-30: a treatment sensitive ward behavior scale. Psychol Rep 19:180–182, 1966

Johnson J, Klingler D, Gianetti R: Band width in diagnostic classification using MMPI as predictor. J Consult Clin Psychol 48:340–349, 1980

Keith S, Gunderson J, Reifman A, et al: Special report: schizophrenia 1976. Schizophr Bull 2:509–565, 1976

Klein D: A proposed definition of mental illness, in Critical Issues in Psychiatric Diagnosis. Edited by Spitzer R, Klein D. New York, Raven Press, 1978

Korchin S: Modern clinical psychology. Principles of intervention, in The Clinic and Community. New York, Basic Books, 1976

Lewine R: Response complexity and social interaction in the psychophysical testing of chronic and paranoid schizophrenics. Psychol Bull 85:284–294, 1978

Lewine R: Stalking the schizophrenia marker: evidence for a general vulnerability model of psychopathology, in Children at Risk for Schizophrenia: A Longitudinal Perspective. Edited by Watt N, Anthony E, Wynne L, Rolf J. Cambridge, UK, Cambridge University Press, 1984, pp 545–550

Lezak M: Neuropsychological Assessment. New York, Oxford University Press, 1976

Liberman R: Assessment of social skills. Schizophr Bull 8:62–83, 1982

Lipton R, Levy D, Holzman P, et al: Eye movement dysfunctions in psychiatric patients. Schizophr Bull 9:13–32, 1983

Lorr M, O'Connor J, Stafford J: The Psychotic Patient Profile. Los Angeles, CA, Western Psychological Services, 1961

Malec J: Neuropsychological assessment of schizophrenia versus brain damage: a review. J Nerv Ment Dis 166:507–516, 1978

Matarazzo J: Wechsler's Measurement and Appraisal of Adult Intelligence. Baltimore, MD, Williams and Wilkins, 1972

McClemore C, Benjamin L: Whatever happened to interpersonal diagnosis? A psychosocial alternative to DSM-III. Am Psychol 34:17–34, 1979

Meehl P, Rosen A: Antecedent probability and the efficiency of psychometric signs, patterns or cutting scores. Psychol Bull 52:194–216, 1955

Moses J, Cardellino J, Thompson J: Discrimination of brain damage from chronic psychosis by the Luria-Nebraska Neuropsychological battery: a closer look. J Consult Clin Psychol 51:441–449, 1983

Newmark C: Psychological assessment: a bird's-eye view. Contemp Psychiatry 4:186–187, 1985

Nuechterlein K, Dawson M: Information processing and attentional functioning in the developmental course of schizophrenic disorders. Schizophr Bull 10:160–203, 1984

Prifitera A, Ryan J: WAIS-R/WAIS comparisons in a clinical sample. Clin Neuropsychol 1983

Reitan R: Manual for administration of neuropsychological test batteries for adults and children. Tucson, AZ, Reitan Neuropsychological Laboratories, 1979

Ricks D: Discussion of Watt-Prentley-Lewine-Fryer paper, in Human Functioning in Longitudinal Perspective. Edited by Sells SB, Crandall R, Roff M, et al. Baltimore, MD, Williams & Wilkins, 1980, pp 29–31

Roy R: The Goldberg Neuroticpsychotic rule and MMPI 2-7-8 patients. J Pers Assess 48:398–402, 1984

Shapiro D: Neurotic Styles. New York, Basic Books, 1954

Trifiletti R: Differentiating brain damage from schizophrenia: a further test of Russell's MMPI key. J Clin Psychol 38:39–44, 1982

Watson C: The schizophrenia-organicity (Sc-O) and psychiatric-organic (P-O) MMPI scales: a review. J Clin Psychol 40:1008–1023, 1984

Watson C, Thomas R, Andersen D, et al: Differentiation of organics from schizophrenics at two chronicity levels by use of the Reitan-Halstead Organic test battery. J Consult Clin Psychol 32:679–684, 1968

Watson C, Gasser B, Schaeffer A, et al: Separation of brain-damaged from psychiatric patients with ability and personality measures. J Clin Psychol 37:347–353, 1981

APPENDIX

SUMMARY OF SELECTED PSYCHOLOGICAL TESTS CITED IN TEXT

Intellectual Functioning

Wechsler Adult Intelligence Scale (WAIS). Appropriate for ages above 16, the WAIS measures intellectual functioning in two broad areas: verbal and performance. The Verbal Scale is made up of Information, Comprehension, Arithmetic, Similarities, Digit Span, and Vocabulary subtests; the Performance Scale consists of Digit Symbol, Picture Completion, Block Design, Picture Arrangement, and Object Assembly subtests. Scale scores are interpreted with respect to appropriate age and sex norms to estimate an individual's general intelligence.

Just as importantly, the patterns of subtest scores are bases for making inferences about deterioration, psychopathology, and neurological disorder, especially as these conditions affect logical reasoning. This latter use of the WAIS should be considered a means of generating hypotheses to be confirmed or disconfirmed by more rigorous testing.

Originally published in 1955, the WAIS has been revised (WAIS-R) to rectify sociocultural biases in the original version. The two forms (WAIS and WAIS-R), although not interchangeable, are quite comparable in the relative scores they yield, with correlations of .74 to .96 for the various subscales. The WAIS-R also consistently yields lower (on the order of 7 points) IQ estimates than the WAIS (Prifitera and Ryan 1983).

Intelligence testing in children is generally conducted with the Wechsler Intelligence Scale for Children (WISC, for ages 6 to 16) and the Wechsler Preschool-Primary Scale (WPPS, for ages 4 to 6 1/2). Intellectual functioning below the age of 4 not only is difficult, but also has only modest power in predicting adult intelligence.

Neuropsychological Functioning

Neuropsychological testing is also conceptualized by many as tapping intellectual functioning, if somewhat more broadly defined. Current neuropsychological testing batteries are actually a selected group of cognitive, perceptual, and motor tasks adopted from experimental psychology. Two major controversies regarding the use of such batteries are the degree to which localization of dysfunction can be determined and the discriminative validity, particularly among neurological patients, poorly educated individuals, and patients with severe psychopathology. Until these issues are resolved, therefore, it is prudent to use neuropsychological testing as only one source of information for making a differential diagnosis in these populations. Although there is not, as yet, a single commonly accepted battery for neuropsychological testing, there are two that have received considerable attention.

Halstead-Reitan. The complete Halstead-Reitan battery is actually composed of three separate batteries: the Wechsler-Bellevue Scale (a predecessor of the WAIS and WAIS-R, for which many testers now substitute either of the latter two tests), the Minnesota Multiphasic Personality Inventory (MMPI) (a modification of the Halstead-Wepman Aphasia Screening Test, a group of sensory-perceptual tests), and the Halstead Neuropsychological Test Battery (frequently what many people mean when they refer to the "Halstead-Reitan"). These batteries, which were selected to sample a broad range of behavior relevant to the assessment of the effects of brain lesions, include "sensory perceptual and motor tasks, psychomotor problem-solving procedures, and higher level psychological functions relating to the symbolic and communicational aspects of language, the ability to deal effectively with visuospatial relationships in manipulatory types of problems, and abstraction and concept function" (Reitan 1979, p. 3).

The Halstead Neuropsychological Battery originally included 27 tests, of which the following are now popularly used: Category Test (concept formation); Tactual Performance Test—Time, Memory and Localization (tactile form discrimination, motor coordination, visualization of shapes, kinesthesis); Rhythm Test (sustained attention, alertness, perception of rhythmic sequences); Finger Oscillation (motor speed); Time Sense Test—Visual and Memory (attention, reaction time, memory, visuomotor coordination); and Critical Flicker Frequency and Deviation (visual acuity and integration).

The sensory-perceptual tasks include Trail Making Test, Sensory Imperception, Tactile Finger Recognition, Finger Tip Number Writing, Tactile Form Recognition, and Handgrip Strength. In addition, lateral dominance (handedness, eyedness, and footedness) is assessed.

The scores from the various tests can be used individually in a profile analysis or the 10 tests of the Reitan can be summed to form the Halstead Impairment Index. This index is the sum of the number of tests on which the individual's score falls in the range of scores exhibited by a standard group of brain-damaged patients. As emphasized in both texts and manuals, no single subtest or even summary score is adequate for determining the presence of brain-damage; the entire performance must be considered in making such judgments.

Order of test administration and scoring have been standardized. Most nonpsychiatric patients and normal controls can complete the entire assessment in a single day. Similar batteries are available for testing children aged 5–8 and 9–14.

Luria-Nebraska Neuropsychological Battery (LNNB). Although there is considerable overlap in specific test items between the LNNB and the Halstead-Reitan, one of the primary differences between the two is the sheer number of tests, with the LNNB having considerably less. In contrast to the 21 individual subtest scores on the Halstead-Reitan (excluding the WAIS and the MMPI), the LNNB yields 11 subtest scores: Motor, Rhythm, Tactile, Visual, Receptive Speech, Expressive Speech, Writing, Reading, Arithmetic, Memory, and Intellectual. Summary scores purportedly pathognomonic of organic disorder and reflecting location (lateralization) of disorder are calculated on the basis of these scores.

The LNNB has been severely criticized for having failed to achieve adequate validity and for making overstated claims of diagnostic accuracy. Given its brevity (in comparison to the Halstead-Reitan), and therefore its considerable savings in time and expense, the LNNB continues to receive research and clinical attention as a potentially viable neuropsychological battery.

Personality Tests

The Rorschach Test. Emerging from a psychoanalytic framework, the Rorschach consists of 10 symmetrical inkblots varying in shape, shading, and color. The inkblots are shown one at a time, in order, and the individual being assessed is asked to report what he or she sees. Following exposure to the complete series, an "inquiry" is conducted, during which the person locates the percepts, clarifies what he or she saw, and explains why the percept looks as it does.

There have been numerous formal scoring systems proposed since Rorschach introduced his text in 1921. Of these, the most rigorously studied and empirically valid is Exner's (1974, 1978) system, which is a compilation and modification of the best elements of the major systems preceding his. As emphasized by Exner, the Rorschach is most useful as a means of attaining a detailed description of an individual's affectivity, response style, motivations, cognitive style, preoccupations, and interpersonal perceptions and response tendencies.

Thematic Apperception Test (TAT). The TAT was originally developed to study motivation in normal personalities, and while it continues to hold a prominent role in this area, it has also gained wide acceptance in the assessment of psychopathology. There are 31 cards, one of which is blank, the remainder depicting interpersonal events or scenes. In practice, only a subset (usually less than 20 and often as few as 10) of cards are used, the selection of which is intended to focus on particular themes chosen by the testing psychologist. The task is to tell as complete and dramatic a story as possible in response to each card.

Although formal scoring systems have been proposed over the years, most clinicians use the TAT stories as raw clinical material from which dynamic themes are deduced. Themes include achievement motivation, sex, aggression, need achievement, and dependency. In addition to content, the structure of the TAT stories provides insight into personality. That is, how the stories are told can be very informative: clearly vs. vaguely, dully vs. interestingly, creatively vs. mundanely, impulsively vs. deliberately, etc.

Minnesota Multiphasic Personality Inventory (MMPI). Originally developed as an aid to psychiatric diagnosis, the MMPI gets considerable use in personality research and assessment. Composed of 550 self-report items ("True," "False," "?"), it is actuarily based. In other words, the items that characterize the various personalities or diagnoses were selected on a strictly empirical basis. A priori defined groups were contrasted on a large number of items; those items that discriminated the criterion groups were retained in the final version.

Ten clinical scales are derived from the 550 items: hypochondriasis, depression, hysteria, psychopathic deviate, masculinity-femininity, paranoia, psychasthenia, schizophrenia, hypomania, and social introversion. Four validity scales reflect the number of items marked "cannot say" (Question Scale), responder's frankness (Lie Scale), attempts to deceive, scoring errors, and carelessness (Validity Scale), and defensiveness of "faking good" (Correction Score).

The diagnoses used in validating the original instrument were based on DSM-II; therefore, the MMPI should be used cautiously until revalidation with DSM-III-R criteria is adequate.

Behavior Observation

Nurses' Observational Scale for In-patient Evaluation (NOSIE). This instrument quantifies everyday observations such as "Is sloppy," "Refuses to speak," and "Talks about his interests," usually for a designated 3-day period. Although usually filled out by nurses, there is nothing to prevent other personnel who have daily contact with the patient from using this rating form.

The items are combined into six scales: Social Competence, Social Interest, Personal Neatness, Irritability, Manifest Psychosis, and Retardation. This behavioral profile has proven to be quite useful in monitoring medication as well as in designating target areas for other sorts of intervention.

Psychotic Reaction Profile (PRP). In many respects the PRP is an expanded NOSIE. Its 85 items quantify similar observable behaviors such as "Usually stays by himself," "Resists suggestions and requests from aides," and "Talk is mostly not sensible." The observing clinician marks each item as either "True" or "Not True," and items are weighted for one of four scales: "Withdrawn," "Thought Disorder," "Paranoid," and "Agitated." Like the NOSIE, the PRP is rated for a 3-day period; but unlike the NOSIE, it emphasizes psychotic behavior. Thus, one might consider the PRP for the monitoring of psychosis and the NOSIE for the monitoring of more broad-based behavior.

Chapter 4

PHARMACOLOGICAL TREATMENT

Ross J. Baldessarini, M.D.
Bruce M. Cohen, M.D., Ph.D.
Martin H. Teicher, M.D., Ph.D.

THE INTRODUCTION OF MODERN psychopharmacological therapy in the 1950s was associated with revolutionary changes in the practice and theory of psychiatry (Baldessarini 1984, 1985). Antipsychotic agents have led to approximately six-fold reductions in the number of patients in public psychiatric hospitals. The use of these agents permits the rapid treatment and rehabilitation of many patients who formerly would have been hospitalized for long periods, encountered prolonged or life-long disability, and suffered relatively high rates of fatality from suicide and medical illnesses. These agents have encouraged dramatic changes in the nature of psychiatric inpatient wards, many of which are now commonly unlocked, located in general hospitals and local community-based centers, and operating with relatively brief median durations of stay.

At the same time, a number of problems and limitations of antipsychotic drug treatment have become increasingly clear. Almost by definition, patients with chronic forms of psychosis re-

This work was supported, in part, by U.S. Public Health Service (NIMH) awards and grants MH-47370, MH-31154, MH-38313, and MH-36224, and by a grant from the MacArthur Foundation. Some portions of this chapter are adapted from material in publications cited in the text. The manuscript was prepared by Mrs. Mila Cason.

spond least satisfactorily to drugs and other treatments. Whereas the short-term effects of antipsychotic drugs are dramatic in acute psychoses and mania, the optimal role of these drugs in long-term treatment of patients with psychiatric disorders other than schizophrenia remains a matter of investigation. All of these groups are at risk of late neurological complications associated with prolonged use of these agents.

In addition to their uncertain benefits in some conditions, the antipsychotic agents induce characteristic forms of immediate and late neurological side effects or toxicity. The very term *neuroleptic* (affecting the nervous system), commonly applied to this class of psychotropic drugs, implies that these agents induce signs resembling neurological disorders, especially of the extrapyramidal system that controls posture and involuntary movement.

These problems and limitations have encouraged thoughtful and critical reappraisal of the clinical applications of available agents as well as a vigorous search for novel agents that might be more selectively antipsychotic and less likely to induce neurological toxicity (Baldessarini 1985; Cohen and Lipinski 1986). Such treatment requires care to assure optimal efficacy and safety. Nevertheless, at present, the neuroleptic agents remain the cornerstone of treatment of psychotic patients.

AVAILABLE ANTIPSYCHOTIC AGENTS AND THEIR INDICATIONS

The antipsychotic drugs in current clinical use in the United States include phenothiazine derivatives with aliphatic and heterocyclic side chains, as well as their thioxanthene analogs. Some structurally dissimilar agents, including the butyrophenones and their diphenylbutylpiperidine analogs, the dibenzazepines, and the indolones, are also used. *Rauwolfia* alkaloids, especially reserpine, were formerly used in high doses to treat psychosis in the 1950s, but their side effects and their possibly limited efficacy relegate them largely to historical interest. The antipsychotic agents currently employed in the United States and their approximate relative potencies are summarized in Table 1.

Even though these drugs are chemically dissimilar, they are quite similar pharmacologically and may share common active structural components ("pharmacophores") (Baldessarini 1985). Almost all of these agents are effective antagonists of dopamine receptors (especially those receptors not associated with the stimulation of adenylate cyclase and referred to as type D-2). Exceptions are reserpine (an amine-depleting agent) and clozapine (an experimental atypical antipsychotic agent with complex actions, weak antidopaminergic and relatively strong antiadrenergic and anticholinergic effects, and a low risk of extrapyramidal side effects). The agents in Table 1 have all been found to be approximately equally effective in treating acute episodes of psychosis, including exacerbations of schizophrenia. (A few agents that have proved to be clinically inferior over the years are not included in Table 1 [see footnote to table] because they are rarely employed at the present time.) The future of the atypical agent clozapine and its congeners remains uncertain because of their association with a relatively high risk of bone marrow suppression and, occasionally, agranulocytosis; the risk:benefit ratio for clozapine may be adequate for use in patients who have responded poorly to other treatments or who have both psychosis and dyskinesia.

The striking pharmacological similarity of these drugs is neither accidental nor coincidental, nor is it convincing evidence that the antidopaminergic activity they share is a uniquely required means to achieve antipsychotic efficacy. (On the other hand, there is as yet no compelling alternative hypothesis concerning antipsychotic actions of available agents other than that they exert antidopaminergic actions in behaviorally crucial cortical and subcortical components of the limbic system and the hypothalamus.) The similarity of these drugs as central antidopaminergic agents arises from a process of pharmaceutical development that has selected agents for clinical study that have behavioral or biochemical actions resembling previously established compounds, such as chlorpromazine. Screening tests for antipsychotic agents almost always have relied on observing antidopaminergic behavioral effects or biochemical actions in brain tissue of laboratory animals. The advent of atypical agents, such as clozapine and its congeners, gives hope that new principles of antipsychotic activity might evolve. However, all the antipsychotic agents now in common clinical use in American medicine (Table 1) to some extent cause side effects via the extrapyramidal nervous system.

Neuroleptic drugs have a broad range of indications among psychotic (and some neuropsychiatric and medical) disorders (see Table 2). It is not correct to consider these drugs either anxiolytic "tranquilizers" or specifically "antischizophrenic" agents. They are inferior antianxiety agents, and can even induce or worsen anxiety by inducing subjective and motor restlessness, termed *akathisia*. Their antipsychotic efficacy is *least* readily demonstrated in chronic idiopathic psychoses (e.g., schizophrenia). The research literature that supports the many possible indications summarized

Table 1. Approximately equivalent doses of commonly used antipsychotic agents by chemical type

Generic name	Commercial name	Approximately equivalent dose (mg)	Relative potency
Phenothiazines			
Aliphatic agents			
Chlorpromazine	Thorazine, etc.[a]	100	Low
Triflupromazine	Vesprin	30	Low
Piperidines			
Mesoridazine	Serentil	50	Low
Thioridazine	Mellaril, etc.[a]	90–100	Low
Piperazines			
Acetophenazine	Tindal	15	Intermediate
Perphenazine	Trilafon	10	Intermediate
Trifluoperazine	Stelazine	3	High
Fluphenazine	Prolixin, Permitil	2–2.5	High
Thioxanthenes			
Aliphatic agent			
Chlorprothixene	Taractan	75	Low
Piperazine			
Thiothixene	Navane	3–4	High
Dibenzazepines			
Clozapine	(Clozaril)[b]	150	Low
Loxapine	Loxitane, Daxolin	10–15	Intermediate
Butyrophenones			
Haloperidol	Haldol	2–2.5	High
Droperidol	Inapsine[c]	1–2	High

Diphenylbutylpiperidine			
Pimozide	Orap	1–2	High
Indolone			
Molindone	Moban, Lidone	8–10	Intermediate

[a]Generic. [b]Experimental. [c]For injection.

Note. Many other agents used elsewhere are not available in the United States. The commercial preparations are available as soluble salts (most are hydrochlorides; Loxitane or Daxolin is a succinate; Tindal is a maleate; Serentil is a benzylate). Other agents not commonly used now or those that are less effective in the treatment of psychoses are not included; for example, butaperazine (Repoise), carphenazine (Proketazine), mepazine (Pacatal), promazine (Sparine), piperacetazine (Quide), and thiopropazate (Dartal). Evidence of the efficacy of some newer agents, such as molindone and loxapine, is not as abundant as for older agents. Droperidol (Inapsine) is an extremely potent, short-acting neuroleptic, now used mainly as a preanesthetic or coanesthetic agent by intramuscular or intravenous injection, although it has powerful antipsychotic–sedative effects that can be useful in psychiatric emergencies. Pimozide (Orap) is a potent anti-psychotic agent currently recommended for Gilles de la Tourette syndrome. In addition, prochlorperazine (Compazine) and thiethylperazine (Torecan), while having typical neuroleptic effects (and probably antipsychotic effects in adequate doses), are mainly used as antiemetic agents. Prochlorperazine carries a high risk of dystonic reactions at antipsychotic doses. Reserpine (Serpasil and generic) and other amine-depleting agents, although inferior antipsychotic drugs, are sometimes used in the management of tardive dyskinesia or akathisia. Although the tabulated drugs vary by more than 100-fold in *potency*, they are similar in clinical *efficacy*.

Data concerning equivalent doses are averages from several sources, some of which vary greatly. These numbers are only an approximate guide, and dosage for each patient must be established by clinical response. In switching from high doses of one agent to those of a dissimilar one, it is wise to proceed gradually over several days to decrease the risk of side effects from the newly introduced drug. These equivalent doses are *not necessarily therapeutic doses* (which are typically several times higher in the treatment of acutely psychotic patients).

Injectable fluphenazine esters are commonly used in doses of 12.5–50 mg intramuscularly every 1 to 4 weeks. The enanthate (derived from a seven-carbon fatty acid) typically acts for 2 weeks, and the currently more popular decanoate (ester of a 12-carbon aliphatic carboxylic acid) for about 3 weeks. As an approximate equivalence, 25 mg (2 ml) of intramuscular fluphenazine decanoate every 2 to 3 weeks resembles in effectiveness about 5–10 mg of fluphenazine HCl (orally) per day (or 200–500 mg of chlorpromazine). The decanoate ester of haloperidol is given every 3 or 4 weeks in intramuscular doses of about 10 to 20 times the daily oral dose.

Source. This material is adapted from tables presented elsewhere (Baldessarini 1984, 1985).

Table 2. Indications for clinical use of neuroleptics

A. Short-term
- Acute psychotic episodes, regardless of type
- Exacerbations of schizophrenia
- Acute manic excitement while deferring use of lithium or awaiting onset of its effects
- Adjunctive therapy for major depression with prominent psychotic symptoms, or when an antidepressant or ECT alone is not successful
- For agitation in delirium, dementia, or severe mental retardation while seeking to identify and treat the primary basis of the problem
- In certain chronic, degenerative, or idiopathic neuropsychiatric disorders with dyskinesias, such as Huntington's disease or Gilles de la Tourette syndrome; or for ballism or hemiballism
- Childhood psychoses or apparently allied conditions marked by severe agitation or aggressive behavior
- Miscellaneous medical indications, notably nausea and vomiting, or intractable hiccups

B. Long-term

Primary indications
- Schizophrenia
- Some degenerative or idiopathic neuropsychiatric disorders (notably, Huntington's disease and Gilles de la Tourette syndrome)
- Childhood psychoses
- Paranoia[a]

Secondary indications
- Otherwise unmanageable, extremely unstable affective (manic-depressive) or other episodic psychoses (unusual)[a]
- Otherwise unmanageable behavior symptoms in dementia, mental retardation, or other brain syndromes[a]

Questionable indications
- Chronic characterological disorders with schizotypal, "borderline," or neurotic characteristics; substance abuse; or antisocial behavior[a]
- Recurrent mood disorder[a]

[a]Efficacy has not been adequately demonstrated in controlled studies, and long-term neurological safety has not been demonstrated.

Note. There may be times when a neuroleptic drug is used in the short-term management of exacerbations and crises of the chronic or recurrent conditions outlined above in section B. Moreover, there may be justification for prolonged use based on clinical judgment in individual cases and objective demonstration of important benefits not achieved otherwise.

in Table 2 is highly variable in quality and quantity (Baldessarini 1985; Baldessarini et al. 1980). Most reports have considered patients with a variety of unclearly defined acute psychoses, or with a collection of diagnostically heterogeneous disorders sometimes called "schizophrenia" but undoubtedly including episodic psychoses of various types, as well as some cases of severe, recurrent affective disorders, personality disorders, "neuroses," dementia, mental retardation, and other neuropsychiatric conditions. Despite the lack of consistent, well-designed, controlled research studies employing contemporary diagnostic criteria, there has been sufficient clinical experience with these agents to support the short-term indications and most of the prolonged uses of antipsychotic agents detailed in Table 2.

Additional impressions arising from research and clinical experience concerning the utility of antipsychotic agents are of clinical interest (Baldessarini 1984, 1985; Baldessarini et al. 1980). No agent has proved to be more effective than the original neuroleptic, chlorpromazine (Baldessarini 1985; Appleton and Davis 1980). There is no compelling evidence that one neuroleptic is more likely than another to be of benefit for treatment of a specific psychotic syndrome in groups of similar patients even though individual patients may seem to do best when given a particular agent (Baldessarini 1985; Platz et al. 1967; Galbrecht and Klett 1968). That is, the *average* clinical outcomes in studies employing sedating low-potency agents (such as chlorpromazine or thioridazine) or high-potency agents (such as a piperazine phenothiazine or thioxanthene, or a butyrophenone) cannot be distinguished (Baldessarini 1985; Appleton and Davis 1980). Moreover, random assignment of either type of agent to groups of patients with psychotic illnesses marked by agitation, excitement, and florid hallucinations, or to those with quiet, withdrawn, and autistic conditions, has also shown

---

Clinical research has not yet provided compelling support for long-term uses in cases other than chronic schizophrenia; nor has it provided evidence that such uses are contraindicated (although there is an emerging impression that risk of tardive dyskinesia may be greater in major affective disorders than in schizophrenia). Clinicians are left to rely on their evaluations of individual patients and on clinical experience as additional research data are assessed. Thus, the recommendations provided above are tentative and based on an attempt to balance the available research literature and clinical experience.

Source. This table is modified from material presented elsewhere (Baldessarini 1985; Baldessarini et al. 1980).

no consistent average difference in efficacy (Platz et al. 1967; Galbrecht and Klett 1968). Nevertheless, it is reasonable to employ the various neuroleptic agents in a commonsense manner by paying attention to their characteristic side effects (sedation and autonomic effects, as well as extrapyramidal toxicity for low-potency agents and prominent extrapyramidal effects for high-potency agents). For example, one can use a relatively sedating agent to treat an otherwise healthy and vigorous manic or excited psychotic patient and use small doses of a high-potency agent to treat a withdrawn autistic patient or a frail elderly demented patient, even though both types of agents are likely to be similarly effective. There is rarely any advantage to mixing different neuroleptic agents, such as using a high-potency agent during the day and a low-potency agent for night-time sedation and sleep.

Recent surveys of clinical practices indicate that older, low-potency neuroleptics, such as chlorpromazine and thioridazine, are still among the most commonly prescribed in the United States, while high-potency agents (notably, haloperidol, fluphenazine, trifluoperazine, thiothixine, and perphenazine) are increasingly becoming popular (Baldessarini et al. 1984). Neuroleptics differ by three- to five-fold in price (several are now available in generic form). Use of a larger unit dose (mg/tablet) is usually more economical.

DOSE-EFFECT RELATIONSHIPS IN ACUTE PSYCHOSIS

In recent years there has been great interest in selecting optimal doses of an antipsychotic agent so as to maximize clinical benefit and minimize neurological and other side effects. This interest has been encouraged by a high level of concern about the frequency and clinical importance of neurological side effects of antipsychotic agents, as well as the occasional difficulty in distinguishing such reactions from the illness being treated (Baldessarini 1984; Baldessarini et al. 1980, 1988). A summary of the salient features of such neurological side effects of neuroleptic agents is given in Table 3.

Studies of dose-effect relationships in the clinical treatment of psychotic patients are remarkably limited in number and variable in the quality of their design. Impressions concerning the relative potencies of antipsychotic agents, as summarized in Table 1, arise by analogy to behavioral dose-response studies in animals. Impressions also arise from clinical trials in which groups of psychotic patients received different mean doses. However, most of these trials have permitted flexible, poorly controlled dosing. It is very

Table 3. Neurological side effects of neuroleptic–antipsychotic agents

Reaction	Features	Period of maximum risk	Proposed mechanism	Treatment
Acute dystonia	Spasm of muscles of tongue, pharynx, face, neck, back; may mimic seizures; *not* hysteria; terrifying; rare fatalities	1–5 days	Dopamine excess? Acetylcholine excess?	Antiparkinsonism agents are diagnostic and curative (im or iv, then po)
Parkinsonism	Bradykinesia, rigidity, variable tremor, mask-like facies, shuffling gait	5–30 days (may persist)	Dopamine blockade	Antiparkinsonism agents (po); dopamine agonists risky?
Akathisia	Motor restlessness; patient experiences severe anxiety or agitation	5–60 days (commonly persists)	Adrenergic excess?	Reduce dose or change drug; moderate doses of propranolol; antiparkinsonism agents or benzodiazepines may help
Malignant syndrome	Catatonia, stupor, fever, unstable pulse and blood pressure, myoglobinemia; can be fatal	Weeks	Unknown	Stop neuroleptic; antiparkinsonism agents usually fail; bromocriptine often helps; dantrolene variable; expert supportive care crucial
Tardive dyskinesia	Oral-facial dyskinesia, choreoathetosis; sometimes irreversible, rarely progressive	6–24 months (worse on withdrawal)	Dopamine excess?	Prevention best; treatment unsatisfactory; slow spontaneous remission
"Rabbit syndrome"	Perioral tremor (late parkinsonism variant?); usually reversible	Months or years	Dopamine blockade?	Antiparkinsonism agents; reduce dose of neuroleptic

Source. This table is adapted from a previous publication (Baldessarini 1985).

unusual to find controlled, prospective studies employing randomized assignment of patients to one of several doses.

In a series of 65 short-term trials of chlorpromazine in psychotic patients, a summary of "success rates" in treating these patients as a function of the dose of chlorpromazine used provides some suggestions of a dose-effect relationship (Appleton and Davis 1980). In all trials that used daily doses of chlorpromazine of 500 mg or more, there was found to be a statistically superior effect of chlorpromazine compared to placebo in treating psychotic (mostly schizophrenic) patients. Doses of 300 mg/day or less yielded results significantly better than placebo in only two-thirds of the trials, and intermediate doses gave an intermediate probability of success of the neuroleptic treatment. In a recent survey involving more than 15,000 U.S. Veterans Administration patients, the average daily dose of neuroleptic was equivalent to approximately 600 mg of chlorpromazine for hospitalized patients and about 300 mg for outpatients (Baldessarini et al. 1984). Other studies indicate that sustained doses equivalent to about 600 mg/day of chlorpromazine are not unusual in schizophrenic outpatients, especially when high-potency agents are employed (Kane et al. 1983; Lehmann et al. 1983).

We have reported that current dosing practices regarding high- and low-potency neuroleptics differ markedly (Baldessarini et al. 1984). The most potent neuroleptics are sometimes used in doses that are two to seven times greater than the apparently equivalent amount of chlorpromazine in acutely psychotic patients. The low-potency agent thioridazine, in contrast, is used typically in doses about half those apparently equivalent to chlorpromazine. These clinical patterns are understandable, if not necessarily scientifically based. Low-potency agents carry an increased risk of sometimes intolerable side effects of sedation, hypotension, autonomic dysfunction, and rare but alarming systemic toxicity (hepatic inflammation, bone marrow suppression, and retinal damage), that may be less common or severe when small doses are used. On the other hand, the characteristic neurological side effects of high-potency neuroleptics evidently are more acceptable to many clinicians.

The apparent rationale for the use of high doses of antipsychotic drugs is to increase the degree and speed of beneficial response. However, as was suggested as early as 1955 by Ayd, there is good evidence that high doses of potent neuroleptics are not more beneficial or more rapidly effective than moderate doses. There is also some basis to suspect that high doses can yield inferior clinical effects as well as excessive neurotoxicity, as was recognized as early as 1960 by Wilkens and Malitz. Moreover, even though typical degrees of extrapyramidal toxicity may not seem to be a medically serious matter, they can be highly distressing and disabling to patients, and dystonic reactions and the neuroleptic malignant syndrome can lead to fatalities (Table 3).

A related problem of the aggressive use of neuroleptics is that the opportunity to evaluate psychotic patients who are completely unmedicated is becoming increasingly rare. Accordingly, clinical impressions of the features of psychosis and mania are now often colored or modified by the effects of neuroleptic or other psychotropic agents. This pattern threatens to become a serious limitation in the psychiatric training of young physicians as well as in the adequate clinical assessment of patients.

A recently popular hypothesis has been that early treatment of acutely psychotic patients with high doses of potent neuroleptics leads to more rapid recovery than conventional treatment, with accompanying savings of morbidity, hospitalization, and lost productivity and income. The practice of using higher than usual doses of high-potency neuroleptics began in the 1960s and 1970s in response to clinical impressions that high doses of low-potency agents were associated with unacceptable side effects, whereas high doses of potent agents were better "tolerated" by patients and clinicians. This practice may also reflect growing pressures to minimize the duration and expense of psychiatric hospitalizations or to avoid them altogether, especially in community clinics and general hospital emergency room settings. The use of high doses of neuroleptics in the short- and long-term treatment of psychotic patients has been reviewed several times in the past decade (Baldessarini 1984, 1985; Baldessarini et al. 1980, 1988; Gardos et al. 1973; Gardos and Cole 1976; Donlon 1976; Donlon et al. 1979; Woggon 1979; Aubree and Lader 1980; Mason and Granacher 1980; Cole 1982; Kirkpatrick and Burnett 1982; Linden et al. 1982).

Perhaps the earliest report of the possible usefulness of rapid increases in doses of antipsychotic drugs ("rapid neuroleptization") in the short-term treatment of acutely ill psychotic patients was by Kinross-Wright (1955); other similar uncontrolled reports appeared in the early 1960s (Danik and Goverdham 1963; Mountain 1963). Later, in the 1970s, there were more than a half-dozen additional reports claiming success in the uncontrolled application of high doses of potent neuroleptics for the treatment of acutely psychotic patients (Oldham and Bott 1971; Polack and Laycob 1971; Sangiovanni et al. 1973; Donlon and Tupin 1974; Carter 1977,

1978; Firling 1978). More recent reports of similar experiences have been less enthusiastic (Zarifian et al. 1982; Bollini et al. 1984).

We have found a series of 19 reports on controlled, mostly prospective, and blindly evaluated trials involving comparisons between two or more randomly assigned doses of neuroleptic or between two types of neuroleptics of dissimilar equivalent doses (see Table 4). We have also found one study comparing a neuroleptic with a sedative benzodiazepine (Lerner et al. 1979). The characteristics of these controlled high vs. low dosage trials were reviewed recently (Baldessarini et al. 1988).

The results of these 19 controlled studies are consistent and illuminating (Table 4). They provide *no* support for regimens employing unusually high doses of injected neuroleptics for special benefits of the treatment of acutely psychotic patients. Dosing at more than the approximate equivalent of 500 or 600 mg of chlorpromazine (or ca. 10–12 mg of haloperidol or fluphenazine) within the first 24 hours after admission or daily during the initial weeks of treatment appeared not to provide additional clinical benefit. This impression is supported by an analysis of 33 paired dosage comparisons arising from the studies already cited. Overall, higher and lower doses gave very similar rates or levels of response. In

Table 4. Comparison of moderate vs. high doses of neuroleptics in acute psychoses

Condition	*N*	Dose: CPZ-eq (mg/24 hr)	Improvement (%)
Paired moderate doses	33	466 ± 47	46.8 ± 4.7
Paired high doses	33	2,384 ± 1,349	53.3 ± 4.2
All doses 600 mg	24	311 ± 31	56.2 ± 4.8
All doses 600 mg	25[a]	3,613 ± 1,757	50.2 ± 4.4

[a]Excludes two aberrantly low responses of 2% at 800 mg and 5% at 1,850 mg, which would have increased the difference even more; 600 mg was the approximate median dose.

Note. Based on data regarding responses in 19 reports on acute psychosis, involving at least two doses of neuroleptic given from 1 hour to 45 days, and providing 33 pairs to compare (Fitzgerald 1969; Slotnick 1971; Ritter et al. 1972; Chien and Cole 1973; Man and Chen 1973; Reschke 1974; Wijsenbeek et al. 1974; Quitkin et al. 1975b; Anderson et al. 1976; Levenson et al. 1976; Gerstenzang and Krulisky 1977; Paprock and Versiani 1977; Stotsky 1977; Donlon et al. 1978; Ericksen et al. 1978; Donlon et al. 1980; Neborsky et al. 1981; Escobar et al. 1983; Dubin et al. 1985). CPZ-eq = chlorpromazine-equivalent. Neither difference is significant by *t*-test ($P > .25$).

addition, in 24 comparisons that could be made of daily doses above or below the median equivalent of 600 mg of chlorpromazine, there was a slight average trend toward *lesser* efficacy of higher doses.

A dose-effect relationship with moderate doses being optimal is especially strongly supported by three controlled studies (Reschke 1974; Anderson et al. 1976; Neborsky et al. 1981) involving random assignment of subjects to one of at least two injected doses of haloperidol. Data from these trials indicate that there was an apparent sigmoid dose-effect relationship between the equivalent of 2 and 10 mg of haloperidol (equivalent to about 100–500 mg of chlorpromazine), with a maximum of about 50% diminution of initial psychopathology scores seen within the first 2–4 hours after dosing (Baldessarini et al. 1988). Higher doses of haloperidol were not associated with additional benefit and may even have yielded lesser degrees of improvement. It is important to point out that these studies utilized intramuscular (im) dosing, as is sometimes done in the immediate and especially the emergency treatment of acutely psychotic and manic patients, and that equivalent oral doses may be somewhat greater, or may yield similar effects somewhat more slowly.

The interpretation of these interesting short-term studies of acutely psychotic patients is not entirely clear. Many of the reports are limited in the richness of their clinical descriptions and details. In addition, their analysis involves combining data obtained using different agents and different times of treatment. The fact that a study by Lerner et al. (1979) demonstrated similar improvement in psychosis following parenteral diazepam or haloperidol may suggest that the major effects obtained were mainly sedative or anxiolytic (or perhaps even anticonvulsant) effects and not "truly antipsychotic" effects. Although patients were described as being obviously sedated by both treatments (Lerner et al. 1979), the distinction between immediate "sedative" and "antipsychotic" effects is rather academic and not necessarily meaningful clinically. A growing number of reports have found clinically useful effects of benzodiazepines in acutely psychotic and manic patients, and the short-term combination of neuroleptic and sedative agents is common in current clinical practice (Guz et al. 1972; Deberdt 1973; Koster van Groos 1973; Shader et al. 1977; Beckman and Haas 1980; Chouinard et al. 1983; Victor et al. 1984; Frykholm 1985; Modell et al. 1985), if only to avoid the use of excessive and potentially toxic doses of neuroleptics or lithium salts (Shader et al. 1977; Modell et al. 1985).

One of the most intriguing aspects of the data from some of the acute studies already cited is the apparently biphasic nature of the dose-effect relationship. This trend appeared to be consistent based on the fact that data from two independent studies involving random assignment to the condition of treatment fell very close together at the highest doses (Anderson et al. 1976; Neborsky et al. 1981). Assuming that the effect is not influenced by artifactual assignment of treatment-resistant cases to high doses, a possible interpretation of this effect is that high doses of neuroleptics, and especially of potent agents such as haloperidol and fluphenazine, exert extrapyramidal or other toxic actions on the central nervous system that may lead to apparent or real loss of benefits or even clinical worsening in psychotic patients (Wilkens and Malitz 1960; Simpson et al. 1976; Marder et al. 1984; Diamond 1985; Keepers et al. 1983; Baldessarini et al. 1988).

Consistent with this hypothesis are clinical impressions, as well as impressions from a study of the dose-effect relationship for the prevalence of identifiable extrapyramidal reactions (Keepers et al. 1983), that the dose-effect curves for antipsychotic benefit and extrapyramidal toxicity are very similar and largely overlapping. The approximately half-maximally effective doses (ED_{50}) in chlorpromazine equivalents for acute antipsychotic benefit and for extrapyramidal effects both appear to be about 250–350 mg/day, suggesting a very narrow therapeutic index of close to 1:1 (side effect:benefit ED_{50} ratio denoting margin of safety).

A related aspect of the above studies of neuroleptic treatment of acutely psychotic patients is that several of these studies (Chien and Cole 1973; Reschke 1974; Quitkin et al. 1975b; Levenson et al. 1976; Donlon et al. 1978; Ericksen et al. 1978; Donlon et al. 1980; Neborsky et al. 1981) provide data concerning improvement at times after the initial hours or days of treatment, to as late as 45 days after this initial period. Again, there was no evidence that higher doses of neuroleptics provided superior results at these later times, or that the speed of improvement or duration of treatment was altered as a result of doses above the equivalent of about 400 or 500 mg of chlorpromazine (Baldessarini et al. 1988). At such later times after the first few days of treatment, it seems less likely that any benefits obtained are merely "sedative" effects, although additional direct comparisons of neuroleptics, sedatives, and a placebo during extended treatment need to be carried out to evaluate this point.

The sometimes marked, apparent antipsychotic effect seen within hours of initiating treatment with a neuroleptic agent may seem inconsistent with a popular view that "truly antipsychotic" actions require treatment for many days or weeks. We suggest that this viewpoint, as well as the sharp distinction between short-term sedative and antipsychotic effects of psychotropic agents, may be an oversimplification. In fact, the time course of response to neuroleptic treatment remains very inadequately studied in well-designed experimental protocols.

An analysis of some available data that may represent a typical pattern of overall clinical response over time in acute psychosis or mania is provided in Figure 1. For comparison, data concerning the response in exacerbations of chronic psychosis (schizophrenia) are also included. The studies summarized in Figure 1 for both acutely psychotic and exacerbated chronically psychotic patients (Appleton and Davis 1980; Neborsky et al. 1981; Lerner et al. 1979; National Institute of Mental Health 1968) are strikingly consistent in indicating that overall clinical improvement follows a complex, multiphasic pattern. This includes a rapid diminution of intense psychopathology, followed by one or more slower phases of recovery. While the precise nature of the changes produced over time is only starting to be investigated carefully (Hurt et al. 1983), the pattern observed seems to be understandable in clinical terms. The early phase of response may represent a rapid decrease in "hot" signs and symptoms of excitement, turmoil, and intense delusions and hallucinations. The later phase may represent the slower return of rationality and improved social relations.

Clearly, the distinction between antipsychotic and sedative or other beneficial neuropharmacological effects may be especially difficult to make in the early phase of treatment. However, it has yet to be demonstrated convincingly that sedatives such as benzodiazepines are effective in the later phases of treatment of acute psychosis, or for maintenance treatment. The pattern of clinical response observed suggests that future dose-finding clinical trials should include late as well as early points of evaluation following the use of low and moderate doses of neuroleptics or other test agents.

Finally, in view of the existing research and clinical experience strongly suggesting that a dose-effect relationship in the neuroleptic treatment of acute psychosis or mania is probably to be found between the daily equivalent of 50 and 500 mg of chlorpromazine, there is no good reason to recommend further trials with high doses of neuroleptics. The next question, then, is whether dosing with neuroleptics can be improved further by the use of plasma assays of drug molecules or of their pharmacological activity.

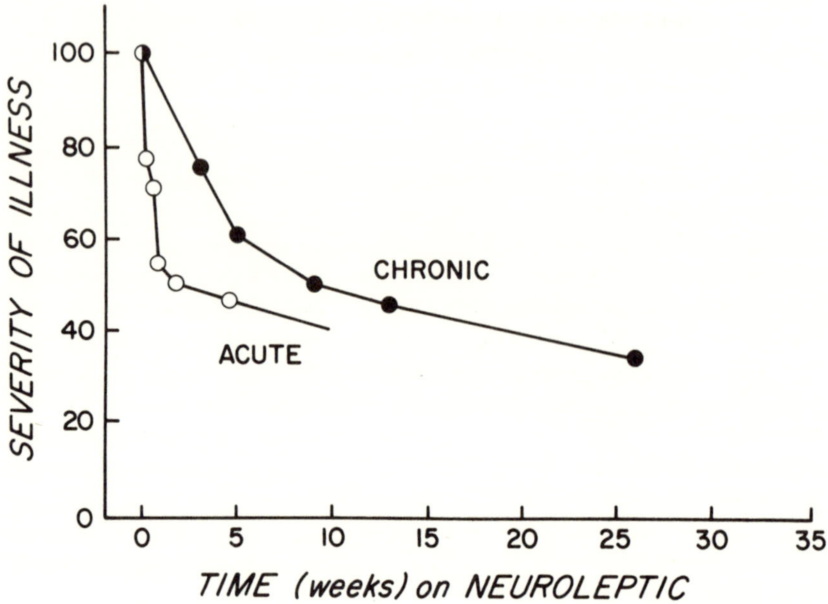

Figure 1. Time course of improvement during neuroleptic treatment. Open circles represent mean trends reported in four studies of early use of a neuroleptic (haloperidol) in acutely psychotic patients (some were schizophrenic). Responses to high and low doses were indistinguishable, so data from seven cohorts were pooled. Closed circles represent mean trends in three NIMH-sponsored studies of phenothiazines in chronic schizophrenia. In both curves, 100 is equated to the most severe initial clinical ratings (usually assessed by the Brief Psychiatric Rating Scale [BPRS]). For both groups of patients there were at least two apparent phases of response: rapid improvement in the first days (acute cases) or weeks (chronic cases), followed by slower improvement thereafter. Early effects probably included calming of acute agitation and florid symptoms, whereas more complete recovery of rationality and function evidently requires a longer time. The data are derived from several studies (Appleton and Davis 1980; Neborsky et al. 1981; Lerner et al. 1979; National Institute of Mental Health 1968) that have been reanalyzed in this way previously (Baldessarini 1985). Reprinted, with permission, from Baldessarini 1985. Copyright 1985, Harvard University Press.

Relationship Between Blood Levels and Clinical Effects of Neuroleptics

Clinical reliance on assays of plasma concentrations of drugs is now routine in the case of digitalis compounds and anticonvulsants, and biological assays are employed routinely to monitor the effects of anticoagulants. In psychiatry, the safe use of lithium salts requires routine monitoring of concentrations of lithium ion in plasma or other body fluids (Baldessarini 1985). Assays of plasma levels of tricyclic antidepressants and their major, active, N-desmethylated metabolites are now widely available and can provide guidelines for treatment (Task Force 1985). Assays also promise to provide early characterizations of drug metabolism and dosage requirements in individual patients following administration of a small test dose of a lithium salt or an antidepressant (Baldessarini 1985; Cooper and Simpson 1976, 1978; Brunswick et al. 1979).

It would be advantageous to know neuroleptic levels in blood if such levels correlate with or predict clinical effects. The blood level of a drug, rather than dose, might then be used to optimize treatment and reduce the time necessary to find an effective dose. Blood levels might also be used for early identification of excessive or toxic doses. Without direct evidence of an excess of drug in tissue, such toxicity (especially akathisia, akinesia, catatonia, or confusion) can be mistaken for symptoms of the underlying illness. Finally, the risk of long-term toxicity, such as tardive dyskinesia, might be reduced.

There has been great interest in monitoring blood levels of neuroleptics since the first practical assay for chlorpromazine became available in the late 1960s (Curry 1968, 1985). At present, chemical assays incorporating gas chromatographic, gas-liquid chromatographic, high-pressure liquid chromatographic, mass fragmentographic, thin-layer chromatographic, and fluorometric techniques, as well as radioimmunoassays, are available for detecting neuroleptics of various chemical classes (Curry 1985; Cohen 1983; Cohen and Baldessarini 1984). Radioreceptor assays are available for estimating the total neuroleptic activity in blood arising from all drug species present (Creese and Snyder 1977; Cohen et al. 1979, 1980a, 1980b, 1980c; Cooper 1985).

Blood levels of neuroleptics have been monitored in more than 100 studies. These studies have been reviewed several times and have produced inconsistent results and no consensus on whether blood levels of neuroleptics correlate with clinical effects (Baldessarini et al. 1988; Curry 1985; Cohen 1983; Cohen and Baldessarini

1984; Cooper et al. 1976; Davis et al. 1978; May and Van Putten 1978; Gelder and Kolakowska 1979; Cohen and Lipinksi 1981; Ko et al. 1985; McIntyre and Gershon 1985; Simpson and Yadalam 1985). Several reviews (Baldessarini et al. 1988; Cohen 1983; Cohen and Baldessarini 1984; May and Van Putten 1978; Simpson and Yadalam 1985; Zarifian et al. 1985) suggest that the lack of agreement may reflect limitations and inconsistencies in the design of most previous studies, as follows:

1. Many studies have used diagnostically and syndromically heterogeneous groups of patients, so improvement cannot meaningfully be compared from patient to patient. Many studies also included chronic patients whose improvement can be expected to be minimal.
2. Blood samples were often collected near times of suspected peak levels (e.g., soon after a dose of medication, when levels change rapidly and are highly variable) rather than at later times of more stable levels.
3. The use of concurrent medications was often not controlled.
4. Usually no allowance was made to eliminate subjects whose condition might have remitted spontaneously. For these subjects (who may represent 25% of a population of acutely psychotic patients [Gottschalk 1979]), blood levels of neuroleptics are irrelevant and will obscure results.
5. More often than not, patients received rather high and individualized doses that were determined by the treating physician. Such practices tend to compensate for individual differences in absorption, distribution, metabolism, and excretion of drugs, and if there is a therapeutic range of plasma levels, individualization of doses brings most patients into or close to that range. This design would place most patients on the flat "plateau" of any blood level vs. clinical effect curve, and any correlation between level and effect over a broader range of levels would not be seen. In addition, this practice virtually ensures that those who do not respond to medication will receive the greatest amounts of medication, thereby biasing the results to show poor response associated with high plasma levels.

Therefore, the contradictory findings of past studies are not strong evidence that a relationship between blood levels and clinical effects of neuroleptics cannot be demonstrated. There is good evidence in animal studies and suggestive evidence in some clinical studies that such a correlation exists. Studies in animals and patients receiving acute (single) doses of drugs provide some of this evidence. The animal studies are few and most have been done with haloperidol; in these cases, blood levels, brain levels, and drug effects on behavior all follow one another quite closely (Janssen and Allewijn 1969; Öhman et al. 1977; Cohen et al. 1980a; Campbell et al. 1980; Neimegeers et al. 1981; Campbell et al. 1982). Similarly, a small number of studies of psychotic patients consistently show that blood levels achieved after a single dose of medication correlate highly with immediate response and later response to medication (Cohen and Baldessarini 1984; May et al. 1981; Yesavage et al. 1983). Furthermore, a few studies of individual patients indicate that patients with aberrantly low or high blood levels can be identified and that they show improvement when their levels are brought closer to the average (Cohen et al. 1979; Curry et al. 1970; Smith et al. 1979). Finally, despite similar doses of medication, patients with lower serum levels of drugs may be at greater risk of relapse (Brown and Silver 1985). Taken together, these findings imply that there may be a measurable relationship between blood levels and clinical effects of neuroleptic treatment.

No extended studies are yet available that satisfy all methodological criticisms. We found 20 studies, involving 603 patients, that employed a fixed dose regimen and a population of overtly psychotic patients (Cohen et al. 1980c; May et al. 1981; Lader 1976; Vanderheeren and Muusze 1977; Clark et al. 1978; Wode-Helgodt et al. 1978; Casper et al. 1980; Dysken et al. 1981; Hansen et al. 1972; Greenberg et al. 1983; Garver et al. 1984; Mavroides et al. 1984a, 1984b; Bigelow et al. 1985; Davis et al. 1985; Potkin et al. 1985; Smith et al. 1985a, 1985b; Van Putten et al. 1983, 1985). In our recent review of this work (Baldessarini et al. 1988), several points are clear. First, few fairly well-designed studies of this kind have been done, and very few of these have focused on any one drug. The neuroleptic most frequently used was haloperidol, and in the seven studies of this drug, only two used the same assay techniques. Chlorpromazine was studied four times, thioridazine three times, and no other drug more than twice. Doses of medication were usually high (mean chlorpromazine-equivalent = 740 mg/day) and only sometimes fixed. Second, all of the studies were small, some exceedingly so (mean N = 30; range = 10–48 subjects completing a protocol). Subjects tended to be diagnostically heterogeneous and often included chronically ill patients who may be poor responders to neuroleptics.

Clearly, it is too early to draw any firm conclusions from these studies. Nevertheless, the presence of at least modest correlations of neuroleptic blood level and effect in many of these studies is encouraging. In fact, of the 12 studies employing acutely psychotic or drug-responsive patients, all report moderate correlations between drug level and clinical improvement. Furthermore, the impression from dose-effect studies (reviewed in the preceding section) that a relationship can be demonstrated at low doses of typical neuroleptics is supported by data arising from these studies of the relationship between plasma levels of a neuroleptic drug and the corresponding clinical benefit (Cohen 1983; Cohen et al. 1980b; Cohen and Lipinski 1981; Yesavage et al. 1983).

Also of interest, and again analogous to findings in dose-response studies, is that many of these studies suggest a relatively limited range of optimal blood levels of neuroleptics. Findings from nine studies that specifically describe such an optimum (Casper et al. 1980; Dysken et al. 1981; Hansen et al. 1972; Mavroidis et al. 1984a, 1984b; Potkin et al. 1985; Smith et al. 1985a, 1985b; Van Putten et al. 1985; Smith et al. 1982; Mavroidis et al. 1983) are summarized in our recent review (Baldessarini et al. 1988). In these reports, 120 of 244 subjects (49%) had levels within a range of blood levels of drug that were associated with a relatively high rate of clinical improvement. In addition to the 26% of patients with low levels, another 25% were above this range and had inferior rates of clinical response. Because the dose of a neuroleptic is rarely decreased in patients who are doing poorly (Dysken et al. 1981; May and Van Putten 1978), patients with excessive blood levels of neuroleptics may continue to receive excessive doses and therefore continue to do poorly.

If these studies are correct, it is important to ask why there is such a narrow range of apparently optimal levels of medication (only two- to three-fold in five out of nine studies and 5.1-fold overall [Baldessarini et al. 1988]). One possibility is that blood levels of neuroleptics that are even moderately higher than optimal levels are associated with untoward neurological side effects (such as akathisia, akinesia, sedation, or confusion) that might mimic or worsen psychiatric illness, as we have already suggested based on dose-effect curves. In support of this hypothesis, the upper limit of doses in all nine of these studies ranged from the daily equivalent of 480 to 1,700 mg of chlorpromazine—doses commonly associated with significant neurological side effects (Baldessarini 1985; Baldessarini et al. 1984; Keepers et al. 1983).

Hansen et al. (1972) specifically addressed this issue in a study of perphenazine. They treated patients with fixed, moderate doses of perphenazine (average 30 mg/day), with or without added antiparkinsonism medication. In the first group of 26 patients, these investigators found apparently optimal plasma levels of perphenazine to be 0.8–2.0 ng/ml. In the second group of 26, they found that side effects increased markedly when plasma levels of perphenazine exceeded 1.6 ng/ml. This striking concordance of the upper end of a "therapeutic range" and levels associated with serious extrapyramidal toxicity suggests that side effects may impair the therapeutic efficacy of neuroleptics even when antiparkinsonism medication is used, and that there are relatively low levels of drug associated with both good therapeutic effects and limited side effects in most patients.

A similar conclusion was reached by Bishop et al. (1965) in their review of studies comparing the development of therapeutic effects and side effects in patients receiving neuroleptics. In summarizing the evidence, the authors suggested that maximal therapeutic effects probably can be achieved at doses that do not lead to more than minimal side effects. Even moderate side effects were associated with less than optimal improvement.

While the results remain preliminary and conclusions somewhat speculative, studies of blood levels of neuroleptic drugs appear to have been useful in defining therapeutic ranges in groups of patients. In particular, the results of these studies add to the growing impression that doses of medication currently common in American psychiatric practice, and the attendant blood levels of drug achieved, are often excessive (Baldessarini 1985; Cohen and Lipinski 1986; Baldessarini et al. 1984; Baldessarini et al. 1988; Cohen and Baldessarini 1984). This impression is consistent with our review of dose-response studies in acutely psychotic patients in the preceding section, as well as our review of long-term treatment in the next section.

Neuroleptic Treatment During Aftercare Following Acute Psychosis

It is customary to continue use of an antipsychotic agent following initial recovery from an acute episode of psychosis, although the research support for this practice is of limited generalizability. Most of the support for beneficial actions of neuroleptic agents following treatment of acute psychosis rests on 44 controlled studies of patients called "schizophrenic" (see footnote to Table 5 for list of studies). These studies used the method of substituting a placebo for an active antipsychotic agent. In addition, few of these studies employed agents other than phenothiazines or followed subjects longer than 6 months. Finally, acceptance into such trials appears to have required some initial clinical responsiveness to treatment. Many of these studies have been reviewed previously (Baldessarini 1984, 1985; Baldessarini et al. 1980; Baldessarini and Davis 1980). The salient features of these controlled trials are summarized in our recent review of this topic (Baldessarini et al. 1988) and in Figure 2 and Table 5. Over a mean period of 10 months, these trials indicate an average risk of exacerbation of psychosis

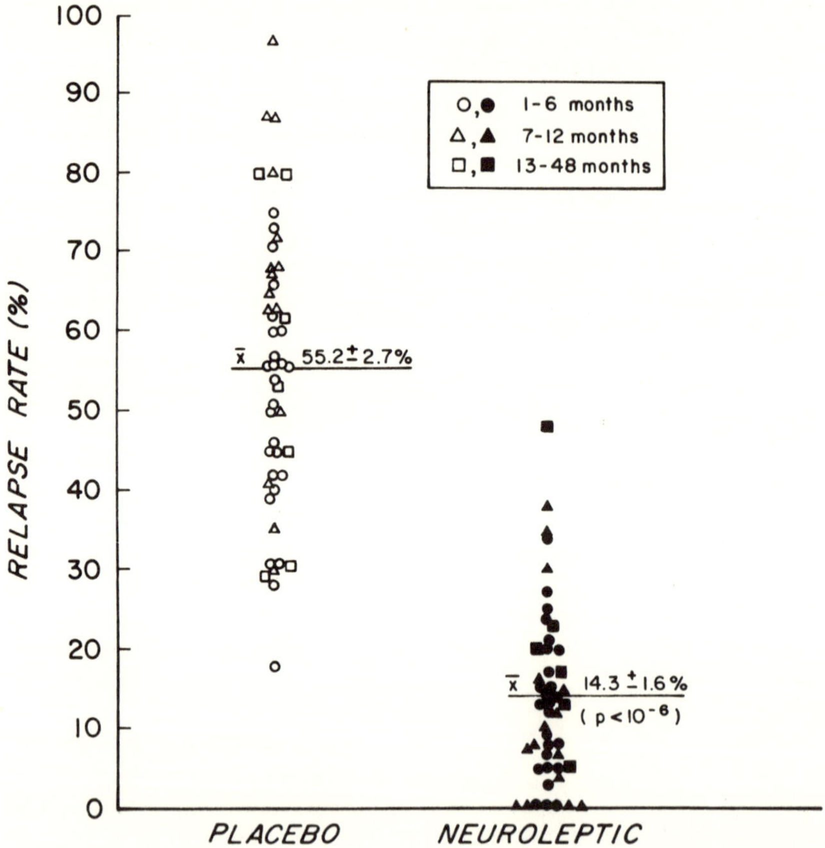

Figure 2. Effects of maintenance treatment in schizophrenia. Data on which this analysis was based are provided in Table 5. There is a highly significant 3.9-fold overall sparing of relapse by active medication (14.3% ± 1.6% [SEM]) compared to placebo (55.2% ± 2.7% [t = 13.0, $P < 10^{-6}$ by paired t-test]). The drug:placebo difference was similar for studies of short (1–6 months), intermediate (7–12 months), or more prolonged periods (13–48 months) of follow-up. Reprinted, with permission, from Baldessarini 1985. Copyright 1985, Harvard University Press.

Table 5. Summary of placebo-controlled studies of protective effects of neuroleptics in schizophrenia

Measure	Results
Number of reports	44
Number of patients (total)	3,939
Proportion of studies using phenothiazine	86%
Mean daily dose (CPZ-eq, mg)	397 ± 51
Mean duration of study (months)	9.8 ± 1.3
Number of studies employing:	
Various phenothiazines	11
Fluphenazine (including depot)	10
Chlorpromazine	8
Trifluoperazine	3
Thioridazine	2
Various agents not defined	2
Flupenthixol	1
Loxapine	1
Penfluridol	1
Pimozide	3
Perphenazine	1
Haloperidol	0
Exacerbation rate on placebo	55.2 ± 2.7%
Exacerbation rate on neuroleptic	14.3 ± 1.6%
Mean ratio of placebo:drug relapse rate	12.8 ± 3.1%

Note. Data are based on 44 reports involving 48 comparisons of one or more neuroleptics vs. a placebo, under double-blind prospective conditions (Shawver et al. 1959; Tuteur et al. 1959; Diamond and Marks 1960; Engelhardt et al. 1960, 1967; Gross 1960; Blackburn and Allen 1961; Schiele et al. 1961; Freeman and Alson 1962; Troshinsky et al. 1962; Whitaker and Hoy 1963; Caffey et al. 1964; Pasamanick et al. 1964; Kinross-Wright and Charalampous 1965; Garfield et al. 1966; Melnyk et al. 1966; Prien and Cole 1968; Prien et al. 1969a, 1969b; Itil and Keskiner 1970; Itil et al. 1970; Leff and Wing 1971; Hershon et al. 1972; Hirsch et al. 1973; Hogarty and Ulrich 1977; Hogarty et al. 1973, 1974, 1976, 1979; Gross 1974; Chien 1975; Clark et al. 1975; Andrews et al. 1976; Johnson 1976; Rifkin et al. 1977; Quitkin et al. 1978; Levine et al. 1980; Muller and Kind 1980; Branchey et al. 1981; Cheung 1981; Wistedt 1981; Kane et al. 1982; Johnson et al. 1983; Nishikawa et al. 1985). These studies have been reviewed in detail elsewhere (Baldessarini et al. 1988). The data showed no significant correlation between drug effect (as relapse rate difference or ratio) and dose or log-dose of drug; placebo relapse rate and dose selected; year of report and dose. Some studies used more than one drug. Data are means ± SEM unless otherwise stated. CPZ-eq = chlorpromazine-equivalent.

of 55.2% on placebo vs. only 14.3% on active medication (a 3.9-fold reduction of risk; $P < 10^{-6}$ by paired *t*-test). However, as noted below, some of the characteristics of these studies suggest that generalization of the results to all types of patients and agents, and to all times of follow-up, would be unwise.

First, some chronically psychotic patients, and many demented patients with psychotic features, are poorly helped by neuroleptic treatment, and may even feel and appear worse clinically with such treatment (Baldessarini et al. 1988; Simpson et al. 1976; Marder et al. 1984; Diamond 1985). Such cases may include a substantial proportion of treatment-resistant schizophrenic patients who are probably under-represented in the follow-up studies cited because of selection designs favoring treatment-responsive patients.

Second, many of the available and commonly used neuroleptic agents have been evaluated minimally or not at all in these studies. Most studies have involved the use of chlorpromazine, thioridazine, or fluphenazine; few studies have been done on other agents, and, notably, none on haloperidol.

Third, the relationship of the time course of relapse and recurrence of psychotic illnesses to their treatment remains imperfectly defined. Three large studies in the United States involving over 1,260 patients diagnosed as schizophrenic (Caffey et al. 1964; Prien et al. 1969a, 1969b; Hogarty and Ulrich 1977) provide data indicating that the risk of relapse after being switched to a placebo followed a semilogarithmic or sinusoidal function for the first 6–12 months of follow-up, with a slope of about 6% or 7% relapse per month (Figure 3). Comparison with cohorts randomly assigned to remain on active medication shows a sparing of relapse of about three- or four-fold over the first year of follow-up (Figure 3). Only two of the 44 follow-up studies persisted for more than a year (Engelhardt et al. 1967; Hogarty and Ulrich 1977), and their results suggest that the risk of exacerbation on placebo may diminish at later times in the second and third year, so that the slopes of functions describing the monthly exacerbation rate in the placebo and neuroleptic-treated cohorts are nearly parallel after 18 months of follow-up (see Figure 3 and Baldessarini et al. 1988; Engelhardt et al. 1967).

In other words, relatively little research has been done concerning the utility of neuroleptic treatment sustained for more than 6–12 months after an acute exacerbation of schizophrenia. One recent long-term observational study even suggests that "tolerance" to antipsychotic effects may have occurred in about 3% of

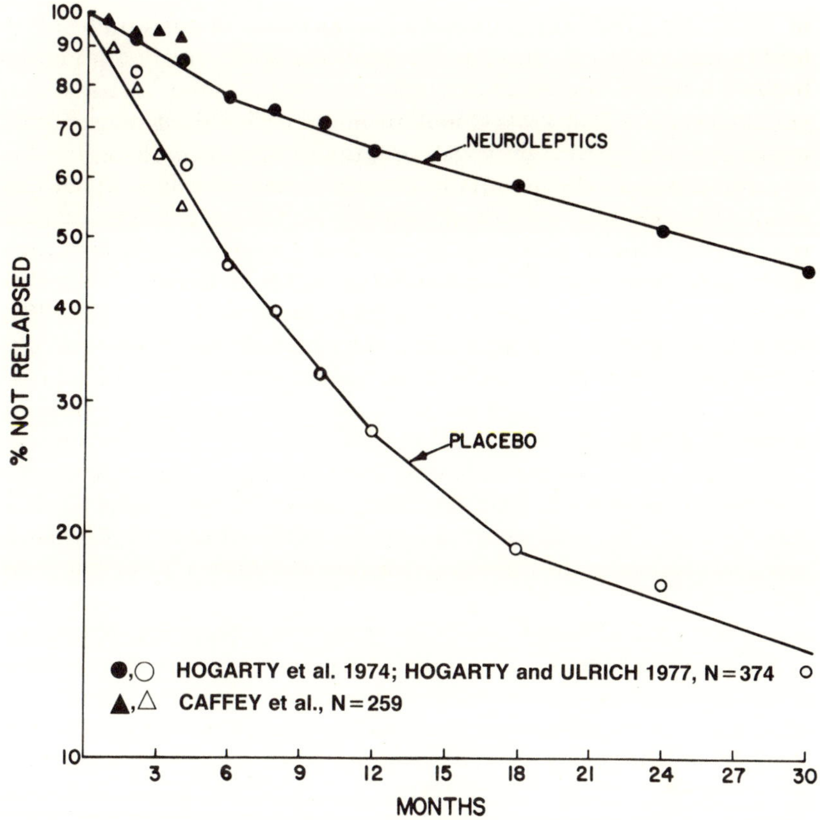

Figure 3. Rate of nonrelapse of schizophrenic patients treated with a neuroleptic or placebo over time. Data are adapted from three large United States studies discussed in the text (Caffey et al. 1964; Prien et al. 1969a; Hogarty and Ulrich 1977), involving over 1,260 patients followed for 6 months or for more than 2 years. The incidence of relapse or exacerbation of illness follows a complex, curvilinear pattern that is not strictly logarithmic, and may diminish in slope at times later than 1 year of follow-up. In the early months, there is a strikingly similar risk of relapse in all studies of placebo, at about 6% to 7% per month. This analysis has been presented previously (Baldessarini 1985). Reprinted, with permission, from Baldessarini 1985. Copyright 1985, Harvard University Press.

patients in a clinic for schizophrenia at times of sustained treatment greater than 2 years, at least following relatively high early doses of a long-acting ester of fluphenazine (Chouinard et al. 1978). Almost nothing is known about prolonged effects of neuroleptic treatment after acute episodes or exacerbations of chronic nonschizophrenic psychosis, mania, or other acute psychoses (Baldessarini 1985; Baldessarini et al. 1980).

An even more troubling aspect of interpreting results of studies of the long-term use of antipsychotic agents is that the range of persons included in studies of schizophrenia in the 1960s and 1970s, when most of this work was done, may be so broad as to severely limit inferences pertinent to current conceptualizations of schizophrenia. The 44 reports on placebo-controlled neuroleptic discontinuation studies in schizophrenia already cited (see footnote to Table 5 for list of studies involved) showed rates of psychotic exacerbation on placebo ranging from below 20% to nearly 100% (Figure 2). This variance is not explained readily by differences between studies in the duration of follow-up (Figure 2), or between definitions of relapse, but might reflect clinical dissimilarities among patients called schizophrenic. The greater breadth of earlier concepts of schizophrenia, especially in American psychiatry, is documented by a well-known study of differential diagnostic practices conducted by psychiatrists in New York and London in the late 1960s (Gurland et al. 1970). Many cases diagnosed by the American clinicians as "schizophrenia" were diagnosed by the English clinicians as affective disorder, personality disorder, or neurosis. Even some current-day European and international diagnostic systems are relatively broad in that they include a category of "acute schizophrenia," the long-term course of which is likely to be dissimilar to that of chronic forms of psychoses and may be similar to affective illness (Stevens and Astrup 1963). The current American Psychiatric Association standards (1987) for the diagnosis of schizophrenia (DSM-III-R), with their 6-month criterion to differentiate (acute) schizophreniform psychosis from (more or less chronic) schizophrenia, and similar diagnostic methods, appear to yield a disorder with a reasonably consistent symptom pattern and course (Robins and Guze 1970; Guze et al. 1983). However, even 6 months of psychotic illness does not necessarily imply a chronic course, nor are all cases of carefully diagnosed schizophrenia necessarily chronic or alike in pathophysiology or treatment response (Cloninger et al. 1985).

The point is not to debate whether older or newer diagnostic concepts and criteria are intrinsically more accurate or valid, but to highlight practical points concerning the clinical application of research findings. Thus, contemporary diagnostic practices may not fit the treatment research literature of the 1960s and 1970s, preventing direct generalizations of past results to contemporary diagnostic categories. By the same token, much more research is now required to obtain closer congruence between treatment responses and contemporary diagnoses.

In summary, it seems that most of the data favoring continued use of an antipsychotic agent following recovery from an acute episode of psychotic illness applies to patients called "schizophrenic" based on relatively broad criteria, and involves follow-up for less than 1 year. Follow-up for 3 to 5 years in one study suggests that the putative prophylactic effects of neuroleptic treatment may undergo tolerance in some patients (Chouinard et al. 1978). This body of research is not a firm basis on which to argue for sustained and aggressive use of neuroleptic agents for all or most psychotic patients. Clinical experience suggests that some chronically psychotic patients (schizophrenic patients) continue to manifest psychotic signs and symptoms indefinitely and to worsen when neuroleptic medication is reduced or removed. However, because not all patients, even those with chronic signs of psychosis, follow this pattern of response, and because the possible prophylactic benefit of neuroleptic treatment in recurrent acute psychoses has not been tested, it remains necessary for clinicians to continue use of antipsychotic agents for more than a few months, only on an empirical, case-by-case basis with repeated reassessments at intervals (Baldessarini 1984, 1985; Baldessarini et al. 1980, 1988).

Dose-Effect Relationships in Follow-up Use of Neuroleptics

Neuroleptics probably are useful in protecting patients for at least several months following an acute episode of psychosis; but are the doses required for maximum toxicity during extended treatment similar to those appropriate for short-term treatment? This question has attracted increased interest in recent years as a result of the suspicion that toxic effects of prolonged use of neuroleptic agents may be, in part, dose-related. In this regard, the lack of convincing epidemiological evidence of a dose-risk relationship in tardive dyskinesia (Baldessarini et al. 1980) is probably a consequence of the excessive doses received by most patients—doses that would overwhelm and obscure any relationship that existed (Kane and Smith 1982).

A particular basis of concern arises from illogical conclusions that may follow from rapid neuroleptization programs and other high-dosage regimens in the treatment of acutely psychotic patients, as discussed above. Acutely psychotic patients tend to improve slowly over time with treatment, and even without treatment they usually improve or recover. However, it is tempting to conclude that the *last* treatment given was necessary for their clinical improvement. If the most recent treatment involved an excessively high dose of a neuroleptic (e.g., 50–100 mg/day of haloperidol or fluphenazine [Baldessarini et al. 1984]), one might be misled into concluding that a correspondingly high dose is required for follow-up treatment, perhaps half as high as the acute dose.

After many attempts in the 1960s and 1970s to find optimal effects of antipsychotic agents at very high doses, it can safely be concluded that this well-intentioned effort to improve treatment of severely chronically ill schizophrenic and other psychotic patients has been a failure. A representative systematic exploration of the upper limits of a dose-effect relationship for long-term antipsychotic benefits in schizophrenia was carried out by Quitkin and colleagues (1975a); they found little or no additional benefit in increasing daily doses of fluphenazine above 20–30 mg, especially when the more moderate dose was sustained for 6 weeks. Similarly, a review by Aubree and Lader (1980) of 11 maintenance studies involving over 700 schizophrenic patients found little benefit in raising mean daily doses of a neuroleptic from typical levels equivalent to about 600 mg of chlorpromazine to over 9,000 mg (usually by the use of high-potency agents). However, a 64% increase in risk of neurotoxic effects was found. Results of such studies indicate that the maximum beneficial effects of neuroleptics are likely to occur at doses not greater than the equivalent of 600 mg of chlorpromazine (or of 10–15 mg of haloperidol or of fluphenazine).

In the past 25 years many studies have explored the effects of very high doses of neuroleptics, especially for the treatment of schizophrenic patients. We found 33 reports of studies (see footnote to Table 6 for list of references) that involved random assignment of over 2,300 chronically psychotic patients to at least two doses of a neuroleptic. The characteristics of these studies are compiled in our recent review (Baldessarini et al. 1988) and the overall results are summarized in Table 6. These results show a consistently higher risk (95%) of neurological side effects at higher doses (equivalent to an average of about 5,200 mg/day of chlorpromazine) than at lower doses (equivalent to about 400 mg/day). In contrast, in only about a third of the comparisons were superior results claimed

Table 6. Effects of neuroleptic dose in maintenance treatment of chronic schizophrenic patients

Measure	Value
Number of studies[a]	33
Number of patients	2,346
Proportion of trials using a phenothiazine (%)	80.0
Mean duration (months)	5.84 ± 0.7
Mean daily low dose (CPZ-eq, mg)	399 ± 85
Mean daily high dose (CPZ-eq, mg)	5,215 ± 2,169
CNS Toxicity, high > low dose (%)[b]	95.0
Antipsychotic benefit, high > low dose (%)[c]	32.0

[a]References: Kane et al. 1983; Lehmann et al. 1983; Simpson et al. 1968, 1976; Caffey et al. 1964; Prien and Cole 1968; Prien et al. 1969b; Chien 1975; Clark et al. 1970, 1972, 1975; Branchey et al. 1981; Schiele et al. 1959; Carscallen et al. 1968; Polvan et al. 1968; Brotman et al. 1969; Williams et al. 1969; Faleni 1970; Itil et al. 1970, 1971; Debuck 1972; Gardos et al. 1974; Quitkin et al. 1975a, 1975b; McClelland et al. 1976; McCreadie and Macdonald 1977; McCreadie et al. 1979; Deneker et al. 1978; Goldstein et al. 1978; Bjorndal et al. 1980; Carpenter et al. 1982; Kane 1985; Hogarty 1984. These references are reviewed elsewhere (Baldessarini et al. 1988).
[b]Involves 22 of the studies reporting on central nervous system (CNS) toxicity, usually as extrapyramidal side effects, confusion, or epileptic seizures.
[c]Involves 50 dose comparisons, in most of which the results are similar for both doses or superior for the *lower* dose; only in 32% of the comparisons were the results of the higher dose claimed to be superior; in 46% of the comparisons the results were similar with both doses; and in 22% of the comparisons the results were possibly or clearly superior at the lower dose. Higher doses tended to be superior when the lower dose was unusually low (<200 mg/day).
Note. Data are means ± SEM. CPZ-eq = chlorpromazine-equivalent.

for the higher dose, whereas lower doses were superior or only equivocally different in two-thirds of the trials.

The significance of these results is open to question, because many of the studies cited involved chronically psychotic patients who had responded relatively poorly to previous treatment and showed small changes in clinical state at either high or low doses of a neuroleptic. In addition, comparisons sometimes involved high vs. very high doses, rather than moderate vs. high doses (Baldessarini et al. 1988). Nevertheless, the results are consistent with the impression that it is unusual to obtain significant additional benefit in chronic psychotic illnesses by the use of doses higher on average than the equivalent of 300–600 mg/day of chlorpromazine.

Explorations of *lower* doses have been infrequent, and only recently have begun to be systematic. Our review of the 44 reports of follow-up studies of psychotic patients (see footnote to Table 5 for a list of studies involved) discussed above and summarized elsewhere (Baldessarini et al. 1988) showed that the trials employed mean daily doses of various neuroleptics ranging from the equivalent of about 200 mg to over 2,000 mg of chlorpromazine. The degree of sparing of illness (difference between rate of exacerbation or relapse on placebo minus that on active medication) bore no discernible relation to dose (r = −0.003 for sparing of relapse vs. dose, and r = −0.083 vs. the log-dose) (Baldessarini et al. 1988). These results may merely reflect the inappropriate post hoc application of these results to the current purpose, because most of these trials were not designed as dose-finding studies and many did not employ strictly controlled doses given by random assignment.

However, if doses over the equivalent of 500 mg/day of chlorpromazine are on the upper plateau of a hypothetical dose-effect curve (possibly as high as the ED_{90}), another possible interpretation of the results is that a dose-effect curve with an ED_{50} below 200 mg/day might exist. Such a relationship would have been missed by the use of doses that were excessive for most patients in most studies. Several recent studies are starting to provide data consistent with the hypothesis that a dose-effect curve for long-term benefits of neuroleptic treatment may lie well "to the left" of doses typically employed in earlier studies and commonly used in clinical practice.

In a provocative report, Lehmann and colleagues (1983) evaluated 94 chronically ill schizophrenic outpatients who were shifted from their usual daily dose of medication (equivalent of 452 mg of chlorpromazine) to a moderate or low dose (equivalent to about 100 or 50 mg). The 1-year results of these modified regimens included rates of exacerbation of just over 28% among those patients kept on the highest full doses, and somewhat higher rates of approximately 45% or 42% among patients receiving the lower doses (Table 7). The lack of a strictly dose-dependent rise in the risk of relapse of psychotic illness reported in this study may reflect the evidently imperfectly random distribution of patients, in that those ending up on the highest average daily doses of medication had previously received the highest daily doses (equivalent to a mean of 609 mg of chlorpromazine), while those with the lowest experimental doses had previously received the lowest daily doses (266 mg). Perhaps some degree of clinical judgment prevailed so that

Table 7. One-year outcome in schizophrenic patients given constant or reduced doses of neuroleptics

Group	*n*	Age	Dose (CPZ-eq, mg/day) Initial	Dose (CPZ-eq, mg/day) Study	Relapse rate (%)
Usual	32	42	609	609	28.1
Medium	31	45	475	100	45.2
Low	31	48	266	50	41.9

Note. Patients were 94 outpatient chronic schizophrenic persons. The term "relapse" includes gross decompensation as well as sufficient worsening to require more medication. Doses are means and indicate lack of perfect randomization; the weighted mean initial dose was 452 mg/day. Data are adapted from Lehmann et al. (1983). CPZ-eq. = chlorpromazine-equivalent.

patients who were apparently "more sick" received higher doses. Lack of random assignment would tend to degrade differences due to drug dosage, as was discussed earlier concerning studies of blood levels of neuroleptics. However, other experiments provide additional support for the hypothesis that there is a dose-dependent antipsychotic effect of neuroleptics at relatively low doses.

Branchey and colleagues (1981) found in chronic schizophrenic patients that most of a previous maintenance dose of loxapine could be replaced by placebo in steps carried out over several months. As the first 80% of the medication was removed in this way, there was less than a 5% increase in exacerbations above a baseline rate initially established by 6 weeks of treatment at full doses that averaged 71 mg/day (equivalent to about 700 mg of chlorpromazine). However, when the last 20% of medication (9 mg/day) was replaced by a pharmacologically inert placebo, there was a dramatic 71% increase in the rate of clinically significant psychotic worsening (Table 8). While this experiment may partly confound effects of time and dose, it suggests that many psychotic patients may do well when given relatively small doses of loxapine.

In another well-designed, double-blind prospective study, schizophrenic patients were randomly assigned by Kane et al. (1983; also see Kane 1985) to continue for a year on previous routine doses of fluphenazine decanoate, or to receive material diluted 5- or 10-fold with an inert oily vehicle. Approximately equivalent doses in terms of daily oral chlorpromazine were 500–600 mg for the full-dose group, and 100–120 mg and 50–60 mg for the lower-dose groups. This study did not include a placebo group, a decision

Table 8. Effect of stepwise substitution of placebo for loxapine in 21 hospitalized schizophrenic patients

Time (wk)	Loxapine dose (%)	Loxapine dose (mg/day)	ca. CPZ-eq. (mg/day)	Relapse rate (%)
6	100	70.9	700	0.0
4	50	35.4	350	0.0
4	25	17.7	175	4.8
4	12.5	8.9	88	0.0
24[a]	0	0.0	0	71.4

[a]All relapses on placebo-only appeared within 17 weeks.
Note. Data are adapted from Branchey et al. (1981). CPZ-eq. = chlorpromazine-equivalent.

based on a prevalent interpretation of the earlier research literature already reviewed—that it would be unethical to withhold treatment altogether. However, analysis of data provided in Table 5 suggests a 1-year risk of recurrence on placebo of about 67%; this value can be used tentatively as a 0 mg point on a dose-effect curve. Full dosing was associated with an unusually low rate of worsening or relapse of 5%, while the intermediate dose gave a rate of just over 22% and the low dose yielded a rate of approximately 42% (Table 9). A similar study was recently reported by Hogarty (1984) in which schizophrenic patients were assigned to receive 20 mg or 4 mg of fluphenazine decanoate by injection every 2 weeks (equivalent to about 400–500 and 80–100 mg/day of chlor-

Table 9. Outpatient treatment of schizophrenic patients vs. dose of fluphenazine decanoate

Treatment (dose)	*n*	Mean dose (mg/2 wk)	ca. CPZ-eq. (mg/day)	One-year relapse (%)	Incidence TD (%)
High	64	31.2	500–600	4.7	6.4[a]
Medium	18	6.2	100–120	22.2	—
Low	62	3.1	50–60	41.9	3.1[a]
Placebo	>500	0	0	ca. 67.4[b]	—

[a]Too few cases for certainty regarding risk of tardive dyskinesia.
[b]Placebo data from reports on 38 cohorts treated with placebo for a mean of 9.8 ± 1.3 months with a mean relapse rate of 55.2 ± 2.7%, suggesting a 1-year rate of ca. 67.6%; among the 10 studies lasting 12 months, the mean relapse rate was 67.1% (see Table 5).
Note. CPZ-eq. = chlorpromazine-equivalent. TD = tardive dyskinesia. Data are adapted from Kane et al. 1983; Kane 1985.

promazine, respectively). The 1-year relapse rate was 25% at the higher dose and only approximately 23% at the low dose (Table 10).

Finally, Nishikawa and colleagues (1984) followed 50 chronic schizophrenic outpatients for a year under double-blind conditions, with random assignment to placebo or daily doses of haloperidol of 1, 3, or 6 mg. Our analysis of their results suggests that 50% prevention of relapse (apparent ED_{50}) corresponds to a dose of 3.8 mg/day (equivalent to about 150 mg of chlorpromazine). A more recent controlled dose study by the same group of Japanese investigators (Nishikawa et al. 1985) employed random assignment of chronic schizophrenic outpatients to a placebo or to one of eight other regimens involving various combinations of doses of thioridazine and pimozide, with follow-up for 1 year. The results (Table 11) showed a dose-dependent increase in risk of extrapyramidal toxicity across doses; but evidence of dose-dependent, beneficial antipsychotic effects was found only at daily doses up to the equivalent of about 200 mg of chlorpromazine.

Another source of support for the hypothesis that less neuroleptic treatment than is commonly employed may be clinically adequate is studies of intermittent treatment given when needed, as determined by the clinician or the patient. One such study by Carpenter and colleagues (1982) involved following a group of 41 chronic schizophrenic patients for 6 months. These investigators found that giving a neuroleptic only when needed could reduce the total time of treatment from 97% to only 34% of the time of follow-up (a 2.9-fold reduction), with a corresponding fall in the amount of medication used from a 6-month mean of 379 mg/day to only 154 mg/day (a 2.5-fold reduction). There was little evidence of an appreciable loss of clinical benefit, as measured by the number of

Table 10. Effect of dose of fluphenazine decanoate on 1-year exacerbation in schizophrenia

Treatment (dose)	*n*	Mean dose (mg/2 wk)	ca. CPZ-eq. (mg/day)	One-year relapse (%)
High	20	20	400–500	25.0
Low	22	4	80–100	22.7
Placebo	>500	0	0	67.4[a]

[a]Placebo data are obtained as in Table 9.

Note. CPZ-eq. = chlorpromazine-equivalent. Data adapted from Hogarty (1984).

Table 11. Effects of randomly assigned doses of neuroleptics on remission in chronic schizophrenic outpatients

ca. CPZ-eq. doses (mg/day)	n	Time in remission (%) ± SEM	Rate of full remission (%)	Risk of toxicity (%)
400–475	36	42.5 ± 6.0	33	33
158–208	22	60.7 ± 9.3	50	23
25–133	35	21.8 ± 3.1	3	11
0 (placebo)	13	16.2 ± 5.0	0	0

Note. Data represent proportion of all days in a year spent in clinically stable status, the proportion of cases remaining in remission for the entire year, and the risk of extrapyramidal reactions. The 106 patients were randomly assigned to various combinations of 0 or 75 mg of thioridazine and 0, 0.2, or 0.6 mg of pimozide (plus trihexyphenidyl for extrapyramidal reactions and nitrazepam as a hypnotic, as needed). Data are adapted from Nishikawa et al. (1985). The difference of time in remission between the two highest doses is nearly significant by one-tailed t-test ($t = 2.64$, $P < .06$).

days of required hospitalization or by clinical rating scores, in the intermittently treated patients.

Taken together, these results suggest that the ED_{50} necessary to protect against relapse of chronic psychosis is between the equivalent of 50 and 150 mg/day of chlorpromazine. These observations, while not definitive, are intriguing. They imply that the *majority* of chronically psychotic patients can be maintained on doses of neuroleptic as low as one-fifth or even one-tenth those usually employed! Nevertheless, many clinicians would argue that such considerations are mainly of academic pharmacological interest because physicians do not usually treat patients at the ED_{50} of a drug, but instead seek the dose most likely to produce the greatest benefit for the greatest number of patients with the smallest risk of serious side effects.

A further analysis of appropriate available data suggests, however, that the consideration of dose-effect relationships may be of more than casual or academic interest (Diamond 1985). We analyzed data arising from several studies employing more than one dose of fluphenazine decanoate for at least 1 year (Kane et al. 1983; Simpson et al. 1976; Hogarty et al. 1976, 1979; Johnson 1976; Kane 1985). The findings are illustrated in Figure 4. Data were fitted by a computer-assisted program (Baldessarini et al. 1988; Packer and Waud 1971; Nedler and Mead 1965) to two simultaneous dose-effect curves, one for beneficial effects and the other for clinical worsening. This computation assumes, as had been suggested by

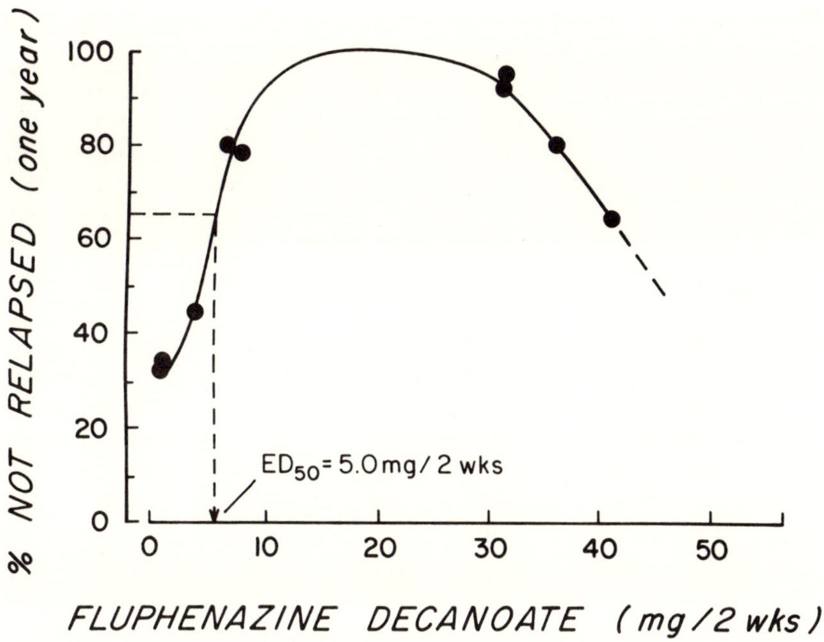

Figure 4. Dose-effect relationship of neuroleptic in chronic psychosis. Data are obtained from six studies (Kane 1985; Kane et al. 1983; Simpson et al. 1976; Hogarty et al. 1976, 1979; Rifkin et al. 1977) involving random assignment of schizophrenic patients to at least two different doses of fluphenazine decanoate (im) during 1 year of follow-up after treatment of a state of acute exacerbation. The data fit a biphasic function having an apparent ED_{50} for beneficial effect (sparing of clinical relapse) of 5 mg/2 weeks, with an interacting negative action having an apparent ED_{50} of 45 mg/2 weeks. The latter "antitherapeutic" effect may be related to neurotoxic effects at higher doses, such as are depicted in Figure 2. This analysis was described previously (Baldessarini et al. 1988). Reprinted, with permission, from *Archives of General Psychiatry*, Vol. 45, 1988, p. 87. Copyright 1988, American Medical Association.

several earlier investigators (Wilkens and Malitz 1960; Simpson et al. 1976; Marder et al. 1984; Diamond 1985), that neurological or other ill-defined side effects of neuroleptics might lead to real or apparent clinical worsening in psychotic patients. While Marder et al. (1984) have recently stressed the untoward effects of akathisia or akinesia on mental status, other effects may also be involved. Our assumption was that two dose-effect curves exist (by analogy to dose-benefit and dose-side effect curves) and overlap so as to interact, especially at the upper end of the dose-benefit curve (Baldessarini et al. 1988). The result predicted, and found, was a biphasic curve with protection increasing to a maximum, followed by decreasing benefits at higher doses. This result is very similar to that found above in examining the acute effects of neuroleptic treatment.

The computed apparent ED_{50} for the beneficial portion of the function in Figure 4 was 5 mg of fluphenazine per 2 weeks, or the approximate equivalent of only some tens of mg per day of oral chlorpromazine (Baldessarini et al. 1988)—a value similar to that suggested in the studies summarized in Tables 6–11. This estimated ED_{50} is somewhat lower than the ED_{50} computed for acutely effective doses (ca. 5–10 mg) (Baldessarini et al. 1988), and much lower than might be expected in view of current treatment practices employing doses typically 10–60 times higher (Baldessarini et al. 1984; Kane et al. 1983; Lehmann et al. 1983; Gardos et al. 1973; Baldessarini et al. 1988; Branchey et al. 1981; Kane 1985; Hogarty 1984). The second function has an apparent ED_{50} of 45 mg per 2 weeks, or the equivalent of approximately 650 mg/day of chlorpromazine (Baldessarini et al. 1988). These results suggest an apparent therapeutic ratio of only nine-fold (45/5 mg). This analysis further implies that doses at or below those commonly used for long-term treatment may have comparable therapeutic and "antitherapeutic" effects! Optimal doses apparently exist, but evidently they occur in a rather limited range, between about 10 and 30 mg of fluphenazine decanoate injected every 2 weeks (Figure 4). The therapeutic index computed for fluphenazine decanoate (9.0) is about six times higher than that found for intramuscular haloperidol (1.5) used in the treatment of acute psychosis (Baldessarini et al. 1988), but the basis of this difference is not known.

The recent study by Nishikawa and colleagues (1985) discussed above and summarized in Table 11 provides data supporting a similar impression. Their observations also suggest a biphasic relationship between dosing and effectiveness of the treatment given, in which optimal benefits were found at the approximate equivalent of about 150–200 mg/day of chlorpromazine, with some loss of efficacy at doses below 150 mg/day, but also at doses above the equivalent of 300 mg/day.

Finally, reports of work by Clark and colleagues (1970, 1972) reveal an interesting disparity in dose-effect relationships, depending on the method of measurement of clinical change. The authors studied 62 chronic schizophrenic patients for periods up to 6 months. When the degree of improvement of the initial presenting signs and symptoms of psychosis was assessed, increasing benefits were seen from daily doses of 150 mg to 600 mg of chlorpromazine. In contrast, assessment of clinical state by the Brief Psychiatric Rating Scale (BPRS) showed an apparently biphasic response, with increasing improvement observed between 0 and 150 mg of medicine per day, a slight additional gain at 300 mg, but substantially less benefit at 600 mg, so much so that clinical state was rated as worse at 600 mg than at 150 mg per day. The BPRS rates many clinical features that might be influenced by side effects of drugs (e.g., "motor retardation," "disorientation," "somatic concern, "anxiety," "emotional withdrawal," and others). Assuming that assignment of doses was not biased by the degree of illness of patients in these reports, it is possible that the biphasic response found with increasing doses of chlorpromazine may reflect neurotoxic or otherwise "antitherapeutic" effects of higher doses of neuroleptic. Some observers have emphasized the importance of akathisia, akinesia, and other extrapyramidal effects of neuroleptics as a basis for the negative impact of medication on some psychotic patients (Van Putten 1983), while others have emphasized putative mood-depressing effects (Hartmann et al. 1980). It is also likely that akinesia can be confused with "depression" and that akathisia can be confused with "agitation" (Baldessarini 1985; Van Putten 1983), and that all of these effects can show up as unfavorable changes in clinical state and its assessment on standard rating scales.

Clearly, these impressions arising from potentially flawed retrospective analyses of a limited number of studies require additional corroboration and testing. For example, even though the studies analyzed claimed random assignment to the doses of fluphenazine given, the experience of one of the studies discussed above (Lehmann et al. 1983) suggests that nonrandom assignment, perhaps of less responsive or more severely ill patients, to higher doses can occur in such studies. Such an artifact could contribute to the biphasic nature of the curves in Figure 4 or of those suggested by other studies already discussed (Table 11; Nishikawa et al. 1985; Clark et al. 1970, 1972). A similar question was raised earlier about the fact that studies of relationships can be generated artifactually if a biased excess of the less responsive patients end up at the higher doses with correspondingly higher plasma levels of drug (Cohen 1983; Cohen and Baldessarini 1984). Despite these caveats, these provocative results strongly suggest not only that further research is required to define optimal doses of neuroleptic agents for short- and long-term use, but also that it is reasonable to seek effective doses for psychotic patients at levels much lower than those currently employed. Not only may higher doses fail to be more effective, but they also may be less therapeutic. They are certainly more toxic, possibly including greater risk of tardive dyskinesia (Gardos et al. 1980; Doongaji et al. 1982).

OTHER ASPECTS OF LONG-TERM NEUROLEPTIC TREATMENT

Now that there are over a dozen long-acting injectable preparations of neuroleptic agents in use worldwide, as well as the enanthate and decanoate esters of fluphenazine and the decanoate ester of haloperidol in North America, it is important to consider the relative advantages of their use. A more generally pertinent question is whether there are significant losses in clinical benefit when control of the treatment shifts from the clinician to the patient. We have already considered the evidence in one relatively small study by Carpenter et al. (1982), which indicated very little loss in the control of chronic psychosis when neuroleptic treatment was given intermittently when needed. Another study on intermittent treatment by Herz et al. (1982) led to similar conclusions, but with some increase in psychotic symptoms. In a 1-year follow-up study of chronic schizophrenic patients, Chien (1975) found an appreciable loss of protection, shown as an increase of relapse from 12% to 38%, when injections of an ester of fluphenazine were scheduled by the patient rather than by the responsible clinician. Several other trials carried out for 1 or 2 years have yielded a variety of outcomes in comparing oral and injected (clinician-controlled) medication (Hogarty et al. 1979; Chien 1975; Rifkin et al. 1977; Quitkin et al. 1978; DelGuidice et al. 1975; Falloon et al. 1978; Johnson 1979; Schooler et al. 1980). Because oral administration of drugs is essentially within the patient's control, it might be predicted that uneven adherence to the recommended treatment would be much more prevalent with oral administration, with a correspondingly poorer outcome. Yet, five of eight comparisons indicated that the results in the first year were virtually indistinguishable between oral and injected medication, or even slightly *better* with oral medication (or patient-elected injections). In the two studies reporting on follow-up for up to 2 years, better results were obtained in the second year when injected medicine was employed (Hogarty et al. 1979; Johnson 1979), suggesting that reduced compliance may eventually have an impact. The results of the eight studies are summarized in Table 12. Overall, there was an approximately 1.7-fold better outcome when injected medicine was employed or when the clinician controlled the schedule. These results, while generally in agreement with conventional wisdom,

Table 12. Effect of patient (Pt)- vs. clinician (MD)-controlled neuroleptic regimen on outcome in schizophrenia

			Relapse rates (%)			
			First year		Two years	
Study	Year	Total *N*	Pt	MD	Pt	MD
Chien[a]	1975	47	38.0	12.4	—	—
DelGuidice et al.[b]	1975	88	92.5	45.0	—	—
Rifkin et al.[c]	1977	73	4.0	5.0	—	—
Falloon et al.[d]	1978	44	20.8	55.0	—	—
Quitkin et al.[e]	1978	56	7.0	10.0	—	—
Hogarty et al.[c]	1979	105	39.5	35.1	64.7	40.3
Johnson[c]	1979	260	43.0	12.0	59.0	34.0
Schooler et al.[c]	1980	214	32.8	24.3	—	—
Kane et al.[c]	1982	11	0.0	0.0	—	—
Total/Mean[f] (±SEM)	9	898	35.4 (±13.0)	21.0 (±6.0)	60.7 (±11.0)	35.8 (±17.8)
Ratio			1.69		1.69	

[a]Fluphenazine (FPZ) enanthate in patient-elected schedule vs. controlled biweekly injections.
[b]Oral FPZ-HCl vs. im FPZ enanthate for 16 months.
[c]Oral FPZ-HCl vs. im FPZ ester for 12 or 24 months.
[d]Oral pimozide vs. im FPZ decanoate.
[e]Oral penfluridol vs. im FPZ decanoate.
[f]Means (weighted by *N*), based on monthly rate × 12.

are sufficiently varied as to suggest that individual, interpersonal, and other factors may play an important role in determining adherence to a treatment regimen and in the eventual outcome (Baldessarini 1985; Johnson 1985).

Additional evidence that subtle, but clinically important, factors enter into the response to antipsychotic treatment over long-term follow-up is provided by a review of the treatment outcome literature by Hogarty (1984). He found that the risk of relapse in chronic schizophrenic patients was not different whether or not the patient had been stable for a year previous to assignment to follow-up on a placebo for 1 year. However, the relapse rate on neuroleptic treatment was lower, and the corresponding neuroleptic: placebo difference stronger, in patients who had remained stable for the year prior to random assignment to continued active medication (4.1- vs. 1.7-fold protection). These observations in a total of nearly 2,000 patients, summarized in Table 13, suggest

Table 13. Exacerbation in schizophrenia vs. recent history

	One-year relapse rates (*N*)	
Treatment	First year	After stable 1 year
Neuroleptic	41% (814)	16% (500)
Placebo	68% (189)	65% (448)
Sparing of relapse	27%	49%
Protection ratio[a]	1.66	4.06

[a]Ratio of relapse on placebo:drug treatment.
Note. Data from review by Hogarty (1984). The results suggest that risk following drug withdrawal continues, but that risk is lower on medication given following a year of stability.

that the beneficial effects of prolonged neuroleptic treatment interact with poorly defined individual factors associated with ability to remain stable. Expressed from a somewhat different point of view, such findings suggest that not all psychotic patients are likely to benefit equally from continued neuroleptic treatment. The current lack of clearly defined criteria with which to select those patients with different requirements for medication calls for an individualized approach to the long-term treatment of patients on a case-by-case basis.

One final point to be made concerning the appropriate comprehensive care of psychotic patients is that optimal improvement and rehabilitation is not likely to arise simply from the optimization of neuroleptic treatment (Baldessarini 1985; Hogarty 1984; Johnson 1985). (See other chapters in this volume for more extensive coverage of this topic.) However, it should be emphasized that recent studies support the impression that, while traditional intensive dynamic psychotherapy is of questionable specific value in the treatment of chronically psychotic patients (Gunderson et al. 1984; McGlashan 1984), and while psychosocial interventions are generally less effective treatment for psychotic symptoms than neuroleptic medication (Hogarty et al. 1973, 1974, 1976, 1979; Hogarty and Ulrich 1977; Chien 1975; Goldstein et al. 1978; Hogarty 1984), the use of supportive and rehabilitative interventions is appropriate on humanitarian and general clinical grounds. Moreover, recent studies provide suggestive evidence that specific psychosocial interventions, especially those with a family therapy and psychoeducational approach, can interact favorably with neuroleptic treatment, at least temporarily (Table 14) (Hogarty 1984; Falloon et al. 1982; Leff et al. 1982).

The data in Table 5, discussed above and reviewed elsewhere

Table 14. Effects of neuroleptics and psychosocial treatment in schizophrenia

Study	Year	*N*	Drug alone	Drug + other	*P*
Falloon et al.	1982	36	44.4%	5.6%	0.02
Leff et al.	1982	24	50.0%	8.3%	0.07
Hogarty	1984	102	25.5%	11.1%	0.11
Total (%)		162	26/78 (33.3%)	8/84 (9.5%)	2.47×10^{-4}

Note. All patients were maintained on similar neuroleptic regimens; half also received psychoeducational family therapy and 10% received social skills training. The pooled results were highly significant (Mantel-Haenszel χ^2 of association = 13.4, $P = 2.47 \times 10^{-4}$) (Janicak et al. 1985), but only the study by Falloon et al. (1982) was statistically significant alone ($P < 0.05$ by χ^2 with Yates' correction), and further follow-up suggested that the 3.5-fold additional early benefits of the psychosocial treatment would diminish later.

(Baldessarini et al. 1988), indicate that even with presumably adequate (or excessive) neuroleptic treatment, 14.3% of schizophrenic patients relapsed within 9.8 months of follow-up, on average. In some studies, these relapse rates on active medication were much higher (up to 38% in 1 year and 48% in 2 years). Clearly, available interventions are far from ideal. Even when neuroleptic treatment can reduce the risk of gross states of exacerbation and the need for rehospitalization, the level of improvement of function, social and family life, work, and productivity is often very limited. Indeed, a trend in contemporary psychiatry is to view schizophrenia again as a severe, chronic illness with many analogies to mental retardation or dementia. One of the effects of sociological and family studies has been to reduce the pressures on such patients and to support compromises and limited expectations (Hogarty 1984; Falloon et al. 1982; Leff et al. 1982).

Conclusions

The treatment of acute psychotic illnesses of various kinds has been revolutionized by the development of neuroleptic agents since the 1950s. Nearly all of these agents in current clinical use in the United States are effective antagonists of dopamine receptors in the basal ganglia, limbic forebrain, and hypothalamus-pituitary. This activity, and the routine association of extrapyramidal and other neurological side effects with antipsychotic effects, probably reflect the conservative nature of the process of developing such drugs by imitation of the characteristics of earlier compounds in the field. While the hope continues that novel agents may be developed that are effectively antipsychotic but lack extrapyramidal and other unacceptable systemic toxic actions, there are few compelling pharmacological theories to guide this process at the present time, and the basis of activity of the few atypical agents that are known remains obscure or controversial (Baldessarini 1985). The search for alternative treatments of acutely psychotic patients has included a revived interest in the use of agents usually considered sedative or antianxiety agents, such as the benzodiazepines (Baldessarini 1985; Cohen and Lipinski 1986), as well as centrally effective antiadrenergic agents, calcium channel-blocking drugs, anticonvulsants, and others. However, the efficacy and possible long-term benefits of these alternative agents remain unclear.

In the meantime, while awaiting the development of better treatments, the use of available antipsychotic agents may be improved by more careful attention to clinical evidence. This includes the observation that moderate doses of neuroleptics are adequate, and that high doses are associated not only with increased risk of side effects but probably also with a loss of clinical benefits. This observation may reflect the behavioral and psychological impact of neurotoxic actions of high doses of neuroleptic agents. Even though attempts to apply assays of blood levels of neuroleptic agents to improve clinical methods of dosing have met only very limited success, they support the impression that excessive as well as low drug concentrations may be associated with inferior clinical benefits. They also strongly suggest that robust relationships between dose or tissue levels of neuroleptic agents and their clinical effects are most likely to be observable when low to moderate doses are employed.

The evidence supporting the long-term benefits of antipsychotic medication remains incomplete. There is a relative lack of very long-term studies in large numbers of reasonably homogeneous populations diagnosed by contemporary criteria. Particular care must be given to separate chronic schizophrenic patients from those with affective, intermittent, organic, and other psychotic illnesses. The available data concerning dose-response relationships in the long-term use of neuroleptic agents now strongly support the impressions arising from acute studies—that, on average, unusually large doses not only fail to provide greater benefits and are associated with greater toxicity, but also tend to yield inferior clinical benefits. It is likely that the risk of tardive dyskinesia and other late neurological complications of prolonged neuroleptic treatment will turn out to be dependent on dose when low, effective doses are evaluated and excessive doses are avoided. Antipsychotic agents, while having the most extensive and compelling support as a major contributor to the care of psychotic patients, are only one aspect of the medically sound and humane treatment of such patients, as is considered in other chapters of this volume.

References

American Psychiatric Association: Diagnostic and Statistical Manual—Third Edition (DSM-III). Washington, DC, American Psychiatric Association, 1980

American Psychiatric Association: Diagnostic and Statistical Manual—Third Edition–Revised (DSM-III-R). Washington, DC, American Psychiatric Association, 1987

Anderson WH, Kuehnle JC, Catanzano DM: Rapid treatment of acute psychosis. Am J Psychiatry 133:1076–1078, 1976

Andrews P, Hall JN, Snaith RP: A controlled trial of phenothiazine withdrawal in chronic schizophrenic patients. Br J Psychiatry 128:451–455, 1976

Appleton WS, Davis JM: Practical Clinical Psychopharmacology, 2nd Edition. Baltimore, MD, Williams and Wilkins, 1980

Aubree JC, Lader MH: High and very high dosage antipsychotics: a critical review. J Clin Psychiatry 41:341–350, 1980

Ayd FJ Jr: Large doses of chlorpromazine in the treatment of psychiatric patients. Dis Nerv Syst 16:146–149, 1955

Baldessarini RJ: Antipsychotic agents, in Psychiatric Therapies. Edited by Karasu B. Washington, DC, American Psychiatric Association, 1984, pp 119–170

Baldessarini RJ: Chemotherapy in Psychiatry: Principles and Practice. Cambridge, MA, Harvard University Press, 1985

Baldessarini RJ, Davis JM: What *is* the best maintenance dose of neuroleptics in schizophrenia? Psychiatry Res 3:115–122, 1980

Baldessarini RJ, Cole JO, Davis JM, et al: Tardive Dyskinesia. Task Force Report 18. Washington, DC, American Psychiatric Association, 1980

Baldessarini RJ, Katz B, Cotton P: Dissimilar dosing with high-potency and low-potency neuroleptics. Am J Psychiatry 141:748–752, 1984

Baldessarini RJ, Cohen BM, Teicher MH: Significance of neuroleptic dose and plasma level in the pharmacological treatment of psychoses. Arch Gen Psychiatry 45:79–91, 1988

Beckman H, Haas S: High dose diazepam in schizophrenia. Psychopharmacology (Berlin) 71:79–82, 1980

Bigelow LB, Kirch DG, Braun T, et al: Absence of a relationship of serum haloperidol concentration and clinical response in chronic schizophrenia: a fixed-dose study. Psychopharmacol Bull 21:66–68, 1985

Bishop MP, Gallant DM, Sykes TF: Extrapyramidal side effects and therapeutic response. Arch Gen Psychiatry 13:155–162, 1965

Bjørndal N, Bjerre M, Gerlach J, et al: High dose haloperidol therapy in chronic schizophrenic patients: a double-blind study of clinical response, side effects, serum haloperidol, and serum prolactin. Psychopharmacology (Berlin) 67:17–23, 1980

Blackburn HL, Allen JL: Behavioral effects in interrupting and resuming tranquilizing medication among schizophrenics. J Nerv Ment Dis 133:303–308, 1961

Bollini P, Andreain A, Colombo F, et al: High dose neuroleptics: uncontrolled clinical practice confirms controlled clinical trials. Br J Psychiatry 144:25–27, 1984

Branchey MH, Branchey LB, Richardson MA: Effects of neuroleptic adjustment on clinical condition and tardive dyskinesia in schizophrenic patients. Am J Psychiatry 138:608–612, 1981

Brotman RK, Musekari LH, Shanken PM: Butaperazine in chronic schizophrenic patients: a double-blind study. Curr Ther Res 11:5–8, 1969

Brown WA, Silver MA: Serum neuroleptic levels and clinical outcome in schizophrenic patients treated with fluphenazine decanoate. J Clin Psychopharmacol 5:143–147, 1985

Brunswick DJ, Amsterdam JD, Mendels J, et al: Prediction of steady-state imipramine and desmethylimipramine plasma concentrations from single-dose data. Clin Pharmacol Ther 25:605–610, 1979

Caffey EM, Diamond LS, Frank TV, et al: Discontinuation or reduction of chemotherapy in chronic schizophrenics. J Chronic Dis 17:347–358, 1964

Campbell A, Herschel M, Cohen BM, et al: Tissue levels of haloperidol by radioreceptor assay and behavioral effects of haloperidol in the rat. Life Sci 27:633–640, 1980

Campbell A, Herschel M, Madsen J, et al: Circadian changes in the distribution and effects of haloperidol in the rat. Neuropharmacology 21:663–669, 1982

Carpenter WT, Stevens JH, Rey AC, et al: Early intervention vs. continuous pharmacotherapy in schizophrenia. Psychopharmacol Bull 18:21–23, 1982

Carscallen HB, Rochman H, Lovegrove TD: High dosage trifluoperazine in schizophrenia. Can Psychiatr Assoc J 13:459–461, 1968

Carter RG: Psychotolysis with haloperidol: rapid control of the acutely disturbed psychotic patient. Dis Nerv Syst 38:237–239, 1977

Carter RG: Use of oral haloperidol following rapid tranquilization of acutely disturbed patients. W Va Med J 74:55–56, 1978

Casper R, Garver DL, Dekirmenjian H, et al: Phenothiazine levels in plasma and red blood cells. Arch Gen Psychiatry 37:301–305, 1980

Cheung HK: Schizophrenics fully remitted on neuroleptics for 3–5 years—To stop or continue drugs? Br J Psychiatry 138:490–494, 1981

Chien CP: Drugs and rehabilitation in schizophrenia, in Drugs in Combination with Other Therapies. Edited by Greenblatt M. New York, Grune & Stratton, 1975, pp 13–34

Chien CP, Cole JO: Depot phenothiazine treatment in acute psychosis: a sequential comparative clinical study. Am J Psychiatry 130:13–17, 1973

Chouinard G, Jones BB, Annable L: Neuroleptic-induced supersensitivity psychosis. Am J Psychiatry 135:1409–1410, 1978

Chouinard G, Young SN, Annable L: Antimanic effect of clonazepam. Biol Psychiatry 18:451–466, 1983

Clark ML, Ramsey HR, Ragland RE, et al: Chlorpromazine in chronic schizophrenia: behavioral dose-response relationships. Psychopharmacologia 18:260–270, 1970

Clark ML, Ramsey HR, Rahdal DK, et al: Chlorpromazine in chronic schizophrenia: the effect of age and hospitalization on behavioral dose response relationships. Arch Gen Psychiatry 27:479–483, 1972

Clark ML, Huber W, Hill D, et al: Pimozide and thioridazine in chronic outpatients. Dis Nerv Syst 36:137–141, 1975

Clark ML, Kaul PN, Whitfield CR: Chlorpromazine kinetics and clinical response. Psychopharmacol Bull 14:43–45, 1978

Cloninger CR, Martin RL, Guze SB, et al: Diagnosis and prognosis in schizophrenia. Arch Gen Psychiatry 42:15–25, 1985

Cohen BM: The clinical utility of plasma neuroleptic levels, in Guidelines for the Use of Psychotropic Drugs. Edited by Stan-

cer HC, Garfinkel PE, Rakoff VM. Jamaica, NY, Spectrum Publications, 1983, pp 246–260
Cohen BM, Baldessarini RJ: Blood neuroleptic levels as a guide to clinical treatment, in Directions in Psychiatry, Vol 4 (part 37). Edited by Flach FF. New York, Hatherleigh Company, 1984, pp 1–7
Cohen BM, Lipinski JF: Radioreceptor assays of blood levels of neuroleptics, in Neuroreceptors—Basic and Clinical Aspects. Edited by Usdin E. New York, Wiley and Sons, 1981, pp 199–214
Cohen BM, Lipinski JF: The treatment of acute psychosis with non-neuroleptic agents. Psychosomatics 527:7–16, 1986
Cohen BM, Herschel M, Aoba A: Neuroleptic, antimuscarinic, and antiadrenergic activity of chlorpromazine, thioridazine, and their metabolites. Psychiatry Res 1:199–208, 1979
Cohen BM, Herschel M, Miller EM, et al: Radioreceptor assay of haloperidol tissue levels in the rat. Neuropharmacology 19:663–668, 1980a
Cohen BM, Lipinski JF, Harris PQ, et al: Neuroleptic blood levels of patients on thioridazine and clinical improvement. Psychopharmacology (Berlin) 70:191–194, 1980b
Cohen BM, Lipinski JF, Harris PQ, et al: Clinical use of the radioreceptor assay for neuroleptics. Psychiatry Res 2:173–178, 1980c
Cole JO: Antipsychotic drugs: is more better? McLean Hosp J 7:61–87, 1982
Cooper TB: Neuroleptic drug monitoring and radioreceptor assays. J Clin Psychopharmacol 5:A15–A16, 1985
Cooper TB, Simpson GM: The 24-hour lithium-level as a prognosticator of dosage requirements: a two-year follow-up study. Am J Psychiatry 133:440–443, 1976
Cooper TB, Simpson GM: Prediction of individual dosage of nortriptyline. Am J Psychiatry 135:333–335, 1978
Cooper TB, Simpson GM, Lee HJ: Thymoleptic and neuroleptic drug plasma levels in psychiatry: current status. Int Rev Neurobiol 19:269–309, 1976
Creese I, Snyder SH: A novel, simple and sensitive radioreceptor assay for antischizophrenic drugs in blood. Nature 270:180–182, 1977
Curry SH: Determination of nanogram quantities of chlorpromazine and some of its metabolites in plasma using gas-liquid chromatography with an electron capture detector. Analyt Chem 40:1251–1255, 1968

Curry SH: Commentary: the strategy and value of neuroleptic drug monitoring. J Clin Psychopharmacol 5:263–271, 1985

Curry SH, Marshall JHL, Davis JM, et al: Chlorpromazine plasma levels and effects. Arch Gen Psychiatry 22:289–296, 1970

Danik JJ, Goverdham M: Haloperidol in the treatment of 120 psychotic patients. Am J Psychiatry 120:389–391, 1963

Davis JM, Erickson SE, Dekirmenjian H: Plasma levels of antipsychotic drugs and clinical response, in Psychopharmacology: A Generation of Progress. Edited by Lipton MA, DiMascio A, Killam KF. New York, Raven Press, 1978, pp 905–916

Davis JM, Erickson SE, Hurt S, et al: Haloperidol plasma levels and clinical response. Basic concepts and clinical data. Psychopharmacol Bull 21:48–51, 1985

Deberdt R: Lorazepam in the treatment of severe anxiety and anxiety associated with psychotic conditions. Curr Med Res Opin 1:296–300, 1973

DeBuck RP: Relative safety and efficacy of high and low dose administration of fluphenazine HCl to psychotic patients, in Proceedings of the Eighth International Congress of Neuropsychopharmacology (CINP, Copenhagen, Denmark), International Congress Series. Amsterdam, Excerpta Medica, 1972, pp 265–272

DelGuidice J, Clark WC, Gocka EF: Prevention of recidivism of schizophrenics treated with fluphenazine enanthate. Psychosomatics 16:32–36, 1975

Deneker SJ, Johanssen R, Lundin L, et al: High doses of fluphenazine enanthate in schizophrenia: a controlled study. Acta Psychiatr Scand 57:405–414, 1978

Diamond LS, Marks JB: Discontinuance of tranquilizers among chronic schizophrenic patients receiving maintenance dosage. J Nerv Ment Dis 131:247–251, 1960

Diamond R: Drugs and the quality of life: the patient's point of view. J Clin Psychiatry 46(No 5, Sec 2):29–35, 1985

Donlon PT: High dosage neuroleptic therapy. Int Pharmacopsychiatr 11:235–245, 1976

Donlon PT, Tupin JP: Rapid "Digitalization" of decompensated schizophrenic patients with antipsychotic agents. Am J Psychiatry 131:310–312, 1974

Donlon PT, Meadon A, Tupin JP, et al: High vs. standard dosage fluphenazine HCl in acute schizophrenia. J Clin Psychiatry 39:800–804, 1978

Donlon PT, Hopkin J, Tupin JP: Overview: efficacy and safety of the rapid neuroleptization method with injectable haloperidol. Am J Psychiatry 136:273–278, 1979

Donlon PT, Hopkin JT, Tupin JP: Haloperidol for acute schizophrenic patients: an evaluation of three oral regimens. Arch Gen Psychiatry 37:691–695, 1980

Doongaji DR, Jeste DV, Jape NM, et al: Tardive dyskinesia in India. J Clin Psychopharmacol 2:341–344, 1982

Dubin WR, Waxman HM, Weiss KJ, et al: Rapid tranquilization: the efficacy of oral concentrate. J Clin Psychiatry 46:475–478, 1985

Dysken MW, Javaid JI, Chang SS, et al: Fluphenazine pharmacokinetics and therapeutic response. Psychopharmacology (Berlin) 73:205–210, 1981

Engelhardt DM, Freedman N, Glick BS, et al: Prevention of psychiatric hospitalization with the use of psychopharmacological agents. JAMA 173:147–149, 1960

Engelhardt DM, Rosen B, Freedman N, et al: Phenothiazines in prevention of psychiatric hospitalization. Arch Gen Psychiatry 16:98–101, 1967

Ericksen SE, Hurt SW, Chang S: Haloperidol dose, plasma levels, and clinical response: a double-blind study. Psychopharmacol Bull 14:15–16, 1978

Escobar JI, Barron A, Kiriakos R: A controlled study of "neuroleptization" with fluphenazine hydrochloride injections. J Clin Psychopharmacol 3:359–362, 1983

Faleni RA: The use of high doses of fluphenazine in the treatment of psychotic patients. Psychosomatics 11:496–499, 1970

Falloon IR, Watt DC, Shepherd M: A comparative controlled-trial of pimozide and fluphenazine decanoate in the continuation therapy of schizophrenia. Psychol Med 8:59–70, 1978

Falloon IR, Boyd JL, McGill CW, et al: Family management in the prevention of exacerbations of schizophrenia: a controlled study. N Engl J Med 306:1437–1440, 1982

Firling RJ: Acutely disturbed psychotic patients treated with parenteral haloperidol. Int Med J 153:117, 1978

Fitzgerald CH: A double-blind comparison of haloperidol with perphenazine in acute psychotic episodes. Curr Ther Res 11:515–519, 1969

Freeman LS, Alson E: Prolonged withdrawal of chlorpromazine in chronic patients. Dis Nerv Syst 23:522–525, 1962

Frykholm B: Clonazepam—Antipsychotic effect in a case of schizophrenia-like psychosis with epilepsy and in three cases of atypical psychosis. Acta Psychiatr Scand 71:539–542, 1985

Galbrecht CR, Klett CJ: Predicting response to phenothiazines: the right drug for the right patient. J Nerv Ment Dis 147:173–183, 1968

Gardos G, Cole JO: Maintenance antipsychotic therapy: is the cure worse than the disease? Am J Psychiatry 133:32–36, 1976

Gardos G, Cole JO, Orzack MH: The importance of dosage in antipsychotic drug administration—a review of dose-response studies. Psychopharmacologia 29:221–230, 1973

Gardos G, Orzack M, Finn G, et al: High and low-dose thiothixene treatment of chronic schizophrenia. Dis Nerv System 35:53–58, 1974

Gardos G, Samu I, Kallos M, et al: Absence of severe tardive dyskinesia in Hungarian schizophrenic outpatients. Psychopharmacology (Berlin) 71:29–34, 1980

Garfield SL, Gershon S, Sletten I, et al: Withdrawal of ataractic medication in schizophrenic patients. Dis Nerv Syst 27:321–325, 1966

Garver DL, Hirschowitz J, Glicksteen GA, et al: Haloperidol plasma and red blood cell levels and clinical antipsychotic response. J Clin Psychopharmacol 4:133–137, 1984

Gelder M, Kolakowska T: Variability of response to neuroleptics in schizophrenia. Compr Psychiatry 20:397–408, 1979

Gerstenzang ML, Krulisky TV: Parenteral haloperidol in psychiatric emergencies: double-blind comparison with chlorpromazine. Dis Nerv Syst 38:581–583, 1977

Goldstein MJ, Rodnick EH, Evans JR, et al: Drug and family therapy in the aftercare of acute schizophrenics. Arch Gen Psychiatry 35:1169–1177, 1978

Gottschalk LA: A preliminary approach to the problems of relating the pharmacokinetics of phenothiazines to clinical response with schizophrenic patients, in Pharmacokinetics of Psychoactive Drugs: Further Study. Edited by Gottschalk LA. New York, Spectrum Publications, 1979, pp 63–81

Greenberg JS, Brown WA, Laughren TP, et al: Neuroleptic levels by radioreceptor assay and clinical response during treatment of acute exacerbations of schizophrenia—some preliminary findings. Psychopharmacol Bull 19:74–76, 1983

Gross HL: A double-blind comparison of once-a-day pimozide, trifluoperazine and placebo in the maintenance care of chronic schizophrenic outpatients. Curr Ther Res 16:696–705, 1974

Gross M: The impact of ataractic drugs on a mental hospital outpatient clinic. Am J Psychiatry 117:444–448, 1960

Gunderson JG, Frank AF, Katz HM, et al: Effects of psychotherapy in schizophrenia. II. Comparative outcome of two forms of treatment. Schizophr Bull 10:564–598, 1984

Gurland BJ, Fleiss JL, Cooper JE, et al: Cross-national study of diagnosis of mental disorders: hospital diagnoses and hospital patients in New York and London. Compr Psychiatry 11:18–25, 1970

Guz I, Moraes R, Sartoretto JN: The therapeutic effects of lorazepam in psychotic patients treated with haloperidol: a double-blind study. Curr Ther Res 14:767–774, 1972

Guze SB, Cloninger CR, Martin RM, et al: A follow-up and family study of schizophrenia. Arch Gen Psychiatry 40:1273–1276, 1983

Hansen CB, Larsen NE, Gulmann N: Dose-response relationship of perphenazine in the treatment of acute psychoses. Psychopharmacology (Berlin) 27:112–115, 1972

Hartmann W, Kind J, Meyer JE, et al: Neuroleptic drugs and the prevention of relapse in schizophrenia: a workshop report. Schizophr Bull 6:536–541, 1980

Hershon HI, Kennedy PF, McGuire RJ: Persistence of extrapyramidal disorders and psychiatric relapse after withdrawal of long-term phenothiazine therapy. Br J Psychiatry 120:41–50, 1972

Herz MI, Szymanski HV, Simon JC: Intermittent medication for stable schizophrenic outpatients: an alternative to maintenance medication. Am J Psychiatry 139:918–922, 1982

Hirsch SR, Gaind R, Rohde PD, et al: Outpatient maintenance of chronic schizophrenic patients with long-acting fluphenazine: double-blind placebo trial. Br Med J 1:633–637, 1973

Hogarty GE: Depot neuroleptics: the relevance of psychosocial factors—a United States perspective. J Clin Psychiatry 45(No 5, Sec 2):36–42, 1984

Hogarty GE, Ulrich RF: Temporal effects of drug and placebo in delaying relapse in schizophrenic outpatients. Arch Gen Psychiatry 34:297–301, 1977

Hogarty GE, Goldberg SC, Collaborative Study Group: Drugs and sociotherapy in the aftercare of schizophrenic patients. I. One year relapse rates. Arch Gen Psychiatry 30:54–64, 1973

Hogarty GE, Goldberg SC, Schooler NR, et al: Drug and sociotherapy in the aftercare of schizophrenic patients. II. Two-year relapse rates. Arch Gen Psychiatry 31:603–608, 1974

Hogarty GE, Ulrich RF, Mussare F, et al: Drug discontinuation among long-term successfully maintained schizophrenic outpatients. Dis Nerv Syst 37:494–500, 1976

Hogarty GE, Schooler N, Ulrich RF, et al: Fluphenazine and social therapy in the aftercare of schizophrenic patients. Arch Gen Psychiatry 36:1283–1294, 1979

Hurt SW, Holzman PS, Davis JM: Thought disorder: the measurement of its changes. Arch Gen Psychiatry 40:1281–1285, 1983

Itil T, Keskiner A: Fluphenazine hydrochloride, enanthate, and decanoate in the management of chronic psychosis. Dis Nerv Syst 31 (suppl):37–42, 1970

Itil T, Keskiner A, Heinemann L, et al: Treatment of resistant schizophrenics with extreme high dosage fluphenazine hydrochloride. Psychosomatics 11:456–463, 1970

Itil T, Saletu B, Hsu W, et al: Clinical and quantitative EEG changes at different dosage levels of fluphenazine treatment. Acta Psychiatr Scand 47:440–451, 1971

Janicak PG, Davis JM, Gibbons RD, et al: A meta-analysis. Am J Psychiatry 142:297–302, 1985

Janssen PAJ, Allewijn FTN: The distribution of the butyrophenones haloperidol, trifluperidol, moperone, and clofluperol in rats, and its relationship with their neuroleptic activity. Arzneimittelforschung 19:199–208, 1969

Johnson DAW: The duration of maintenance therapy in chronic schizophrenia. Acta Psychiatr Scand 53:298–301, 1976

Johnson DAW: Further observations on the duration of depot neuroleptic maintenance therapy in schizophrenia. Br J Psychiatry 135:524–530, 1979

Johnson DAW: Antipsychotic medication: clinical guidelines for maintenance therapy. J Clin Psychiatry 46(No 5, Sec 2):6–15, 1985

Johnson DAW, Pasterski G, Ludlow JM, et al: The discontinuance of maintenance neuroleptic therapy in chronic schizophrenic patients: drug and social consequences. Acta Psychiatr Scand 67:339–352, 1983

Kane JM: Antipsychotic drug side effects: their relationship to dose. J Clin Psychiatry 46(No 5, Sec 2):16–21, 1985

Kane JM, Smith JM: Tardive dyskinesia: prevalence and risk factors, 1959 to 1979. Arch Gen Psychiatry 39:473–481, 1982

Kane JM, Rifkin A, Quitkin F, et al: Fluphenazine vs. placebo in patients with remitted, acute first-episode schizophrenia. Arch Gen Psychiatry 39:70–73, 1982

Kane JM, Rifkin A, Woerner M, et al: Low-dose neuroleptic treatment of outpatient schizophrenics. Arch Gen Psychiatry 40:893–896, 1983

Keepers GA, Clappison VJ, Casey DE: Initial anticholinergic prophylaxis for neuroleptic-induced extrapyramidal syndromes. Arch Gen Psychiatry 40:1113–1117, 1983

Kinross-Wright J, Charalampous KD: A controlled study of a very long-acting phenothiazine preparation. Int J Neuropsychiatry 1:66–70, 1965

Kinross-Wright V: The intensive chlorpromazine treatment of schizophrenia. Psychiatry Res Rep 1:53–62, 1955

Kirkpatrick B, Burnett GB: Observations on neuroleptic use in acutely psychotic patients. J Clin Psychopharmacol 2:205–207, 1982

Ko GN, Korpi ER, Linnoila M: On the clinical relevance and methods of quantification of plasma concentrations of neuroleptics. J Clin Psychopharmacol 5:253–262, 1985

Koster van Groos GA: The treatment of neurotic and psychotic anxiety with lorazepam. Curr Med Res Opinion 1:288–290, 1973

Lader M: Monitoring plasma concentrations of neuroleptics. Pharmakopsychiatrie 9:170–177, 1976

Leff J, Wing JK: Trial of maintenance therapy in schizophrenics. Br Med J 3:599–604, 1971

Leff J, Kuipers L, Berkowitz R, et al: A controlled trial of social intervention in the families of schizophrenic patients. Br J Psychiatry 141:121–134, 1982

Lehmann H, Wilson WH, Deutsch M: Minimal maintenance medication: effects of three dose schedules on relapse rates and symptoms in chronic schizophrenic outpatients. Compr Psychiatry 24:293–303, 1983

Lerner Y, Lwow E, Levitan A, et al: Acute high-dose parenteral haloperidol treatment of psychosis. Am J Psychiatry 136:1061–1064, 1979

Levenson AJ, Burness GB, Nottingham JD, et al: Speed and rate of remission in acute schizophrenia: a comparison of intramuscularly administered fluphenazine HCl with thiothixene and haloperidol. Curr Ther Res 20:695–700, 1976

Levine J, Schooler NR, Severe J, et al: Discontinuation of oral and depot fluphenazine in schizophrenic patients after one year of continuous medication: a controlled study. Adv Biochem Psychopharmacol 24:483–493, 1980

Linden R, Davis JM, Rubenstein J: High vs. low dose treatment with antipsychotic agents. Psychiatr Annals 12:769–781, 1982

Man PL, Chen C: Rapid tranquilization of acutely psychotic patients with intramuscular haloperidol and chlorpromazine. Psychosomatics 14:59–63, 1973

Marder SR, Van Putten T, Mintz J, et al: Costs and benefits of two doses of fluphenazine. Arch Gen Psychiatry 41:1025–1029, 1984

Mason AS, Granacher RP: Rapid tranquilization methods, in Clinical Handbook of Antipsychotic Drug Therapy. New York, Brunner/Mazel, 1980, pp 109–141

Mavroidis ML, Kanter DR, Hirschowitz J, et al: Clinical response and plasma haloperidol levels in schizophrenia. Psychopharmacology (Berlin) 81:354–356, 1983

Mavroidis ML, Kanter DR, Hirschowitz J, et al: Clinical relevance of thiothixene plasma levels. J Clin Psychopharmacol 4:155–157, 1984a

Mavroidis ML, Kanter DR, Hirschowitz J, et al: Therapeutic blood levels of fluphenazine: plasma or RBC determinations? Psychopharmacol Bull 20:168–170, 1984b

May PRA, Van Putten T: Plasma levels of chlorpromazine in schizophrenia: a critical review of the literature. Arch Gen Psychiatry 35:1081–1087, 1978

May PRA, Van Putten T, Jenden DJ, et al: Chlorpromazine levels and the outcome of treatment in schizophrenic patients. Arch Gen Psychiatry 38:202–207, 1981

McClelland HA, Farquharson RG, Leyburn P, et al: Very high dose fluphenazine decanoate. A controlled trial in chronic schizophrenia. Arch Gen Psychiatry 33:1435–1439, 1976

McCreadie RG, Macdonald IM: High dosage haloperidol in chronic schizophrenia. Br J Psychiatry 131:310–316, 1977

McCreadie RG, Flanagan WL, McKnight J, et al: High dose flupenthixol decanoate in chronic schizophrenia. Br J Psychiatry 135:175–179, 1979

McGlashan TH: The Chestnut Lodge Follow-up Study. II. Long-term outcome of schizophrenia and affective disorders. Arch Gen Psychiatry 41:586–601, 1984

McGlashan TH, MacDonald IM: High dosage haloperidol in chronic schizophrenia. Br J Psychiatry 131:310–316, 1977

McIntyre IM, Gershon S: Interpatient variations in antipsychotic therapy. J Clin Psychiatry 46(No 5, Sec 2):3–5, 1985

Melnyk WT, Worthington AG, Laverty SG: Abrupt withdrawal of chlorpromazine and thioridazine from schizophrenic inpatients. Can Psychiatr Assoc J 11:410–413, 1966

Modell JG, Lenox RH, Weiner S: Inpatient clinical trial of lorazepam for the management of manic agitation. J Clin Psychopharmacol 5:109–113, 1985

Mountain HE: Crash tranquilization in a milieu therapy setting. J Fort Logan Health Center 1:43–44, 1963

Muller P, Kind J: A study on the prophylaxis of relapse. Reported by Hartmann W, Kind J, Meyer JE, et al: Neuroleptic drugs and the prevention of relapse in schizophrenia: a workshop report. Schizophr Bull 6:536–541, 1980

National Institute of Mental Health, Psychopharmacology Research Branch Collaborative Study Group: Short-term improvement in schizophrenia: the contribution of background factors. Am J Psychiatry 124:900–909, 1968

Neborsky R, Janowsky D, Munson E, et al: Rapid treatment of acute psychiatric symptoms with high-low-dose haloperidol. Arch Gen Psychiatry 38:195–199, 1981

Nedler JA, Mead R: A simplex method for function minimization. Computer J 7:308–313, 1965

Neimegeers CJE, Heykauts JJP, Janssen PAJ: Antiemetic effect of haloperidol in the dog as related to plasma level and dose. Psychopharmacology (Berlin) 75:240–244, 1981

Nishikawa T, Tsuda A, Tanaka M, et al: Prophylactic effect of neuroleptics in symptom-free schizophrenics: a comparative dose-response study of haloperidol and propericiazine. Psychopharmacology (Berlin) 82:153–156, 1984

Nishikawa T, Tsuda A, Tanaka M, et al: Prophylactic effects of neuroleptics in symptom-free schizophrenics: roles of dopaminergic and noradrenergic blockers. Biol Psychiatry 20:1161–1166, 1985

Öhman R, Larsson M, Nilsson IM: Neurometabolic and behavioral effects of haloperidol in relation to drug level in serum and brain. Naunyn Schmiedebergs Arch Pharmacol 229:105–114, 1977

Oldham AJ, Bott M: The management of excitement in a general hospital psychiatric ward by high dosage haloperidol. Acta Psychiatr Scand 47:369–376, 1971

Packer R, Waud D: Pharmacological estimation of drug-receptor dissociation constants. J Pharmacol Exp Ther 177:1–12, 1971

Paprock J, Versiani M: A double-fluid comparison between loxapine and haloperidol by parenteral route in acute schizophrenia. Curr Ther Res 21:80–100, 1977

Pasamanick B, Scarpitti FR, Lefton M, et al: Home vs. hospital care for schizophrenics. JAMA 187:177–181, 1964

Platz AR, Klett CJ, Caffey EM Jr: Selective drug action related to chronic schizophrenic subtype (a comparative study of carphenazine, chlorpromazine, and trifluoperazine). Dis Nerv Syst 28:601–605, 1967

Polack P, Laycob L: Rapid tranquilization. Am J Psychiatry 128:640–643, 1971

Polvan N, Vagcioglu V, Itil F, et al: High and very high dose fluphenazine in the treatment of chronic psychosis, in Proceedings of the Sixth International Congress of Neuropsychopharmacology (CINP, Terragona, Spain), International Congress Series No 180. Amsterdam, Excerpta Medica, 1968, pp 495–497

Potkin SG, Shen Y, Zhou D, et al: Does a therapeutic window for plasma haloperidol exist? Preliminary Chinese data. Psychopharmacol Bull 21:59–61, 1985

Prien RF, Cole JO: High dose chlorpromazine therapy in chronic schizophrenia. Arch Gen Psychiatry 18:482–495, 1968

Prien RF, Cole JO, Belkin NF: Relapse in chronic schizophrenics following abrupt withdrawal of tranquilizing drugs. Br J Psychiatry 115:679–686, 1969a

Prien RF, Levine J, Cole JO: High dose trifluoperazine therapy in chronic schizophrenia. Am J Psychiatry 126:305–313, 1969b

Quitkin F, Rifkin A, Klein DF: Very high dosage vs. standard dosage fluphenazine in schizophrenia. Arch Gen Psychiatry 32:1276–1281, 1975a

Quitkin F, Rifkin A, Kaplan JH, et al: Treatment of acute schizophrenia with ultra-high dose fluphenazine: a failure at shortening time on a crisis-intervention unit. Compr Psychiatry 16:279–283, 1975b

Quitkin F, Rifkin A, Kane J, et al: Long-acting oral vs. injectable antipsychotic drugs in schizophrenics: a one-year double-blind comparison in multiple episode schizophrenics. Arch Gen Psychiatry 35:889–892, 1978

Reschke RW: Parenteral haloperidol for rapid control of severe, disruptive symptoms of acute schizophrenia. Dis Nerv Syst 35:112–115, 1974

Rifkin A, Quitkin F, Robiner DJ, et al: Fluphenazine decanoate, fluphenazine hydrochloride given orally, and placebo in remitted schizophrenics. I. Relapse rates after one year. Arch Gen Psychiatry 34:43–47, 1977

Ritter RM, Davidson DE, Robinson TA: Comparison of injectable haloperidol and chlorpromazine. Am J Psychiatry 129:78–81, 1972

Robins E, Guze SB: Establishment of diagnostic validity in psychiatric illness: its application to schizophrenia. Am J Psychiatry 126:983–987, 1970

Sangiovanni F, Taylor MA, Abrams R, et al: Rapid control of psychotic excitement states with intramuscular haloperidol. Am J Psychiatry 130:1155–1156, 1973

Schiele BC, Mendelsohn RM, Penman AS, et al: Comparison of low and high dosage procedures in chlorpromazine therapy. Psychiatr Q 33:252–259, 1959

Schiele BC, Vestre ND, Stein KE: A comparison of thioridazine, trifluoperazine, chlorpromazine, and placebo: a double-blind controlled study on the treatment of chronic hospitalized, schizophrenic patients. J Clin Exp Psychopathol 22:151–162, 1961

Schooler NR, Levine J, Severe JB, et al: Prevention of relapse in schizophrenia: an evaluation of fluphenazine decanoate. Arch Gen Psychiatry 37:16–24, 1980

Shader RI, Elkins R, Ciraulo D: On guidelines for maximum dosages. Am J Psychiatry 135:499–500, 1977

Shawver J, Gorham DR, Leskin LW, et al: Comparison of chlorpromazine and reserpine in maintenance drug therapy. Dis Nerv Syst 20:452–457, 1959

Simpson GM, Yadalam K: Blood levels of neuroleptics: the state of the art. J Clin Psychiatry 46(No 5, Sec 2):22–28, 1985

Simpson GM, Amin M, Kurz-Bartholini E, et al: Problems in the evaluation of the optimal dose of a phenothiazine (butaperazine). Dis Nerv Syst 29:478–484, 1968

Simpson GM, Varega E, Haber EJ: Psychotic exacerbations produced by neuroleptics. Dis Nerv Syst 37:367–369, 1976

Slotnick VB: Management of the acutely agitated psychotic patient with parenteral neuroleptics: a comparative symptom effectiveness profile of haloperidol and chlorpromazine, in Proceedings of the Fifth World Congress of Psychiatry, Mexico City, 1971

Smith RC, Crayton J, Dekirmenjian H, et al: Blood levels of neuroleptic drugs in nonresponding chronic schizophrenic patients. Arch Gen Psychiatry 36:579–584, 1979

Smith RC, Vroulis G, Shvartsburd A, et al: RBC plasma levels of haloperidol and clinical response in schizophrenia. Am J Psychiatry 139:1054–1056, 1982

Smith RC, Baumgartner R, Shvartsburd A, et al: Haloperidol and thioridazine drug level and clinical response in schizophrenia: comparison of gas-liquid chromatography and radioreceptor drug level assay. Psychopharmacol Bull 21:52–58, 1985a

Smith RC, Baumgartner R, Shvartsburd A, et al: Comparative efficacy of red cell and plasma haloperidol as predictors of clinical response in schizophrenia. Psychopharmacology (Berlin) 85:449–455, 1985b

Stevens JH, Astrup C: Prognosis in "process" and "non-process" schizophrenia. Am J Psychiatry 119:945–953, 1963

Stotsky BA: Relative efficacy of parenteral haloperidol and thiothixene for the emergency treatment of acutely excited and agitated patients. Dis Nerv Syst 38:967–973, 1977

Task Force on the Use of Laboratory Tests in Psychiatry: Tricyclic antidepressants—blood level measurements and clinical outcome: an APA Task Force Report. Am J Psychiatry 142:155–162, 1985

Troshinsky CH, Aaronson HG, Stone RK: Maintenance phenothiazines in aftercare of schizophrenic patients. Penn Psychiatr Quart 2:11–15, 1962

Tuteur W, Stiller R, Glotzer J: The discharged mental hospital chlorpromazine patient. Dis Nerv Syst 20:512–517, 1959

Vanderheeren FAJ, Muusze RG: Plasma levels and half-lives of thioridazine and some of its metabolites. Eur J Clin Pharmacol 11:135–140, 1977

Van Putten T: The clinical management of noncompliance, in The Chronic Psychiatric Patient in the Community: Principles of Treatment. Edited by Barvosky I, Budson RD. New York, Spectrum Publications, 1983, pp 383–395

Van Putten T, May PRA, Marder SR, et al: Plasma levels of thiothixene by radioreceptor assay: clinical usefulness. Psychopharmacology (Berlin) 79:40–44, 1983

Van Putten T, Marder SR, May PRA, et al: Plasma levels of haloperidol and clinical response. Psychopharmacol Bull 21:69–72, 1985

Victor BS, Link NA, Binder RL, et al: Use of clonazepam in mania and schizoaffective disorders. Am J Psychiatry 141:1111–1112, 1984

Whitaker CB, Hoy RM: Withdrawal of perphenazine in chronic schizophrenia. Br J Psychiatry 109:422–427, 1963

Wijsenbeek H, Steiner M, Goldberg SC: Trifluoperazine: a comparison between regular and high doses. Psychopharmacologia 36:147–150, 1974

Wilkens B, Malitz S: Some problems of dose variations in the use of tranquilizing drugs. Am J Psychiatry 117:23–29, 1960

Williams JR, Solecki RT, Puttkammer S: Effects of single, combined and non-drug treatments of chronic mental patients. Dis Nerv Syst 30:696–701, 1969

Wistedt B: A depot neuroleptic withdrawal study: a controlled study of the clinical effects of the withdrawal of depot fluphenazine decanoate and depot flupenthixol decanoate in chronic schizophrenic patients. Acta Psychiatr Scand 64:65–84, 1981

Wode-Helgodt B, Borg S, Fryo B, et al: Clinical effects and drug concentrations in plasma and cerebrospinal fluid in psychotic patients treated with fixed doses of chlorpromazine. Acta Psychiatr Scand 58:149–173, 1978

Woggon B: Neuroleptika-Absetzversudie bei chronisch schizophrenen patienten. I. Literaturzuzammenfassurg. Int Pharmacopsychiatr 14:34–56, 1979

Yesavage JA, Holman CA, Cohn R, et al: Correlation of initial thiothixene serum levels and clinical response. Arch Gen Psychiatry 40:301–304, 1983

Zarifian E, Scatton B, Bianchetti G, et al: High doses of haloperidol in schizophrenia. A clinical biochemical and pharmacokinetic study. Arch Gen Psychiatry 39:212–215, 1982

Zarifian E, Scatton B, Bianchetti G, et al: Comparative efficacy of red cell and plasma haloperidol as predictors of clinical response in schizophrenia. Psychopharmacology (Berlin) 85:449–455, 1985

Chapter 5

NEUROLEPTIC MALIGNANT SYNDROME

Christopher C. Colenda III, M.D., M.P.H.
Salley S. Jessee, M.D.

NEUROLEPTIC MEDICATIONS ARE a cornerstone in the management of acute psychotic episodes, including schizophrenic decompensations. However, the use of neuroleptic medications may lead to significant side effects such as acute dystonias, akathisia, and neuroleptic-induced parkinsonism. Even more problematic complications are tardive dyskinesia and neuroleptic-induced catatonia. However, the most serious complication of neuroleptic medications is the potentially fatal neuroleptic malignant syndrome (NMS). The essential features of this syndrome are hyperthermia, muscular rigidity (lead-pipe rigidity), Parkinsonian symptoms, altered consciousness, and autonomic dysfunction. The syndrome was originally described in the French literature by Delay et al. (1960), and subsequently addressed by Delay and Deniker (1968) in the English literature. In the United States, Preston (1959) reported several cases with symptoms suggestive of NMS, indicating that the symptoms were not limited to one geographic region or neuroleptic class.

Neuroleptic malignant syndrome was thought to be rare, having an estimated incidence of 0.5–1.0% in patients who had been exposed to neuroleptic medications. This estimated exposure incidence of NMS was determined by Delay et al. (1963) from several

The authors appreciate the help of Kathryn Colenda for French translations.

hundred patients receiving haloperidol, as cited by Caroff (1980). Pope et al. (1986) reported on a survey of nearly 500 neuroleptic-treated patients admitted during a single year and noted a prevalence of NMS of 1.4%. Addonizio et al. (1986) found a prevalence of NMS of 2.4% in a retrospective chart review study of 82 consecutive male inpatients. Another 9.8% of the patients developed some symptoms of NMS that resolved without neuroleptic treatment being discontinued. The authors suggested that the full-blown syndrome of NMS lies at one end of the spectrum of extrapyramidal side effects of neuroleptics. Levinson and Simpson (1986a, 1986b), based on their review of the literature, concluded that NMS was a heterogenous group of conditions that were not necessarily "malignant" and hence should be termed "extrapyramidal symptoms (EPS) with fever." They observed that only a minority of the cases reported had EPS and fever without a medical explanation for the fever.

The variance in prevalence rates among the above studies might be due to their retrospective design and to differences in NMS case definitions. More recently, Gelenberg et al. (1988) in a prospective study found that only one patient developed NMS out of 1,470 patients admitted to a short-term private psychiatric hospital (a rate of 0.07%). Such a low incidence of NMS could be the result of a tendency to use lower dosages of neuroleptics or the nature of the facility (private, median length of stay = 13 days). The only other prospective study of NMS (Keck et al. 1987) found a prevalence of 0.9%. Thus, the two prospective studies have shown a similar frequency of NMS in patients exposed to neuroleptics that mirrors early work by Delay et al. (1963).

Within recent years, clinicians have become sensitized to this complication of neuroleptic administration and case reports have become more frequent in the literature. Comprehensive clinical and pathophysiological reviews of NMS have been written by Caroff (1980), Kurlan et al. (1984), Mueller (1985), Levenson (1985), Fricchione (1985), and Pearlman (1986).

CLINICAL FEATURES

The clinical symptoms associated with NMS, as well as their frequency, have been summarized in reviews by Levenson (1985) and Kurlan et al. (1984) (see Table 1). It is important to note that the case reports cited by these authors overlap considerably.

Kurlan et al. (1984) summarized the cardinal features of NMS, hyperthermia, and muscle rigidity, with associated mental status

Table 1. Clinical features associated with neuroleptic malignant syndrome

Signs/Symptoms	Frequency
Movement disorders	
Parkinsonism	98%
Rigidity	92
Tremor	56
Sialorrhea	31
Other movement disorders	
Dystonia	33
Chorea	15
Other neurological problems	
Dysphagia	40
Akinetic mutism	38
Autonomic dysfunction	
Fever	100
Tachycardia	79
Diaphoresis	60
Labile blood pressure	54
Mental status changes	
Coma	27
Stupor	27
Lethargy	12
Confusion/agitation	8

Source. Table abbreviated from Kurlan et al. 1984.

changes occurring in about 73% of patients. Levenson (1986) emphasized an elevation of serum creatine phosphokinase (CPK) to a level greater than 1,000 U/liter as a further major manifestation of NMS. Other important symptoms include tachycardia, excessive perspiration, labile blood pressure, resting tremor, dystonia, sialorrhea, dysphagia, and akinetic mutism. Delay and Deniker (1968) felt that respiratory insufficiency was an additional cardinal manifestation of the disorder. However, Kurlan et al. (1984) and Caroff (1980) believed that the pulmonary abnormalities were secondary complications as a result of prolonged debilitation and immobility, aspiration, changes in consciousness, and autonomic dysfunction.

Kurlan et al. (1984), Levenson (1985), and Pearlman (1986) have reviewed the demographic risk factors associated with NMS. They report the following: (a) NMS occurs most often in young patients (median age 36 years; 80% of the cases occur in patients below the age of 40); (b) it is more frequent in males (male/female ratio is approximately 1.4:1); (c) it occurs primarily in patients being treated for psychotic disorders (schizophrenia, 46%; affective disorders, 25%); (d) it may occur in patients who have intercurrent neurological disorders along with behavioral disturbances; (e) it is associated with patients who have been debilitated and dehydrated; (f) it has on rare occasions occurred in patients receiving neuroleptics prior to the induction of anesthesia; (g) there is a suggestion that patients receiving chlorpromazine-equivalent doses in excess of 1,000 mg/day are at increased risk for NMS; (h) depot administration of neuroleptics was found in 22% of the cases and was associated with prolonged morbidity; and (i) rechallenge of patients with neuroleptics has produced symptoms of NMS in 20 of 54 reported cases. Because the analyses by these authors are retrospective and based on case reports in the literature, it is quite possible that these findings are not generalizable to the total patient population treated with neuroleptics.

Laboratory findings in patients with NMS include a leukocytosis ranging from 12–30,000 cells, generalized abnormalities of liver function, acidemia, hypoxemia, and hypercarbia. An intriguing report of low serum iron in 19 of 20 patients with NMS (Rosebush and Mazurek 1988) awaits replication. The summary of NMS case reports by Kurlan et al. (1984) reveals that computerized tomography of the head and CSF examination yield nonspecific findings. High levels of dopamine metabolites have been reported in the CSF of a patient with NMS (Tollefson and Garvey 1984). Electroencephalograms do not show focal findings, but generalized slowing of cortical activity may be present. Elevated plasma and urinary catecholamines have been reported in patients with NMS (Feibel and Schiffer 1981). As summarized by Kurlan et al., postmortem examinations of three patients with NMS did not demonstrate diagnostic lesions, though more recently hypothalamic pathology was reported in one patient (Horn et al. 1988).

Neuroleptic malignant syndrome has been associated most frequently with high-potency neuroleptics such as piperazine derivatives and haloperidol. However, NMS has also been described in patients receiving chlorpromazine and thioridazine. The extensive reviews by Kurlan et al. (1984) and Pearlman (1986) found that cases of NMS were associated with both high and low doses of neuroleptic medications. Kurlan et al. reported that a single neuroleptic was used in 60% of the cases and more than one neuroleptic was used in 40% of the cases. The syndrome was most often associated with single or combined administration of haloperidol (63%), fluphenazine (27%), or chlorpromazine (19%). This finding suggested that patients who are treated with high-potency neuroleptics such as haloperidol are at higher risk of developing NMS. However, because high-potency neuroleptics, especially haloperidol, are used much more frequently than low-potency neuroleptics, one would expect that the former would be more frequently implicated in NMS. Further, because high-potency neuroleptics are often used at higher chlorpromazine-equivalent doses than those at which low-potency neuroleptics are used (Baldessarini et al. 1984), high-potency neuroleptics would be expected to have an even greater disproportionate frequency for the development of NMS.

Symptoms similar to NMS have been described in patients with neurological disorders who are not receiving neuroleptic medications. The syndrome has been described in patients with Parkinson's disease in association with the withdrawal of dopaminergic indirect agonists (L-dopa/carbidopa and amantadine, and amantadine alone). Mueller (1985) speculates that the incidence of this variant of NMS may be higher than previously thought, and may be associated with the "on-off" phenomenon in patients with Parkinson's disease on drug holidays from L-dopa. The "on-off" phenomenon found in patients with Parkinson's disease refers to rapid and random fluctuations in motor performance with seemingly little relation to the timing of L-dopa administration. Pharmacokinetic factors relating to absorption and delivery of L-dopa to the brain, as well as pharmacodynamic factors regulating dopamine-receptor functions, have been postulated to cause the variation in motor performance. In addition, Burke et al. (1981) described a patient with Huntington's disease who received dopamine-depleting medication (alpha-methyltyrosine and tetrabenazine) and then developed a syndrome similar to NMS.

Caroff (1980) noted that NMS may occur after prior asymptomatic exposure to neuroleptic medication. Once the syndrome develops, the clinical signs and symptoms escalate over the ensuing 24–72 hours. In the 52 cases that Kurlan et al. (1984) summarized, the duration of the illness ranged from 8 hours to 30 days, with a mean duration of 12 days. The mean onset of NMS symptoms occurred 3–9 days after initiation of neuroleptics (Pearlman 1986). Addonizio et al. (1987) reported that two-thirds of NMS patients developed the syndrome within 14 days of initiating neuroleptics.

Complications from NMS include the following: rhabdomyolysis (secondary to myonecrosis resulting from sustained muscle contraction), which can lead to myoglobinuria and acute renal failure; pulmonary embolism; acute myocardial infarction; disseminated intravascular coagulation; sepsis; and neurological sequelae such as parkinsonism, dyskinesia, dementia, and ataxia.

The estimated mortality rate for NMS was 20% in the review by Kurlan et al. (1984). Pearlman (1986) noted that the mortality rate dropped to 4% in cases reported after 1980. Caroff (1980) reported a calculated mortality rate of 14% in patients receiving only oral neuroleptics; he found a calculated mortality rate of 38% in patients receiving im long-acting fluphenazine with or without oral supplements. Shalev et al. (1989) estimate that the mortality from NMS has fallen considerably since 1984 to 11.6%. Mortality decreased in patients who developed NMS from the use of haloperidol, whereas mortality increased in patients with organic brain syndromes. The decrease in mortality is possibly the result of early recognition of NMS. Myoglobinemia and renal failure increase the risk of mortality, although the cause of death is most often cardiopulmonary problems.

DIFFERENTIAL DIAGNOSIS

The differential diagnosis for NMS is extensive, because the syndrome has symptoms that mimic many other disorders. The clinician should strongly suspect the disorder when a patient presents with the cardinal manifestations of the syndrome, and when there is a simultaneous history of neuroleptic use, withdrawal of indirect dopamine agonists, or use of dopamine-depleting agents. A thorough physical and neurological examination should be performed by the clinician, along with a gathering of laboratory data such as muscle CPK isoenzyme, blood chemistries, blood cultures, and CSF analysis. Intercurrent medical conditions may complicate the presentation of NMS and will make its management more difficult.

The differential diagnosis for NMS may be conceptualized along medical, neurological, and psychiatric parameters.

Medical

Systemic collagen vascular diseases such as polymyositis and systemic lupus erythematosis may produce signs similar to NMS but can be distinguished from NMS by appropriate laboratory studies. Metabolic disorders such as diabetic ketoacidosis, hypercalcemia, acute intermittent porphyria, and hepatic encephalopathy may produce catatonic-like symptoms that mimic NMS, but the history and laboratory examinations help distinguish these entities. Volatile substance abuse (toluene, airplane glue, acetone, gasoline) (Ron 1986) and hallucinogenic substances (mescaline, PCP, LSD) may also cause catatonic-like reactions that could be confused with NMS; usually, such reactions do not include hyperthermia or lead-pipe rigidity as found in NMS.

Heat stroke and heat exhaustion are important clinical conditions that mimic NMS. Usually, a history can be obtained of recent exercise or agitation under hot and humid conditions. Anticholinergic medications such as benztropine mesylate inhibit peripheral mechanisms for heat loss, leading to rapid increase in core body temperature, decreased sweating, and changes in mental status. In contradistinction to NMS, patients with heat stroke usually do not present with muscle rigidity. In addition, patients with NMS frequently sweat profusely.

Malignant hyperthermia (MH) is a disorder of skeletal muscle that shares some clinical features with NMS. It is a pharmacogenetic disorder affecting individuals who are exposed to halogenated inhalation anesthetics and to the depolarizing muscle relaxant succinylcholine (Nelson and Flewellen 1983). Although MH may have a multifactorial etiology, a common form appears to have an autosomal dominant inheritance pattern. The primary pathophysiological defect in MH appears to be dysfunction of the sarcolemma and sarcoplasmic reticulum, which leads to an increased concentration of intracellular calcium ions, resulting in muscle contracture and secondary muscle rigidity, aerobic and anaerobic respiration, and acidosis (Kurlan et al. 1984; Nelson and Flewellen 1983). Malignant hyperthermia has a mortality rate that approaches 60% (Butt and Kalow 1970), whereas the mortality rate of NMS was about 20% and has been reduced to 4% with wider recognition of the syndrome (Pearlman 1986). Dantrolene is the treatment of choice for MH.

Clinical and laboratory differences exist that help distinguish NMS from MH. In MH the onset of symptoms is usually precipitous and occurs within minutes to hours after exposure to the offending agent. In NMS, symptoms usually take longer to develop. The administration of curare or pancuronium will produce flaccidity in patients with NMS but will have no effect in patients with MH. Baseline muscle creatinine kinase is mildly elevated in patients with MH and their relatives but is not elevated in patients who are between episodes of NMS (Kurlan et al. 1984).

Some evidence suggests that NMS and MH have similar pathophysiological mechanisms. Muscle from patients with MH will show a hypercontractile response to caffeine and/or halothane, and this response has been used as a diagnostic test to determine patient susceptibility to MH. Caroff et al. (1983) reported a case in which a NMS patient had an abnormal in vitro contractile response to halothane as well as to fluphenazine, and they suggested that the two disorders may have pathogenic mechanisms in common. (It may have been that this patient with NMS was also at risk to develop MH.) Caroff et al. (1986) have found that the in vitro contractile response of rat diaphragm that had been exposed to haloperidol was inhibited by dantrolene and the phospholipase inhibitors indomethacin and spermine. Abnormal phospholipase activity has been implicated in the pathogenesis of MH (Caroff et al. 1986). Based on his clinical and experimental work, Caroff speculates that the pathogenesis of NMS is related to a direct neuroleptic effect on skeletal muscle.

Neurological

Several neurological conditions may have symptoms similar to NMS. Central nervous system infections, such as viral encephalitis, bacterial or fungal infections, or parasitic infestations, may present with symptoms similar to NMS and must be eliminated as diagnostic possibilities by CSF fluid examination. Postinfectious encephalopathies such as encephalitis lethargica can mimic NMS. Today, encephalitis lethargica is an extremely rare disorder, but in the wake of the influenza pandemic after World War I, it was a serious problem, producing symptoms similar to those of NMS.

Akinetic mutism is a neurological syndrome in which patients have rudimentary muscle movement but wakeful unresponsiveness to environmental stimuli. Ross and Stewart (1981) note that akinetic mutism may arise from damage to the brain stem reticular formation as well as from lesions to the anterior cingulate gyrus, globus pallidus, and medial forebrain bundle as it passes through the anterior hypothalamus. The "locked-in" or de-efferented syndrome is a neurological disorder that inhibits a patient's ability to express an awareness of his or her surroundings by word or movement, but leaves him or her with full consciousness of his or her environment. Both disorders may stem from central nervous system trauma, surgery, and/or tumors, or from peripheral neurological lesions such as polyneuritis, poliomyelitis, or myasthenia gravis. Postsurgical or traumatic central hyperthermia may also mimic NMS.

Basal ganglia disorders with rigidity, such as severe forms of parkinsonism, must be distinguished from NMS by history and physical examination. Because NMS may also be associated with the withdrawal of agents used to treat Parkinson's disease, the clinician needs to be especially sensitive to the possibility of NMS in these patients.

The muscle rigidity found in patients with NMS may mimic disorders of muscle hypertonicity, such as decerebrate and decorticate rigidity, hypertonia associated with tetanus, strychnine poisoning, and tetany secondary to metabolic abnormalities such as hypercalcemia. Paratonia, or *gegenhalten*, is a neurological disorder usually found in patients with diffuse forebrain dysfunction that may be associated with metabolic encephalopathy, diffuse cerebral atrophy, or hypertensive disease. The physiological basis of paratonia is unknown, but the symptoms mimic the extrapyramidal rigidity of parkinsonism. Patients demonstrate a "plastic-like" increase in their resistance to muscle movement of the extremities, trunk, and head that diminishes with slow movement and is exacerbated with rapid movement.

The stiff man syndrome is a rare central nervous system disorder of uncertain etiology that in the early stages of its clinical course may mimic NMS. It is characterized by intermittent but progressive muscle rigidity and spasm, with an eventual development of muscle contractures of the trunk, back, and lower limbs. This syndrome is usually not accompanied by hyperthermia.

Psychiatric

Clinical disorders that have catatonic symptoms must be differentiated from NMS. Catatonic signs such as stupor, mutism, waxy flexibility, and negativism may be associated with psychotic disorders, including acute schizophrenic episodes, manic psychosis, schizophreniform disorder, reactive psychosis, and conversion disorders. Patients with catatonic symptoms associated with these disorders usually do not show the intense muscle stiffness, hyperpyrexia, and severe autonomic dysfunction that is found in patients with NMS.

In the preneuroleptic era, a syndrome of hyperpyrexia and autonomic dysfunction was described in catatonic patients and dubbed "acute lethal catatonia" (Stauder 1934). Caroff (1980) and Fricchione (1985) speculate that lethal catatonia probably represents a hypothalamic crisis in catatonic patients that is associated with heat exhaustion, dehydration, and fatigue secondary to manic or catatonic excitement. Peele et al. (1986) consider NMS to be a medicated form of lethal catatonia. However, Castillo et al. (1989)

have pointed out the significant clinical differences between lethal catatonia and NMS. In lethal catatonia, the prominent symptom often is continued uncontrolled agitation, which fluctuates with catatonic mutism and rigidity, symptoms that are associated with limited fluid and food ingestion. This condition results ultimately in an exhaustive state that could become terminal. Fever and complications such as rhabdomyolysis and elevated CPK are not prominent symptoms of lethal catatonia. NMS, on the other hand, is not prominently characterized by severe agitation and exhaustion. Mann et al. (1986) add that altered dopaminergic transmission in a major hypothalamic heat loss pathway accounts for temperature elevation, whereas catatonic symptoms reflect changes in mesostriatal-mesolimbic pathways.

Gelenberg and Mandel (1977) described the "catatonia-parkinsonian" syndrome as a potential side effect associated with the administration of high-potency neuroleptics. Patients with this syndrome displayed posturing, waxy flexibility, negativism, incontinence, and Parkinsonian symptoms such as stiffness and bradykinesia. Stoudemire and Luther (1984) used the term "neuroleptic-induced catatonia" to describe the same syndrome. They noted that although NMS and neuroleptic-induced catatonia were precipitated by neuroleptic usage, patients with neuroleptic-induced catatonia did not have the severe hyperthermia or autonomic dysfunction that characterizes patients with NMS. However, Stoudemire and Luther added that patients may develop fever secondary to medical complications such as pneumonia and dehydration. They also suggested that timely discontinuation of the neuroleptic may avert the development of NMS, thereby implying that the difference between neuroleptic-induced catatonia and NMS may involve whether or not the patient experiences a hypothalamic crisis.

PATHOPHYSIOLOGY

A precise understanding of the complex pathogenesis of NMS has not been developed and remains speculative to date. Because dopamine receptor blockade, withdrawal of dopamine indirect agonists, or administration of dopamine-depleting agents can lead to NMS, a leading hypothesis focuses on the pharmacological dysregulation of the dopaminergic systems of the central nervous system. Fricchione (1985) describes this as hypodopaminergia involving dopaminergic systems in the hypothalamus, the mesostriatal-mesolimbic system, and the brain stem. Kurlan et al. (1984) feel that central nervous system blockade of dopamine receptors in the preoptic-anterior hypothalamus, the striatum, and the spinal cord is crucial to the development of NMS.

The report by Tollefson and Garvey (1984) of a patient with NMS who had a high CSF dopamine metabolite level adds evidence to a dopaminergic dysregulation hypothesis of NMS. They speculate that the finding of elevated dopamine metabolites supports their premise that NMS occurs during an accelerated period of dopamine turnover. (However, in the absence of pre- and post-NMS levels, other possibilities cannot be ruled out.) Tollefson and Garvey present evidence that neuroleptics acutely block dopamine sites, inducing a transient increase in dopamine turnover via neuronal feedback loops. From these researchers' perspective, NMS appears to be an idiosyncratic reaction whereby the normal neuroleptic-induced increase of dopaminergic neuronal firing and turnover is exaggerated, leading to possible reduced affinity of dopamine at postsynaptic striatal or mesolimbic receptors. The net effect would be a relative hypodopaminergia. If their hypothesis were correct, one would expect NMS to be associated with the initiation or increase in dose of neuroleptics. Addonizio et al. (1987) report that 66% of patients who developed NMS did so within 14 days of neuroleptic treatment being initiated. Levenson (1985) and Caroff (1980) have emphasized the general medical condition of the patient (e.g., fluid status, fatigue, or intercurrent illness) as an important determinant of whether a patient develops NMS. It may be that the patient's condition influences the development of a hypothalamic crisis that then extends neuroleptic-induced catatonia to NMS.

Thermoregulation

The dramatic hyperpyrexia found in patients with NMS may be associated with abnormalities of central thermoregulation and excessive heat production (Kurlan et al. 1984; Pearlman 1986). These abnormalities may be related to dopamine receptor blockade in the preoptic-anterior hypothalamus, striatum, and spinal cord. Although central thermodetection and thermoregulation involve noradrenergic, serotonergic, and cholinergic systems, there is considerable experimental evidence indicating that dopamine receptors located in the preoptic-anterior hypothalamus play a major role in hypothalamic thermodetection (Cox et al. 1978; Henderson and Wooten 1981). Experimental evidence suggests that hypothalamic thermoregulation involves a complicated relationship between afferent dopamine receptors in the preoptic-anterior hypothalamus and the posterior hypothalamus, and vasomotor efferents from the posterior hypothalamus.

Although a detailed understanding of the exact anatomic and/or neurochemical pathways does not exist, experimental evidence suggests that the preoptic-anterior hypothalamus is concerned with integrating neural afferents from the periphery concerned with thermal detection. These inputs are compared to a "set-point" in the posterior hypothalamus (Henderson and Wooten 1981). The preoptic-anterior hypothalamus initiates impulses to the posterior hypothalamus, which in turn initiates efferent physiological/behavioral impulses to the periphery that modulate heat dissipation (Cox et al. 1978).

Although the following summary may be an oversimplification, dopamine blockade of the thermodetection function of the preoptic-anterior hypothalamus disrupts the neurophysiological relationship between the anterior hypothalamus and the posterior hypothalamus. This disruption inhibits posterior hypothalamic efferents controlling vasomotor thermoregulation. In the face of the heat load seen in NMS, the normal peripheral shunting of blood to dissipate the heat load does not occur, leading to an elevation of core body temperature. Clinical evidence supports this hypothesis: patients with NMS are pale despite profuse perspiration (indicating shunting of blood away from the periphery).

Heat Production

The heat load found in patients with NMS may also result from shivering and nonshivering thermogenesis (Kurlan et al. 1984). Shivering thermogenesis results from muscle rigidity and is a consequence of central dopamine receptor blockade in the striatum, causing extrapyramidal Parkinsonian side effects (stiffness and tremor). Whether neuroleptics have an additional direct effect on skeletal muscle remains speculative. Different classes of neuroleptics have contradictory effects on muscle physiology. Chlorpromazine has been shown to facilitate the contractile response of muscle, but the butyrophenones retard the response (Rosenberg 1977). This finding led some commentators to speculate that intrinsic abnormalities of muscle contractility may not play a major role in the pathogenesis of the hyperthermia associated with NMS. However, as mentioned above, Caroff (1986) has presented data that shows haloperidol does increase resting contractile tension in vitro in rat diaphragms, an effect that is blocked by dantrolene and the phospholipase inhibitors indomethacin and spermine.

Nonshivering thermogenesis is associated with increased cellular metabolic rate independent of muscle contraction (Kurlan et al. 1984). It consists of mobilizing caloric energy reserves, which is facilitated by enhanced sympathetic nervous system activity. Clinically, patients with NMS have signs and symptoms of enhanced sympathetic nervous system activity (tachycardia, labile blood pressure, etc.). In addition, Feibel et al. (1981) report a case of NMS with elevated urinary and plasma catecholamines. Experimentally, a diencephalo-spinal dopamine projection system designed to inhibit thoracolumbar sympathetic preganglionic outflow has been described (Lindvall et al. 1983). It has been proposed that neuroleptic blockade of the dopamine receptors may enhance sympathetic nervous system activity, leading to increased cellular metabolic rate and subsequent hyperpyrexia (Kurlan et al. 1984).

Treatment: A Rational Approach

In the past, the treatment for NMS has consisted of (a) prompt recognition of the syndrome, (b) immediate cessation of neuroleptic medication, and (c) aggressive use of supportive measures. In recent years, clinicians have developed treatment strategies based upon an improved understanding of the pathophysiology of the syndrome. Although positive results have been reported, these reports are anecdotal and lack scientific validation through systematic clinical trials. Levenson (1986) has questioned the efficacy of specific treatment at this point in our understanding of NMS. Shalev et al. (1989) do not find a protective effect when specific pharmacological agents such as bromocriptine and dantrolene are used to treat NMS. However, others have provided strong arguments to the contrary. In our opinion, in addition to general supportive measures, specific treatment options should be employed.

Based on a summary of existing evidence, the following treatment strategy is suggested for treating patients diagnosed as having NMS.

General

1. Stop all neuroleptic medication.
2. Check patient's airway, measure arterial blood gases, and administer oxygen if indicated.
3. Continuously monitor the patient's vital signs.

4. Begin intravenous fluids.
5. Measure serum electrolytes and correct imbalances.
6. Measure serum CPK and monitor CPK throughout the course of the syndrome.
7. Measure fluid input and output, and periodically check urine for myoglobin casts.
8. Consider additional clinical tests, including chest X-ray, ECG, EEG, and blood and urine cultures if infection is suspected.
9. Consider lumbar puncture, which may be indicated for diagnostic purposes if therapeutic intervention does not improve the patient's clinical status after 24–36 hours.
10. Consider treating hyperpyrexia with antipyretics and cooling blankets, in addition to the specific treatment strategy listed below.
11. If intercurrent infections, such as a urinary tract infection, pneumonia, or septicemia, are detected, administer the appropriate antibiotics.

Specific

Specific treatment measures, as outlined below, are based upon improving dopaminergic activity and reducing muscle rigidity. Because NMS is etiologically related to direct or indirect dopamine blockade, one cannot overemphasize the importance of discontinuing the neuroleptics and initiating treatment with dopamine agonists.

(a) Bromocriptine is a direct dopamine agonist. Its mechanism of action in NMS may center on correcting the pharmacological insult produced by neuroleptic administration. According to Mueller's treatment regimen (Mueller et al. 1983; Mueller 1985), if the patient is able to swallow, bromocriptine, 5 mg po tid, should be initiated. This dose may need to be increased up to 20 mg qid in order to achieve a therapeutic effect. A response to the medication, characterized by improvement in rigidity and akathisia, can be seen within 2 to 4 hours of administration. Once a therapeutic response has been achieved, bromocriptine should be continued for 10 days and then gradually tapered over a week's time. As Levenson (1986) has pointed out, hypotension and reactivation of a psychotic process are potential side effects of bromocriptine administration, but this has not been Mueller's experience.

(b) Dantrolene sodium is a muscle relaxant that uncouples excitation/contraction of muscle by interfering with the release of calcium from the sarcoplasmic reticulum. Its primary use in treating NMS is to reduce the hyperthermia associated with muscle rigidity and shivering thermogenesis (Coons et al. 1982; Khan et al. 1985). If the patient is moribund and cannot take medication by mouth, dantrolene is especially useful given intravenously. The starting dose ranges from 0.25 mg/kg to 1.0 mg/kg body weight given qid by slow intravenous infusion. The dose may be increased to as much as 3 mg/kg body weight qid as needed to alleviate symptoms. Note that hepatic toxicity may occur with doses above 10 mg/kg per day, and other complications such as seizures and pleural effusions with pericarditis have been reported in patients using dantrolene on a long-term basis.

(c) A rational approach to the therapy of NMS would be to utilize dantrolene and bromocriptine simultaneously. Granato et al. (1983) reported clinical success in using the combination of dantrolene and bromocriptine to treat NMS.

Additional Treatments

(a) Amantadine given 100 mg po bid has been reported to benefit a patient with NMS. However, the withdrawal of amantadine has also precipitated NMS (Henderson and Wooten 1981). Hence, we feel that amantadine should not be the immediate drug of choice for treatment of NMS, but it may be considered if bromocriptine and/or dantrolene fail to alleviate the symptoms.

(b) Electroconvulsive therapy has been reported to be beneficial in three cases of NMS. The reason why ECT works in treatment of this disorder is not clearly understood. Jessee and Anderson (1983) postulated that ECT may be beneficial because it increases the turnover of brain dopamine. Fricchione (1985) adds that ECT may benefit patients with NMS as a result of ECT's positive effect on GABA transmission, which in turn increases dopamine activity. Electroconvulsive therapy might also be effective by treating the underlying catatonic state, thus reducing thermogenesis in patients with NMS. Treatment with ECT should be considered if all other treatment options have failed.

PREVENTION

Is NMS a preventable disorder? This is a difficult question to answer, because all of the clinical information about the syndrome has been compiled from case reports and the pathophysiology remains speculative. Because the disorder appears to be relatively rare, conducting longitudinal studies would be difficult and might not significantly add to our understanding of the disorder. However, over the last few years the frequency of case reports has increased, reflecting an increased awareness of the syndrome by clinicians.

Currently, preventative strategies are general and nonspecific. Mueller (1985) recommends to clinicians that they be sensitive to certain patients who may be at high risk of developing NMS:

1. Patients who do not have a diagnosis of schizophrenia.
2. Patients who have not responded well to neuroleptics.
3. Patients who are receiving neuroleptics for the first time.
4. Patients who have neurological impairments, particularly parkinsonism.
5. Patients who are fatigued, dehydrated, and chronically ill.
6. Patients who are young males.
7. Patients who are being withdrawn from dopaminergic agonists.

Preventing the syndrome from recurring is of particular interest to clinicians, because the patient's primary psychiatric illness usually needs continued treatment. Challenging patients with neuroleptic agents after the syndrome has resolved has led to the re-emergence of NMS symptoms in some patients but not in others (Pelonero et al. 1985). Recently, Rosebush et al. (1989) reported that 13 of 15 patients were able to take neuroleptics again after suffering from an episode of NMS. Successful reinstitution of medication was more likely to occur when there was at least a 2-week hiatus between the episode of NMS and reintroduction of medication. In the authors' small series, the relative potency or dosage of the successfully reintroduced neuroleptic did not have strong correlation with the dose or the potency of the original agent. At the present time, the best strategy for clinicians is to look for alternative treatments that may improve the patient's condition. For psychotic disorders, this may require switching to a different class of neuroleptic, treatment with lithium or carbamazepine, or ECT.

References

Addonizio G, Susman VL, Roth SD: Symptoms of neuroleptic malignant syndrome in 82 consecutive inpatients. Am J Psychiatry 43:1587–1590, 1986

Addonizio G, Susman VL, Roth SD: Neuroleptic Malignant Syndrome: review and analysis of 115 cases. Biol Psychiatry 22:1004–1020, 1987

Baldessarini RJ, Katz B, Cotton BP: Dissimilar dosing with high potency and low potency neuroleptics. Am J Psychiatry 141:748–752, 1984

Burke R, Fahn S, Mayeaux R, et al: Neuroleptic malignant syndrome caused by dopamine-depleting drugs in a patient with Huntington's disease. Neurology 31:1022–1026, 1981

Butt BA, Kalow W: Malignant hyperthermia: a statistical review. Can Anaesth Soc J 17:293–315, 1970

Caroff SN: The neuroleptic malignant syndrome. J Clin Psychiatry 41:79–83, 1980

Caroff SN, Rosenberg H, Gerber J: Neuroleptic malignant syndrome and malignant hyperthermia. Lancet 1:244, 1983

Caroff SN, Rosenberg H, Fletcher J: Haloperidol induced muscle contractures and NMS, in Symposium 95: Neuroleptic Malignant Syndrome: Recent Advances. APA Annual Meeting, Washington, DC, May 1986

Castillo E, Rubin RT, Molsboer-Trachsler E: Clinical differentiation between lethal catatonia and neuroleptic malignant syndrome. Am J Psychiatry 146:324–328, 1989

Coons DJ, Hillman FJ, Marshal RW: Treatment of neuroleptic malignant syndrome with dantrolene sodium: a case report. Am J Psychiatry 134:944–945, 1982

Cox B, Kerwin R, Lee TF: Dopamine receptors in the central thermoregulatory pathways of the rat. J Physiol (Lond) 282:471–483, 1978

Delay J, Deniker P: Drug-induced extrapyramidal syndromes, in Handbook of Clinical Neurology, Vol 6. Edited by Viken PJ, Bruyn GW. Amsterdam, North Holland, 1968, pp 248–266

Delay J, Pichot P, Lemperieré T: Un neuroleptique majeur non phenothiazine et non reserpinique l'haloperidol dans le traitment des psychoses. Ann Med Psychol (Paris) 118:145–152, 1960

Delay J, Pichot P, Lemperieré T: L'emploi des butyrophenones en psychiatrie. Etude statistique et psychometrique, in Proceedings of the Sumpos Internazionale sull l'Haloperidol e Triperidol, Milan, 1963, pp 305–319

Feibel JH, Schiffer RB: Sympathoadrenomedullary hyperactivity in the neuroleptic malignant syndrome: a case report. Am J Psychiatry 138:8–9, 1981

Fricchione GL: Neuroleptic catatonia and its relationship to psychogenic catatonia. Biol Psychiatry 20:304–313, 1985

Gelenberg AJ, Mandel MR: Catatonic reactions to high-potency neuroleptic drugs. Arch Gen Psychiatry 34:947–950, 1977

Gelenberg AJ, Bellinghausen B, Wojcik JD, et al: A prospective survey of neuroleptic malignant syndrome in a short-term psychiatric hospital. Am J Psychiatry 145:517–518, 1988

Granato JE, Stern BJ, Ringel A, et al: Neuroleptic malignant syndrome: successful treatment with dantrolene and bromocriptine. Ann Neurol 14:89–90, 1983

Henderson VW, Wooten GF: Neuroleptic malignant syndrome: a pathogenic role for dopamine receptor blockade? Neurology 31:132–137, 1981

Horn E, Lach B, Lapierre Y, et al: Hypothalamic pathology in neuroleptic malignant syndrome. Am J Psychiatry 145:617–620, 1988

Jessee S, Anderson GF: ECT in the neuroleptic malignant syndrome: case report. J Clin Psychiatry 44:186–188, 1983

Keck PE, Pope MG, McElroy SC: Frequency and presentation of neuroleptic malignant syndrome: a prospective study. Am J Psychiatry 144:1344–1346, 1987

Khan A, Jaffe JH, Nelson WH, et al: Resolution of neuroleptic malignant syndrome with dantrolene sodium: a case report. J Clin Psychiatry 46:244–246, 1985

Kurlan R, Hamill R, Shoulson I: Neuroleptic malignant syndrome. Clin Neuropharmacol 7:109–120, 1984

Levenson JL: Neuroleptic malignant syndrome. Am J Psychiatry 142:1137–1145, 1985

Levenson JL: Reply to comments: diagnosing and treating neuroleptic malignant syndrome (letter). Am J Psychiatry 143:675, 1986

Levinson DF, Simpson GM: Diagnosing and treating neuroleptic malignant syndrome (letter). Am J Psychiatry 143:673–674, 1986a

Levinson DF, Simpson GM: Neuroleptic-induced extrapyramidal symptoms with fever. Arch Gen Psychiatry 43:839–848, 1986b

Lindvall O, Bjorklund A, Skagerberg G: Dopamine containing neurons in the spinal cord: anatomy and some functional aspects. Ann Neurol 14:255–260, 1983

Mann SC, Caroff SN, Bleirr HR, et al: Lethal catatonia. Am J Psychiatry 143:1374–1381, 1986

Mueller PS: Neuroleptic malignant syndrome. Psychosomatics 26:654–662, 1985

Mueller PS, Vester JW, Fermaglich J: Neuroleptic malignant syndrome: successful treatment with bromocriptine. JAMA 249:386–388, 1983

Nelson TE, Flewellen EH: The malignant hyperthermia syndrome. N Engl J Med 309:416–418, 1983

Pearlman CA: Neuroleptic malignant syndrome: a review of the literature. J Clin Psychopharmacol 6:257–273, 1986

Peele R, de Veau L, Zanni G: Is neuroleptic malignant syndrome a myth? in Paper Session No. 1. New Perspectives in Biological Psychiatry. APA Annual Meeting, Washington, DC, May, 1986

Pelonero AL, Levenson JL, Silverman JJ: Neuroleptic therapy following neuroleptic malignant syndrome. Psychosomatics 26:946–948, 1985

Pope HG, Keck PE, McElroy SL: Frequency and presentation of neuroleptic malignant syndrome in a large psychiatric hospital. Am J Psychiatry 143:1227–1233, 1986

Preston J: CNS reactions to small doses of tranquilizers. Am Prac Digest Treatment 10:627–630, 1959

Ron MA: Volatile substance abuse: a review of possible long-term neurological, intellectual and psychiatric sequelae. Br J Psychiatry 148:235–246, 1986

Rosebush PI, Mazurek MF: Serum abnormalities in neuroleptic malignant syndrome. Abstract #78, New Research, APA Annual Meeting, Montreal 1988

Rosebush PI, Stewart TD, Gelenberg AJ: Twenty neuroleptic rechallenges after neuroleptic malignant syndrome in 15 patients. J Clin Psychiatry 50:295–298, 1989

Rosenberg H: Malignant hyperthermia syndrome. Anesth Analg 56:466, 1977

Ross ED, Stewart RM: Akinetic mutism from hypothalamic damage. Successful treatment with dopamine agonists. Neurology 31:1435–1439, 1981

Shalev A, Harmesh H, Munitz M: Mortality from neuroleptic malignant syndrome. J Clin Psychiatr 50:18–25, 1989

Stauder KH: Die todliche katatonia. Arch Psychiatr Nervenkr 102:614–634, 1934

Stoudemire A, Luther JS: Neuroleptic malignant syndrome and neuroleptic-induced catatonia: differential diagnosis and treatment. Int J Psychiatry Med 14:57–63, 1984

Tollefson GD, Garvey MJ: The neuroleptic malignant syndrome and central dopamine metabolites. J Clin Psychopharmacol 4:150–153, 1984

Chapter 6

THE TREATMENT ALLIANCE

Lawrence B. Inderbitzin, M.D.

> No patient must ever be completely given up; the doctor must always be prepared to take action and to offer the patient the chance to abandon his pathological way of thinking.
>
> E. Bleuler

DESPITE THE DRAMATIC THERAPEUTIC effects of antipsychotic medications, comprehensive treatment of schizophrenia remains one of the psychiatrist's most challenging and difficult tasks. Pharmacotherapy and psychosocial interventions require thoughtful integration. There is no single treatment model applicable to all schizophrenic patients. A flexible approach, utilizing different therapeutic modalities at different times under varying circumstances, is essential. Goals of treatment include fostering and supporting healthy mental functioning while minimizing disorganizing anxiety, feelings of vulnerability, and nonadaptive regression.

The doctor-patient relationship is always a crucial variable in determining therapeutic outcome. Establishing a relationship by making emotional contact with the acutely psychotic schizophrenic patient is the first task of treatment. A comprehensive diagnostic understanding will facilitate this process. Even with an acutely psychotic patient, emotional contact and a therapeutic at-

The author wishes to gratefully acknowledge James A. Ryan, M.D., for his conceptual contributions and clinical examples.

titude will lead to further information that clarifies crucial diagnostic questions. Interviews that are conducted exclusively by fact gathering and "cataloging of symptoms" are likely to further alienate a terrified and suspicious patient, leading to diagnostic confusion and treatment failures or stalemates.

In this chapter the treatment alliance will be emphasized as a crucial variable in work with schizophrenic patients. The historical and conceptual roots of the treatment alliance concept will be described, the relationship and importance of the therapeutic attitude will be discussed, and a methodology for establishing a treatment alliance with an acutely psychotic patient will be explained and illustrated. In addition, some related issues concerning individual psychotherapy will be explored.

Historical and Conceptual Issues

Hippocrates, Galen, Plato, and others emphasized that the relationship between the physician and the patient is itself a therapeutic factor that underlies the effectiveness of all the physician's other skills. The Hippocratic doctrine asserted that the art of medicine consists of three things: the disease, the patient, and the physician. According to Hippocrates, "The physician is the servant of the art and the patient must combat the disease with the physician" (Hutchins 1952, p. 117). The physician must know about diseases (causes, symptoms, course), but individual cases are all different. Therefore, in *The Book of Prognostics* and the treatise *Of the Epidemics*, Hippocrates insisted that the physician know his patient "as an individual and [know] all the relevant circumstances of his life" (Hutchins 1952, p. 117).

The attempt to study the doctor-patient relationship in detail began in earnest with Freud (1911). He elucidated the concept of transference in therapeutic relationships. In essence, transference is the displacement of ideas, feelings, and attitudes from important persons in the patient's past to the relationship with the therapist. Transference was first considered an obstacle to psychotherapeutic treatment and later a primary means (via interpretation) to cure. Freud divided transference into positive and negative types and further divided positive transference into the "unobjectionable" positive transference that attached the patient to the doctor, and the erotic transference that functioned as a resistance to the treatment. Regarding the former, Freud said that it was necessary to wait "until an effective transference has been established in the patient, a proper rapport with him. It remains the first aim of the treatment to attach him to it and to the person of the doctor" (Freud 1911–1913, p. 139).

Differences between transference and other aspects of the doctor-patient relationship have always been recognized. More recently the terms treatment alliance, therapeutic alliance, working alliance, etc., have been applied to the "nonneurotic, rational, reasonable rapport which the patient has with the analyst and which allows him to work purposefully" (Greenson and Wexler 1969). Although all these terms refer to the joint efforts of the patient and therapist to work together to understand and resolve the patient's problems, they have been used by different authors in conflicting ways and have been fraught with controversy. Sandler et al. (1973), Brenner (1979), and Schafer (1983) have reviewed and criticized the concept of the treatment alliance on several grounds. For instance, they have pointed out that too much emphasis on the alliance aspect of the therapeutic relationship may encourage unnecessary, noninterpretive interventions. The experience of relationship with the therapist may come to be viewed as more important than the therapist's interpretive efforts. Conversely, the role of interpretation in fostering the treatment alliance is often overlooked (Levy 1984). Transference elements cannot always be separated from the reality-based elements of the treatment alliance. These criticisms are valid and important. It is useful to conceptualize the treatment alliance as comprised of both rational and irrational components (Gutheil and Havens 1979). Both can contribute positively to the treatment. In most instances the irrational (i.e., belief in the therapist's magical powers of healing) components predominate early in the treatment. As treatment progresses, these are surrendered in favor of the more rational components.

In recent years psychotherapy research has focused new attention on the alliance concept, especially in relation to treatment outcome. Recent reviews suggest that the strength of the alliance correlates positively with therapeutic outcome (Hartley and Strupp 1983; Hartley 1985; Docherty 1985; Luborsky and Auerbach 1985). However, problems exist in defining the concept, particularly regarding the interrelationships among component elements, including the doctor/therapist-patient relationship as a whole, the therapist's technical interventions, the cooperative efforts of patient and therapist, and transference phenomena. Furthermore, the therapeutic alliance concept is thought by some to cut across different theoretical models of therapy as well as to be uniformly applicable to the treatment of patients with widely divergent kinds of psychopathology. These views are critically examined by Freebury (1986) in a manner that highlights the need for greater conceptual clarity and more precise definitions.

In discussing the therapeutic alliance in relation to the treatment of acutely psychotic schizophrenic patients, it is useful to opt for an inclusive rather than a narrow or restricted approach. The alliance develops in stages, although there may be considerable overlap among them. Consenting to work together, agreeing on problems to be tackled, defining the limits of the relationships, as well as the more traditional nurturing of joint objective observing and subjective experiencing perspectives, constitute components of the treatment alliance to be discussed below. In working with psychotic patients, none of these components can be taken for granted, because they can to some extent work with less disturbed individuals who seek therapy voluntarily and whose problems are at least superficially well defined. What occurs in the early or preparatory stages of alliance formation with psychotic individuals is crucial if later observation, exploration, and resolution of intrapsychic and interpersonal conflicts are to occur. These early stages in the development of the treatment alliance require more comprehensive study in therapies involving schizophrenic patients that often begin involuntarily, in crisis situations with psychotic distortions of reality, and in situations in which various therapeutic modalities are implemented simultaneously. As described here, the treatment alliance is closely related both historically and conceptually to the doctor-patient relationship as a whole and is not limited by a narrow definition that would restrict it to a purely expressive psychotherapeutic relationship. Everything that occurs between doctor and patient impacts on the treatment alliance.

THE THERAPEUTIC ATTITUDE

The term "therapeutic attitude" refers to the nontechnical manner in which the therapist approaches the patient. It includes such important features as honesty, concern, empathy, and respect for privacy and confidentiality. These features will not be discussed in detail here. Instead, the focus will be on those aspects of the therapeutic attitude that seem especially pertinent to the development of a treatment alliance with schizophrenic patients and that have perhaps received less attention.

In order for treatment to begin in a manner that holds promise for continuing toward and resulting in a positive outcome, the patient must feel that the therapist's main interest is in being helpful. This will only occur if the patient perceives that there is a congruence between his or her own current, crucial interests and the interests of the therapist. As Friedman (1969) describes this dilemma, if the therapist does not accept the patient on his or her own terms, the patient will feel he or she is being asked to be someone else and will have little cause for hope. Conversely, if the therapist merely settles for the patient's current terms (psychosis), the concealed nonpsychotic part of the patient's personality will be ignored. Friedman also warns, as did Fenichel (1941), that if therapists *begin* treatment by looking too eagerly for the development of a therapeutic alliance to rely on as a *fulcrum* of treatment, they will interfere with the slow and gradual development of mutual trust and acceptance. This is particularly true with schizophrenic patients who are especially sensitive to being imposed upon or having demands (i.e., for cooperation in a joint effort) made upon them. Hill (1955) recommends that the therapist maintain an "intransitive mood," the emphasis being on attempting to understand the patient rather than on communicating an interest in bringing about changes in the patient. He also thought that the schizophrenic patient should be "dealt with closely, directly, naturally and without hesitation or embarrassment" (p. 42).

Optimism about treatment is an important aspect of the therapeutic attitude. This does not imply any denial of the seriousness of the patient's problems. An optimistic attitude conveys to the patient that the therapist wants to help despite the severity of the psychopathology, the time required, and the pain to be endured on the path to recovery. Of course, there will be times when the therapist will feel discouraged, anxious, and angry. When it seems as though nothing is being accomplished, it is common either to declare the patient untreatable or to consider oneself unsuitable as a therapist. These attitudes, if maintained, are indicators for obtaining consultation and supervision with an experienced colleague.

Neutrality

Neutrality is usually considered to be synonymous with a nonjudgmental therapeutic stance and has been almost universally considered a cornerstone of the treatment alliance. However, neutrality as a guiding principle of treatment is open to easy misinterpretation and misunderstanding. The term neutrality usually refers to a mode of listening and focus of attention upon which psychotherapeutic interventions are based. Anna Freud (1936) recommended a position equidistant from id, ego, and superego, and we might now add external reality. By this she meant that the therapist should not "join forces" with any of these agencies (i.e., encourage instinctual discharge or function as the patient's conscience). In practical clinical terms, this translates into avoiding either a seductive or a critical therapeutic stance. However, it does *not* mean that the therapist should remain passive and never take a stand. It is not neutral for a therapist to stand by idly and silently while the patient is involved in self-destructive or assaultive behavior. Under the guise of neutrality, physicians and others in emergency rooms sometimes enter into prolonged and intense arguments about hospitalization or the need for medication with reluctant, fearful, acutely disturbed patients. The result is usually an escalating conflict with an exacerbation of psychotic symptoms or a violent outburst that "proves" to the ambivalent staff members who are conflicted about their own aggressive responses to the patient that hospitalization really is required.

Manfred Bleuler (1976) recommended that the schizophrenic patient be accepted "as a brother" rather than watched "as a person who has become unintelligible and different from the therapist." The therapeutic attitude conveys that the therapist wants to understand and to help a fellow human being. While striving to do this by combating the psychosis, the therapist must maintain respect for the patient whose psychotic thinking is his or her current attempt at adaptation.

THE BEGINNING OF TREATMENT

Although general principles of good treatment can be described, treatment of each patient must be individualized. Skill is acquired through experience and practice with good supervision. The focus here will be on the beginning of treatment because this phase is particularly difficult with the acutely psychotic patient. Initially the patient's ability to contribute to the treatment alliance is often minimal, and this must be expected and accepted. However, the establishment of the treatment alliance between therapist and patient is so crucial that it must be foremost in the clinician's mind. Only a life-threatening situation should take precedence over the therapist's concern about the alliance. From the moment the patient first comes into contact with the mental health system, everything that occurs will impact on the treatment alliance.

Not infrequently, the first challenge to the treatment alliance occurs around the issue of informed consent. It is not easy to provide the acutely psychotic schizophrenic patient with the information necessary to enable him or her to arrive at a logical decision about treatment. Nevertheless, this is often the first task confronting the physician. Failure to achieve informed consent can spell disaster for the whole treatment process. Freud's concept of splitting of the ego describes the process of thinking along two contradictory lines at the same time (rational and irrational). There is always some rational portion of the patient's mind, regardless of how concealed it may be by psychosis. A careful, tactful investigation of the reasons leading to the patient being brought to the hospital often leads to a shared rational basis for informed consent. An attempt must always be made by the therapist to carefully explain the reasons for hospitalization and to outline in general terms what kind of help the patient can expect. Often a patient's irrational fears about hospitalization can be moderated by a visit to the ward to "see for himself" and talk with both patients and staff there.

The therapist's first contact with the patient's family is also extremely important and can tip the balance of the treatment alliance in either direction. The guilt and anxiety experienced by the family are often different from what the patient is feeling. The therapist must recognize that the family can either support or undermine the treatment alliance, and that if the family members feel understood by the therapist they are more likely to support the treatment plan. Attempts early in the treatment to foster the patient's "independence" and "separation" from the family often disrupt the treatment alliance. The following example is illustrative: Donnie, a 15-year-old boy, was admitted to a psychiatric hospital because be began hearing "soap opera" stars talking to his mother. He had been an avid fan of these programs for years and had viewed them daily after school with his mother. Donnie developed an elaborate delusional system about the stars visiting his home and conversing with him and his mother and was perplexed when his mother denied these events. After admission, he gradually improved on phenothiazines but continued to be preoccupied with the "soap stars." His mother discussed the "soap stars" with him and brought magazines about them. Consequently, the staff became increasingly aware of the relationship between Donnie and his mother and recommended to both that they become more independent of each other. Their reply was simultaneous: "But we like it like this." Both Donnie and his mother insisted that there was nothing wrong with their relationship, and his mother immediately decided to remove Donnie from the hospital for "financial reasons."

The treatment begins as soon as the patient reaches the hospital. It is important to remember that entering any new social system, especially a hospital, is an anxiety-provoking experience, even for the nonschizophrenic person. Every attempt should be made to minimize ambiguity and confusion in the environment. Often patients are not told why they are brought to the hospital. Usually it is best to share with them what is known. Carefully explaining who we are, what we are doing, and why we are doing it may seem self-evident, but it is too often forgotten in practice. Acutely psychotic patients not uncommonly have been neglectful of themselves physically and often present dehydrated, in poor nutritional status, and with other intercurrent illnesses. Dramatic psychological symptoms should not deter the clinician from attending to pressing physical needs. Those patients who are agitated, overstimulated, and highly distractible require a calm environment and perhaps solitude; immediate group activities are contraindicated. Self-destructive and/or assaultive behavior is best dealt with in a firm, direct, and protective manner. If seclusion is necessary, the reason for it should always be explained along with the requirements necessary for the patient to be able to leave seclusion. In all these situations, the first task is to provide protection and safety.

Unfortunately, many hospital environments offer multiple assaults on the patient's self-esteem, which has already been battered from within. Every attempt should be made to minimize the indignities and insensitivities that inevitably occur in an institutional environment. Such simple things as allowing the patient to keep personal belongings that are of no danger can make a great difference. Requests for telephone privileges, writing materials, cigarettes, or other such items should, whenever possible, be granted without fanfare. In this initial phase, the most common errors made by therapists are participating in the dehumanizing processing of a patient, being unnecessarily and inappropriately withholding, and not taking a firm, active stand when the patient's anxiety or agitated behavior calls for it.

Medication

Although the conflict between psychotherapy and psychopharmacologic interventions seems to have subsided, some of the underlying issues are of more than historical interest. Early criticisms by Szasz (1957) and others focused on the use of medications as instruments of restraint and coercion that were prescribed more for the benefit of therapists than patients. These concerns receded as the effectiveness of neuroleptics in relieving psychotic symptoms became increasingly apparent. However, many continued to believe that medications would interfere with psychotherapy. This issue was reviewed in a Group for the Advancement of Psychiatry 1975 publication. At that time and to this date, there is no clear evidence that appropriately prescribed psychotropic agents interfere with psychotherapy. In fact, existing data support the contrary view that medications are often useful adjuncts and facilitators of psychotherapy. As early as 1966, Zetzel pointed out that neuroleptics reduced projections and delusions, helped patients form therapeutic alliances, and thus facilitated psychotherapy.

A positive perspective on integrating psychotherapy and psychopharmacologic treatment is now more prevalent, but this does not mean that earlier antagonistic points of view were without any foundation. Medications and the act of prescribing them are full of meaning for both patient and physician. Whether this meaning is the same or different for patient and physician, and whether it is conscious or unconscious, have profound implications for the treatment alliance. Psychological responses to the prescription and taking of medication can affect the patient and the treatment in a manner unexplained by the medication's pharmacological actions.

Psychiatric patients, and particularly psychotic ones, differ in significant ways from patients who seek treatment for medical conditions. Although medical patients may also use denial, the psychiatrist must confront profound denial routinely, especially with acutely psychotic patients. Frequently such patients are brought to the emergency room against their will by relatives, friends, or the police. Although it is common for someone who is acutely psychotic to admit to great distress, denial, projection, and externalization often combine to attribute the cause of this distress to outside circumstances. Attempts to recommend medications under these circumstances may challenge the patient's defensive beliefs too soon and in a way that is alienating. For this reason, it is wise to reconsider the practice of routine rapid neuroleptization of psychotic patients in emergency rooms. There are advantages to observing a patient in the hospital for a day or two without any medications unless an emergency situation dictates otherwise.

Many patients and their families consider antipsychotic medications to be "drugs" or "tranquilizers." They fear an addictive potential and/or have "moral objections," as discussed by Greenfield (1985, pp. 113–116). Taking medication may be experienced as a confirmation of "weakness" or "sickness." It is important to explain early that the purpose of the medication is to relieve *specific symptoms that are troubling to the patient*. Symptoms such as "difficulty concentrating," feeling "confused," or "not like myself" may not be the manifestations of psychosis that seem most significant to the clinician. However, discussion of such complaints in relation to medication benefits offers the best possibility for beginning treatment with medications in a collaborative and cooperative way that will be least threatening to the patient and family. This, in turn, will foster the treatment alliance.

Recently there has been much emphasis on the importance of educating patients about medications and obtaining informed consent before treatment is begun. The reasons for these recommendations are not only legal. A careful discussion of benefits, side effects, risks, dosage changes, and informed consent can have a potent facilitating effect on the treatment alliance. However, tact and timing are essential, and it is often not possible for either the patient or the family to listen to these facts and make an informed decision during the acute crisis. In such instances, elaborating details, especially about disturbing side effects, should be postponed until they are not heard as an overloading assault that jeopardizes the alliance. Informed consent must be discussed as an *ongoing* issue throughout the treatment. Goals will change as symptoms subside. Even if compliance with drug regimens has not been a problem during earlier stages of treatment, the clinician should not assume that the patient understands the prophylactic function of medication that is important during later phases of treatment.

Although education about medication is extremely important, the doctor who assumes that education is sufficient to ensure compliance does so at his or her own peril. Because the giving and taking of medication is so frequently highly charged with meanings for both doctor and patient, didactic methods alone result in a high rate of noncompliance. These meanings are often unconscious and symbolic, and manifest medication issues serve as a vehicle of expression for powerful transference and countertransference reactions. It is especially easy to miss these important reactions in clinics and other situations where medication is viewed as the primary treatment and the doctor-patient relationship is not conceptualized as psychotherapeutic. A common misconception is that if one is not "doing psychotherapy," transference and countertransference reactions will not occur. The variety of possible fantasies about medications, both positive and negative, is limited only by the human imagination; thus a cataloging of all the manifestations of transference and countertransference meanings expressed through medication is not feasible.

As with any other kinds of transference or countertransference reactions, the impact on the treatment alliance of distortions related to medications can be decisive, especially when unrecognized and therefore not understood. Common examples cited in the literature include patients experiencing medication as proof of the doctor's love, as an attempt to seduce or fuse, and as a means of intrusion or poisoning. Patients sometimes stop medications, complain about side effects, or make suicide attempts to express hostile feelings toward their doctor. Countertransference aspects of pharmacotherapy have received less attention. Levy (1977) described the use of prescribing drugs "as a concrete enactment of establishing interpersonal boundaries, a disavowal of frightening feelings, a guilty renunciation or secret fostering of forbidden regressive pleasures, or a means of establishing control over a seemingly uncontrollable situation" (p. 29). He used case examples to illustrate these responses as defending against the regressive pull of symbiosis on the therapist in the psychotherapeutic treatment of schizophrenic patients. Careful inquiry into these psychological issues is essential to the maintenance and stability of the treatment alliance. It is also important to remember that decreasing or stopping a neuroleptic can be just as psychologically important as prescribing one.

Making Emotional Contact

A crucial issue in the treatment of schizophrenia is the establishment of emotional contact with the patient as soon as possible. MacKinnon and Michels (1971) have pointed out that the development of shared understanding between patient and therapist is the best criterion for judging whether a successful interview has taken place. Although this task can be especially difficult with a schizophrenic patient, it is of critical importance. In part, the difficulty can be attributed to the psychosis itself. It is not easy to approach a patient who is uninterested in reality, uncommunicative, or speaking only in a primary process way. The problem may be compounded further by a patient's flat or inappropriate affect and preoccupation with delusions and/or hallucinations. Because the patient is in the hospital and the therapist wants to help, it is often assumed, incorrectly, that the schizophrenic patient correctly interprets the therapist's intentions. Many of these patients have long ago given up expecting another person to be helpful to them. Furthermore, many have had prior experiences in clinics and hospitals with mental health professionals whose main aim was to gather information, get rid of patients' symptoms, and discharge them as soon as possible. Karon and VandenBos (1981) and others have pointed out how the structure of the modern mental health system tends to reinforce this problem by rewarding high-volume, high-speed treatment while de-emphasizing the quality of care. Any disappointing, frustrating, dehumanizing human contacts may result in the patient retreating even farther from reality. Thus the first encounters with the patient are critical.

In order to more closely examine what is meant by "making emotional contact," it is necessary to reiterate that virtually all students of schizophrenia agree that some portion of a healthy person remains within the psychosis. In conceptualizing the psychopathology of schizophrenia as a "psychical split," Freud (1940) wrote, "Even in a state so far removed from the reality of the external world as one of hallucinatory confusion, one learns from the patients after their recovery that at the time in some corner of their mind (as they put it) there was a normal person hidden who like a detached spectator watched the hubbub of illness go past him" (pp. 201–202). The therapeutic task is to emphatically seek out this nonpsychotic portion of the ego, establish meaningful communication with it, and nurture its growth and expansion. Conveying to the psychotic patient a sense of understanding of the patient's experience even though he or she has not and perhaps cannot express it clearly in words, is very much like what Winnicott (1958), Mahler et al. (1975), and others have described as occurring between mother and infant during early development. To be effective, the contact must center on some aspect of inner or outer reality *in which the patient has maintained a current interest*. This kind of approach, which involves an active reaching out to the patient, is similar to that described by Jacobson (1967). It is, however, in sharp contrast to the methods described by Rosen (1953) (entering into the patient's psychosis) and Searles (1965) (symbiotic fusion). If the reaching out is not active and persistent, the therapist will be easily kept away; if it is too forceful, the patient will withdraw further. In order to locate and focus on some area in which the patient has maintained an interest in the real world, the therapist must allow both his conscious and unconscious perceptions to roam freely and neutrally over the almost infinite range of possibilities. Neutral in this context means an absence of preconceived notions about what *should* be the patient's interest; such a bias could interfere with observing what the patient is actually presenting at the moment. A useful guideline is to be alert for something that the patient is currently experiencing as a problem. Although this may differ sharply from what looks *most* problematic to the therapist, not surprisingly, it often leads directly to the patient's "chief complaint" and to why hospitalization occurred. What is likely to be missed are those interests that appear to be trivial. For instance, a lack of cigarettes might represent a "chief complaint" and offer the best opportunity at the moment to be helpful.

Making emotional contact is neither a kind of fuzzy-minded love treatment nor an abstract theoretical concept. Rather it is a clinical phenomenon with clear behavioral referents that can be reliably observed. When we are with an acutely psychotic schizophrenic person who is immersed in primary-process thinking, and whose affect is flat or inappropriate, we may feel a remoteness and strangeness about the patient (praecox feeling of Rumpke). If an abrupt change is perceived in the patient in direct response to something the therapist has just said, this juncture represents "making emotional contact." This phenomenon is characterized by a sudden increased contact with reality accompanied by a change from primary-process to secondary-process thinking and/or some sign of affect, especially warmth. Not only the interviewer, but impartial observers can perceive the change. My experience has been like Ryan's (personal communication), who notes that if observers were asked what they had seen and felt during the interview, they were in agreement. Typical comments were, "He warmed up at such and such a point," or "It seemed like you were interviewing two people; one before such and such a point and one afterwards." Also, the observers themselves experienced an emotional "turning on" to the patient at the same juncture. They had sensed something missing in the patient and recognized that "something" when it returned during the interview. The following three vignettes are illustrative:

> A 36-year-old severely delusional woman who was markedly guarded in her speech and suspicious in her demeanor only communicated with brief verbal responses and with a flat affect. When asked what was troubling her, she indicated that something had been going on in her neighborhood for some time and that people had said some nasty things about her. Now there was something else that she could only allude to vaguely, with hints that there had been some further abuses by others. She responded (still with

flat affect) to a question about her job by saying that she had worked for a restaurant chain for the past 15 years until 2 days prior to admission. She had been at the same restaurant for more than 5 years, and most of her previous employment was at another restaurant in the same chain. At this point the interviewer asked her what it was like to work in these two places, including some details with which the interviewer was vaguely familiar from personal experience. In response, there was a perceptible and gradually increasing warmth in her voice and an understanding was reached that she had liked her work; it was her "whole life." She wanted to return but was afraid. This led to a brief discussion of her fears. People had begun to say that she was homosexual; she had heard voices accusing her of homosexual acts, and a number of people were involved in a plot to transform her into a homosexual. Her fears were worse at night, and so it was arranged for her to return to work by day and stay in the hospital at night. She did this for several days while taking a low dosage of thorazine and was discharged to the Outpatient Clinic. Although she continued to show indications of delusional thinking, she also gained the capacity to question the reality of some of her delusional thoughts.

A 29-year-old divorced mother who had been admitted to the hospital because of seizures following an insulin overdose was presented at a weekly staff conference. The interviewer knew of her fixed delusion that she was diabetic, and that she had been administering insulin to herself for an undetermined period of time. She was evasive, guarded, and suspicious during the interview and responded to questions briefly, tangentially, or not at all. The interviewer's attempts to gain some understanding of the events leading up to her hospitalization and of her interesting and unusual delusion were to no avail. Throughout the interview her affect remained blunted and the interviewer sensed no rapport. However, she mentioned several times that she wanted to leave the hospital. She felt guilty about being there and not taking care of her son. At this point she was asked how long it had been since she had seen her son. As she responded appropriately to the question she began crying. She said that her son was not allowed to visit on the ward because it was against hospital rules. The issue was discussed with her in a forthright manner and the misunderstanding about visiting rules was cleared up. She appeared relieved and grateful and did not mention leaving the hospital again during the remainder of the interview.

A 38-year-old schizophrenic man with four previous hospitalizations was admitted in an acutely psychotic state and spoke only "word salad" during the first hospital day. On the second day, he insisted on leaving, refusing to discuss why or reveal anything else about himself to any staff member. He spoke through clenched teeth, no feeling tone accompanying his verbal productions. However, his taut jaw musculature suggested a struggle with intense feelings. Throughout the beginning of the interview the patient repeatedly commented that he wanted to leave right away and that he had a right to leave. The reason for his wish to leave the hospital could not be elicited nor would he say why he had come. However, he did mention that he had been in a veteran's hospital once and knew all about psychiatry; that there was the "ego, the superego, and the lid." The interviewer responded, "You know, what you say is not quite right. The ego and the superego are the lid, and I think that's what your trouble is, that you are having trouble keeping the lid on." The patient's jaw relaxed immediately and he laughed. He repeated the comment that the ego and the superego are the lid several times, and he said that he thought this had been very funny. He then repeated the part about his own trouble keeping the lid on and said that he had been afraid that he would murder the other patients in his bedroom. The patient began to talk about his long-standing difficulties with his wife; their frequent separations and threats of separation, and finally his feeling of panic that he would murder her with an ax or a pistol. It was this fear that had led him to come to the hospital. Immediately following his acknowledgment of his problem with violent impulses, the patient spoke earnestly and with appropriate affect. He agreed to continue his treatment in the hospital and subsequently maintained a good working relationship with the staff.

The last vignette deserves special comment for two reasons. First, it represents an example of a situation in which the interviewer was able to detect that the patient was aware of, interested in, and very concerned about an aspect of his *inner reality*. Second, this example illustrates the fear of loss of control over violent impulses that is commonly encountered in acutely psychotic patients. When perceived, such fears should always be discussed and controlling measures such as medication and seclusion should be offered.

The techniques described and illustrated above do not result in magical cures. Hopefully, it is equally apparent that "making emotional contact" with a patient is essential and central to the process of forming a treatment alliance. No special talent or unusual personality characteristics are necessary. However, patience, persistence, and repetition are required. Thus it is not surprising that those who spend the most time with the patient, such as nurses, mental health assistants, and other patients, sometimes provide the most meaningful therapeutic encounters. Many "spontaneous cures" and psychotherapeutic triumphs can be traced retrospectively to just such relationships on the ward. The importance of consistent availability cannot be overemphasized. An acute psychotic disturbance is an indication for at least daily visits by the primary caretaker. When a regular schedule of appointments is established, it should be adhered to as carefully as possible. Any departure from this schedule, particularly if unexpected and unexplained, can be extremely disruptive to the therapeutic relationship and cause significant regressions.

Exploratory or insight-oriented approaches are usually least helpful during the acute psychotic phase. Psychotherapeutic efforts during this period should emphasize the establishment of a relationship, and interventions should support and strengthen failing ego functions such as reality testing. A here-and-now focus is usually most helpful.

Just as there is no psychopathology that is unique to schizophrenia, there are no transference and countertransference problems that occur only in the treatment of these patients. However, some problems do seem to be more common and intense. They center around the patient's wishes for and fear of symbiotic union, and his or her struggles with murderous rage. These issues tend to stir up countertransference feelings of fear, impotence, isolation, withdrawal, and despair on the one hand, and grandiose, omnipotent control on the other. When chronic, such feelings in the therapist can be dealt with best in supervision or in a combination of supervision and personal treatment. The ability to tolerate transferences and countertransferences is essential. As the treatment alliance develops, the patient's conflicts often become increasingly focused in the transference relationship. The understanding of this new version of the past becomes the fulcrum of the treatment.

INDIVIDUAL PSYCHOTHERAPY

Despite many positive case reports and an extensive clinical literature on individual psychotherapy with schizophrenic patients, there have been very few systematic, methodologically sound, long-term outcome studies investigating the efficacy of psychotherapy in schizophrenia. The enormous resources required, as well as the methodological challenges and complexities, have discouraged most investigators. Controlled studies that have been completed, such as the well-known studies of May et al. (1981) and the more recent Chestnut Lodge (McGlashan 1984) and Boston University (Gunderson et al. 1984) investigations, have failed to demonstrate the efficacy of individual, psychodynamically oriented psychotherapy. One noteworthy exception is the Michigan State University project. In their book *Psychotherapy of Schizophrenia*, Karon and VandenBos (1981) maintain that psychotherapy has been demonstrated to be helpful for schizophrenic patients when careful quality control of the psychotherapy has been provided. However, this study, like most, has been criticized on methodological grounds. Reviews by Gomes-Schwartz (1984) and McGlashan (1984) provide a detailed consideration of the methodological issues and controversies. Regarding these outcome studies, Cancro (1983) has pointed out that negative findings have been interpreted incorrectly by many people as a positive demonstration of ineffectiveness. The best-known studies utilized "psychoanalytically oriented psychotherapy," but this says very little about what was actually done in the treatment. Unfortunately, there has been much confusion between psychoanalysis as a theory and psychoanalysis as a method of treatment. Psychotherapy that is informed and guided by psychoanalytic theory does *not* necessarily make extensive use of the primary treatment techniques of psychoanalysis. Furthermore, the dichotomy between supportive and insight-oriented or expressive therapy is misleading. All psychotherapy has both supportive and expressive elements. Schlesinger (1969) has framed this issue in a useful way: exactly "what needs to be supported and when and why, and what needs expression and why" (p. 268). He has also emphasized that the patient defines what is supportive. The technique, according to Schlesinger, "is a supportive technique if the patient experiences it as supportive" (p. 268). Interpretations, which are usually associated with expressive techniques, are sometimes experienced by the patient as very supportive. Schizophrenic patients most often need support of their reality testing, self-esteem, and anxiety management associated with sexual and especially aggressive conflicts.

It is important to note that even those investigators whose results have been the most pessimistic believe that individual psychotherapy has a role in the treatment of schizophrenia (Gomes-Schwartz 1984). As McGlashan (1984) has emphasized, none of the research results mitigate against the importance of the individual relationship between doctor and patient. The clinical relationship between the patient and the professional who is meaningfully and empathically involved should be at the center of all treatment (McGlashan 1986). It is also important to note that the research findings are not unequivocally negative. Katz et al. (1984), in their treatment dropout study involving schizophrenic patients, found marked heterogeneity in terms of reasons for dropping out and subsequent outcomes. Of particular relevance here is their finding of significant interhospital differences. In a study of three Boston area hospitals, McLean Hospital had a lower dropout rate than

Boston University Hospital or Bedford VA Hospital. McLean emphasized individual psychotherapy and long-term treatment, whereas Boston University and Bedford VA emphasized rapid discharge. A direct relationship was found between length of hospitalization and likelihood of remaining in therapy for more than 6 months. In addition, recoveries and functionally adequate outcomes occur in one of every three of the schizophrenic patients studied. Some of these patients were chronic and so called "hopeless cases" (McGlashan 1984). Luborsky (1984) has recently outlined methods for evaluating and facilitating the treatment alliance. His manual, *Principles of Psychoanalytic Psychotherapy*, for the first time provides a detailed method for documenting what actually transpires in psychoanalytic psychotherapy. Therefore, it could provide a foundation for more meaningful and much needed outcome studies. Given our current state of knowledge, we are unable to predict in advance which patient will benefit most from psychotherapy. Therefore, psychotherapy should always be considered in the overall treatment planning for schizophrenia, particularly when other modalities have been ineffective.

CONCLUSIONS

Although the purpose of psychotherapy is to facilitate growth, it has potential for harm as well as for help. In order to assist the nonpsychotic ego in its struggle for dominance, we must demonstrate that the current reality, as painful as it often seems, is nevertheless better than psychosis. To be successful we must find that normal person within the psychosis and provide for him what he needs and cannot provide for himself. At the same time, we must avoid doing for him what he can do for himself. The challenge is to accept the patient wherever he is, while at the same time combating his psychosis.

A powerful statement by a recovering schizophrenic patient about the value of psychotherapy used in conjunction with medication was included by the editor in a recent issue of the *American Journal of Psychiatry*:

> The question of whether the fragile ego of the schizophrenic patient can withstand the rigors of intensive therapy seems to me an unfortunate hindrance to the willingness of psychiatrists to attempt psychotherapy with schizophrenic individuals. A fragile ego left alone remains fragile. It seems there must be some balance that can be achieved so that schizophrenic patients can receive the benefits of psychotherapy with therapists who are sensitive

> to their special needs and can help their egos emerge, little by little. Medication or superficial support alone is not a substitute for the feeling that one is understood by another human being. For me the greatest gift came the day I realized that my therapist really had stood by me for years and that he would continue to stand by me and to help me achieve what I wanted to achieve. With that realization my viability as a person began to grow. I do not profess to be cured–I still feel the pain, fear, and frustration of my illness. I know I have a long road ahead of me, but I can honestly say that I am no longer without hope. (Anonymous 1986, p. 70)

References

Anonymous: "Can We Talk?" The schizophrenic patient in psychotherapy: a recovering patient. Am J Psychiatry 143:69–73, 1986

Bleuler M: The long-term course of the schizophrenic psychoses, in Annual Review of the Schizophrenic Syndrome, Vol 14. Edited by Cancro R. New York, Brunner/Mazel, 1976, pp 435–452

Brenner C: Working alliance, therapeutic alliance, and transference. J Am Psychoanal Assoc 27 (suppl):137–157, 1979

Cancro R: The treatment of the severe schizophrenic patient, in Treatment of the Seriously Ill Psychiatric Patient. Edited by Gralnick A. Gralnick Foundation, Port Chester/Rye Brook, NY, 1983, pp 113–127

Docherty J: The therapeutic alliance and treatment outcome, in American Psychiatric Association Annual Review, Vol 4. Edited by Hales R, Frances A. Washington, DC, American Psychiatric Press, 1985, pp 527–531

Fenichel O: Problems of Psychoanalytic Technique. Albany, NY, Psychoanalytic Quarterly, 1941

Freebury D: The therapeutic alliance in psychotherapy research: unsolved problems. Psychiatr J Univ Ottawa 11:72–76, 1986

Freud A: The Ego and Mechanisms of Defense. Revised edition. New York, International Universities Press, 1966 (original work published 1936)

Freud S: Papers on technique, in Standard Edition of the Complete Psychological Works of Sigmund Freud, Vol 12. Edited by Strachey J. London, Hogarth Press, 1911–1913, p 139

Freud S: Outline of psychoanalysis, in Standard Edition of the Complete Psychological Works of Sigmund Freud, Vol 23. Edited by Strachey J. London, Hogarth Press, 1940, pp 201–202

Friedman L: The therapeutic alliance. Int J Psychoanal 50:139–153, 1969

Gomes-Schwartz B: Individual psychotherapy of schizophrenia, in Schizophrenia. Edited by Bellack A. Orlando, FL, Grune & Stratton, 1984, pp 307–335

Greenfield D: The Psychotic Patient. New York, Free Press, 1985

Greenson R, Wexler M: The non-transference relationship in the psychoanalytic situation. Int J Psychoanal 50:27–40, 1969

Group for the Advancement of Psychiatry, Committee on Research: Pharmacotherapy and Psychotherapy: Paradoxes, Problems and Progress, Vol 9, Report No 93, March 1975

Gunderson J, Frank A, Katz H, et al: Effects of psychotherapy in schizophrenia. II. Comparative outcome of two forms of treatment. Schizophr Bull 10:564–584, 1984

Gutheil T, Havens L: The therapeutic alliance: contemporary meanings and confusions. Int Rev Psychoanal 6:467–481, 1979

Hartley D: Research on the therapeutic alliance in psychotherapy, in American Psychiatric Association Annual Review, Vol 4. Edited by Hales R, Frances A. Washington, DC, American Psychiatric Press, 1985, pp 532–549

Hartley D, Strupp H: The therapeutic alliance: its relationship to outcome in brief psychotherapy, in Empirical Studies of Psychoanalytic Theories, Vol 1. Edited by Masling J. Hillsdale, NJ, Erlbaum, 1983, pp 1–37

Hill L: Psychotherapeutic Intervention in Schizophrenia. Chicago, University of Chicago Press, 1955

Hutchins RM (ed): Medicine, in Great Books of the Western World, Vol 3. Chicago, University of Chicago Press, 1952

Jacobson E: Psychotic Conflict and Reality. New York, International Universities Press, 1967

Karon B, VandenBos G: Psychotherapy of Schizophrenia. Northvale, NJ, Jason Aronson, 1981

Katz H, Frank A, Gunderson J, et al: Psychotherapy of schizophrenia: what happens to treatment dropouts? J Nerv Ment Dis 172:326–331, 1984

Levy S: Countertransference aspects of pharmacotherapy in the treatment of schizophrenia. Int J Psychoanal Psychother 6:15–30, 1977

Levy S: Principles of Interpretation. Northvale, NJ, Jason Aronson, 1984

Luborsky L: Principles of Psychoanalytic Psychotherapy. New York, Basic Books, 1984

Luborsky L, Auerbach A: The therapeutic relationship in psychodynamic psychotherapy: the research evidence and its meaning for practice, in American Psychiatric Association Annual Review, Vol 4. Edited by Hales R, Frances A. Washington, DC, American Psychiatric Press, 1985, pp 550–561

MacKinnon R, Michels R: The Psychiatric Interview in Clinical Practice. Philadelphia, WB Saunders, 1971

Mahler M, Pine F, Bergmann A: The Psychological Birth of the Human Infant. New York, Basic Books, 1975

May P, Tuma A, Dixon W: Schizophrenia: a follow-up study of the results of five forms of treatment. Arch Gen Psychiatry 38:776–784, 1981

McGlashan T: The Chestnut Lodge Follow-up Study II. Long-term outcome of schizophrenia and the affective disorders. Arch Gen Psychiatry 41:586–601, 1984

McGlashan T: Schizophrenia: psychosocial treatment and the role of psychosocial factors in its etiology and pathogenesis, in American Psychiatric Association Annual Review, Vol 5. Edited by Frances A, Hales R. Washington, DC, American Psychiatric Press, 1986, pp 96–111

Rosen J: Direct Analysis. New York, Grune & Stratton, 1953

Sandler J, Dare C, Holder A: The Patient and the Analyst. London, George Allen and Unwin, 1973

Schafer R: The Analytic Attitude. New York, Basic Books, 1983

Schlesinger H: Diagnosis and prescription for psychotherapy. Bull Menninger Clin 33:268, 1969

Searles H: Collected Papers on Schizophrenia and Related Subjects. New York, International Universities Press, 1965

Szasz T: Some observations on the use of tranquilizing drugs. Arch Neurol Psychiatry 77:86–92, 1957

Winnicott D: Collected Papers. London, Tavistock Publishers, 1958

Zetzel E: Discussion, in Psychiatric Drugs. Edited by Solomon P. New York, Grune & Stratton, 1966, pp 75–85

Chapter 7

MILIEU TREATMENT

Bandupriya P. Vidanagama, M.D.
Hugo J. Zee, M.D., F.A.P.A.
Steven T. Levy, M.D.

PSYCHIATRIC HOSPITALS FUNCTION in a variety of ways. They serve as humane shelters for the troubled, shield their inhabitants and the public from each other, and provide a location for "treatment" in a strict medical sense. These hospitals may themselves become a therapeutic tool by virtue of their organization and structure. The notion that the structure and organization of an institution can by itself be beneficial is not new. Religious monasteries and some Victorian public schools are examples of institutions in which this occurs. This chapter will explore the way a psychiatric inpatient unit can function as a therapeutic tool in the care of deeply disturbed patients.

HISTORY OF THE MILIEU CONCEPT

Traditionally, society has viewed psychiatric patients with distrust and fear. They have been isolated, ostracized, and frequently eliminated from general society's interactions. Humanistic approaches to the management of mentally ill patients, including provision of an environment for treatment conducive to self-understanding and eventual recovery leading to reintegration into society, was championed by Phillipe Pinnel and William Tuke in the early nineteenth century. This approach to the mentally ill is described by Main (1946) as a "fine traditional mixture of charity and discipline given in a practiced technique to help patients" (p. 66). The development of psychoanalysis in the late-nineteenth and twentieth centuries fostered an emphasis on humane attitudes toward the mentally ill, but was based on the assumption that psychological disturbances resided primarily within the individual. Treatment was to be carried out based on a medical model of one-to-one interaction, downplaying the significance of social and other environmental factors.

Sullivan (1931) was among the earliest and most important psychiatrists in this century to focus on the social environment in which treatment took place. Sullivan supported a form of treatment in which psychiatric workers deliberately formulated and controlled a sympathetic environment for the total body of patients and staff involved in the treatment process. He believed that psychotic patients who are surrounded by affection and intimacy rather than by dislike and humiliation were better able to organize themselves. Sullivan stressed that environment, including what can be learned from communal experiences in treatment units, contributes in a positive way to recovery.

The significance of the social structure and organization of the psychiatric ward in relation to patients' behavior and outcome of treatment was increasingly recognized in response to the experiences of psychiatrists and other mental health professionals during World War II and the postwar period, particularly in the United Kingdom and the United States. T.F. Main (1946) and Maxwell Jones (1966), among others, emphasized that the immediate psychological environment in which patients function determines their attitudes, behavior, and symptoms and is a critical factor in determining the outcome of treatment.

Social psychiatrists like Maxwell Jones thought that psychosocial breakdowns were related to disordered interactive patterns and maladaptive modes of communication. The psychiatric ward environment was therefore shaped to make these maladaptive patterns of communication and interaction more easily observable. Once these patterns were observed, they could be clarified and understood, and changes could be made in them.

We will focus in this chapter on the role of various milieu factors in carrying out the treatment of acutely psychotic patients in a short-term treatment setting. A short-term unit treating such patients should address many issues, among which are the following: (1) clinical diagnosis, psychodynamics, and precipitating events; (2) understanding of psychotic manifestations with a view toward their integration with ongoing life experiences; and (3) overall psychosocial functioning, especially postdischarge functioning. All patients should be rapidly assessed in terms of present illness, clinical diagnosis, and current psychodynamics. During this period, every attempt should be made to engage the patient in psychological dialogue in order to understand the personal meaning of his or her difficulties. In addition, regular meetings with family members and involved outside agencies should be scheduled to attend to current and postdischarge needs of the patient. Day-to-day living issues, financial problems, and socialization skills need to be addressed within the safety of the hospital community. We will define and clarify the basic principles of the milieu in relation to the above goals and functions. We will also address problems in the conceptualization of milieu principles as well as the task of adapting milieu treatment to acutely psychotic schizophrenic patients during brief psychiatric hospitalizations.

Sullivan (1931) believed that patients within hospital settings should not be hurried out to unfavorable life situations. However, most discussions of milieu treatment, its impact and problems, assume longer inpatient stays than are customary today. During the last 50 years, there have been many social, political, economic, and philosophical changes with regard to psychiatric hospitalization. The detrimental effects of prolonged hospitalization have led to widespread deinstitutionalization and to an increasing focus on short-term treatment units, where the emphasis is on early return of the patient to the community. Most acutely psychotic patients now receive their inpatient treatment on such short-term treatment units.

Types of Milieus

Psychiatric milieus vary in their form and function. They can be open or closed, large or small, in a traditional setting or in an unconventional setting such as a halfway house or other community-based rather than hospital-based setting. Some milieus can be designed for residential (long-term) treatment, while others may be suitable for patient stays of only a few days. Cumming and Cumming (1962) view the role of the milieu as "to present challenges in the form of problem solving in a protected environment, without producing high anxiety" (pp. 71–77). They believe milieu treatment should offer a well-organized structure, including supportive groups, in a variety of settings in which patients are encouraged to solve problems with guidance from trained personnel.

Gunderson (1978a, 1978b) describes five processes that regularly take place in a psychiatric milieu program: containment, support, structure, involvement, and validation. Containment is the ability of the unit to contain the patient's unacceptable impulses and poorly controlled behavior. Support refers to the unit providing supportive, empathic, and caring attitudes. Structure means the use of time and space in the patient's day in a productive, helpful, organized fashion. (Space refers to control of patient movement on the unit.) Involvement refers to the ability of the unit to actively engage patients in a psychological fashion and to observe patterns of interaction and ability to relate to others. Validation involves an examination and exploration of intrapsychic events and their relationship to current realities. Gunderson believes that the successful milieu unit will utilize one or more of the above processes in the care of each patient. He stresses that what is therapeutic for a particular patient has to be determined by the milieu in each instance rather than the milieu expecting all patients to fit into a particular model. This general approach serves as a useful guide to which we will refer in describing an optimal treatment setting for the care of acutely psychotic patients.

PHILOSOPHY OF THE MILIEU

The traditional medical hospital model is composed of a nurturing, omnipotent, hopefully benevolent, and highly parental staff, and of incapable, irresponsible, passive, recipient patients. Current notions of shared responsibility for treatment between patient and caretaker, and joint examination and exploration of events rather than unilateral interventions, directly conflict with this more traditional model. A careful review of current treatment philosophies leads to the conclusion that this conflict has been handled in a dichotomous fashion in the structuring of psychiatric treatment units.

The concept of a therapeutic environment has different meanings in various settings. Tucker and Maxmen (1973) state, "Although every inpatient unit says it has a therapeutic community or 'milieu,' nobody agrees on what it actually is, for these terms may mean anything from homelike furnishings to elaborate behavior modification programs with specific motives and goals" (p. 888). Wilmer (1958) points out that "the milieu community may use any form of therapy, but the basic therapy is the milieu" (p. 825). In this case, the milieu is viewed as a therapeutic tool by itself. In contrast, Abroms (1969) describes the milieu as "a social arrangement within which treatment can be carried out" (p. 336). In other words, milieu is a social setting that aims at reducing destructive, disorganized, deviant, and inappropriately dependent behavior by setting limits and teaching new skills. It is within such an environment that other treatment procedures take place. The milieu can thus be thought of as either a treatment setting or a treatment.

Despite this dichotomous view, both approaches include viewing all transactions within the social structure as important sources of information. Currently, in most psychiatric settings, milieus that are part of brief treatment programs are thought of as facilitating environments rather than as totally independent treatment systems. The two views of milieu need not be mutually exclusive. Milieus can function both as an integral therapeutic part of a multimodal therapy program and as a facilitating treatment setting.

An Atmosphere of Safety

Behavioral dyscontrol and thought disorganization in acutely psychotic patients make them extremely difficult to reach psychologically. Intense resistances develop to the milieu's efforts. These resistances include difficult-to-understand interpersonal reactions based upon the extensive use of primitive defensive operations that significantly distort reality. Given such difficulties, building a therapeutic alliance may becor. e a monumental task (see Chapter 6 of the present volume). With acutely psychotic schizophrenic patients, short-term hospitalization should not be viewed as a comprehensive curative procedure but rather as an effort to establish a therapeutic alliance for long-term ongoing care of chronic difficulties, care that will take place primarily outside of hospital settings. This effort will include in-hospital and posthospital rehabilitation services and psychoeducational modalities.

The psychological discovery process occurs best in a setting where the patient experiences an atmosphere of safety, where his or her projections are safely "held" by essentially constant, reliable caretakers offering steady support while simultaneously insisting that psychological work continue in spite of hatred and periods of failure. In such settings, the patient does not experience malicious retaliation in response to his or her sometimes primitive aggressive feelings and behavior. Clarifications are sought and tendered in the face of the patient's bewilderment, confusion, and suspiciousness, inevitable by-products of the disorganization caused by psychotic processes. The milieu becomes a holding environment. It is in such a responsive and empathic atmosphere that the patient must begin to regain the capacity for confident expectations (trust in others) so that psychotherapeutic confrontation and clarifications offered by staff can be accepted and used profitably rather than merely suffered as persecutory attacks.

The staff needs to meet regularly in order to systematically study each patient as well as the interpersonal, group, and intersystemic dynamics (i.e., between disciplines, between hospital administration and the milieu) in order to understand each patient's interactions from different therapeutic perspectives as well as to assess functional capability and plan for the future. Such self-scrutiny by staff requires considerable leadership, because painful issues among the staff invariably must be dealt with. Staff may feel embarrassed to learn that their interactions with the patient are more personally than professionally motivated, that interpersonal, interdisciplinary, and hierarchical rivalries, primitive sexual and aggressive wishes, jealousies, guilt, pride, and conflicts over trust and power among staff are major determinants in patient/staff interactions. Considerable trust among team members must develop in order for them to feel comfortable enough to reveal to other staff members detailed personal reactions related to patients. Such trust and openness among staff is essential for the unit to become a safe place for patients to begin to reveal and explore their own fears, fantasies, and conflicts. In addition to trust and openness, regular meetings are essential for posthospital planning in terms of family intervention and rehabilitation functions.

Reinforcement of the team's maturity must come from educational endeavors such as supervision, case conferences, and interdisciplinary educational meetings, as well as from support given by higher administrative levels. This "therapy" for the staff has much to do with reinforcing the sense of hope, excitement, and curiosity about the work among an enlightened social network of caretakers (supervisors, administrators, and coworkers). Hidden staff "burn out" can be detected in the common occurrence of flight toward more casual involvement with disturbed patients. By having only superficial interaction with the acutely psychotic patient, the staff member has less appreciation of what such patients are struggling with intrapsychically. While frequently attributed to limited time and "appropriately" limited goals, such subtle abandoning of patients is more frequently due to countertransference anxieties stirred up by attempts at more intense involvement with psychotic individuals.

The gratification for staff from psychodynamic work with acutely psychotic patients is very different from that derived from other therapeutic activities with patients in milieu settings that focus on objective and quantitative factors such as symptom removal and number of patients treated. In psychodynamic work, gratification evolves from a deeper understanding of the human condition and from the creative process taking place within the supportive social context. On short-term units working with psychotic patients, the focus is on the struggle for mutual engagement. This engagement, which centers on joint recognition of a serious illness requiring intensive, long-term treatment, may make up the bulk of the work that can take place during the brief hospital stay. Nonetheless, both staff and patients benefit from such an experience. Sometimes it is not until long periods of time have passed after hospitalization that the merits and gratifications inherent in such therapeutic efforts are fully realized. This mutual engagement motivates the patient to work towards his or her optimum functional level.

The ward must tolerate symptomatic behavior within certain time, spatial, hygienic, administrative, and legal limits. Conversely, there should be an intolerance for certain other behaviors; for example, when sheer hatred or chaos renders treatment chronically ineffective, or when verbal interaction is replaced by physical harm to self or others. More difficult to detect is when a regressive adaptation becomes chronic and nonproductive. Setting of limits and use of medication are interventions in which the patient's participation should be actively sought. This is particularly true of medications, which patients often experience as intrusive and unwanted in spite of demonstrably useful effects. Containment of behavior so that it can be mutually observed, experienced, and understood is a desired goal; disintegration, fragmentation, and deepening psychosis and a chronically regressive adaptation must be struggled against on a continuous basis.

Individualizing Treatment Approaches

Gunderson's (1978a, 1978b) hierarchy of therapeutic milieu processes (i.e., containment, support, structure, involvement, and validation, in that order), described earlier, are arranged temporally with regard to hospital course as well as in order of progressively greater complexity. There is an increasing requirement for more patient participation and initiative. In the past, milieus have customarily had broad and definitive goals for all patients. However, in a unit with a mixed psychiatric population, as is common in most hospitals (both general and psychiatric), what is therapeutic has to be defined for each patient. Most acutely psychotic patients, in their disorganized state, are not immediately available for explorative, insight-oriented interventions. Clearly, the initial need is for containment. This may be provided in many ways. The ward should be comfortable and safe. The use of medication, restraints, and seclusion help to reinforce internal controls and reality testing in the face of omnipotent and other psychotic distortions. Such reinforcement should be carried out in a therapeutic fashion. Many patients initially view containment procedures as punitive. The treatment team should be in close contact with the newly admitted patient to clarify that such procedures are for purposes of safety and group comfort, and are designed to reduce the distress caused by psychotic experiences. Failure of such efforts at clarification will alienate the patient. Treatment will come to be viewed with suspicion and distrust, endangering the building up of any therapeutic alliance.

In most cases of acute psychosis, containment and support should be viewed together. Support can be provided around concrete issues such as food, cigarettes, personal belongings, direct advice about daily routines, help with reality testing, and education about the hospital and about mental illness in general. When support is combined with containment, patients usually begin to feel safe and more comfortable. The hospitalization experience eventually must be viewed as a positive one. The patient's individual therapist as well as other staff will seek to convey a message of intrinsic interest and caring for the patient, essential ingredients for the development of any long-term relationship. Posthospital issues of daily functioning must be addressed along with outpatient management of medication and other follow-up care. Patients generally have various misconceptions about their medications and side effects that need to be clarified. Education about medications through medication groups can be very helpful.

The patient, after discharge, usually moves into a family or community living arrangement. If other supportive groups are available and motivated, they should be included in the discharge planning. This may involve several meetings with the family or other supports to discuss issues of medication, socialization, activities, and work (see Chapter 8 regarding family treatment). During hospitalization, the patient's interests and capabilities in terms of social interactions, day-to-day survival skills, and work and educational capabilities should be assessed. The milieu can be helpful in identifying dysfunctional areas and allowing the patient to practice newly learned skills. Carefully timed insight-oriented efforts and psychosocial rehabilitation approaches can complement each other as long as both are genuinely valued by staff. The treatment program must be individualized to the specific and changing needs of each patient. Consequently, ward activities must be directed with individualized treatment goals in mind. The milieu must function in a manner similar to an investigative, curious therapist as well as provide a supportive, educational structure.

Glick et al. (1974) examined the efficacy of short-term (21–30 days) versus long-term (90–120 days) hospitalization. Long-term treatment was not found to be superior to short-term hospitalization for the schizophrenic patients studied, although a "longer period of inpatient hospitalization allowed long-term patients to plan better for discharge and, in some way, accept the necessity for continued treatment" (p. 369). In a subsequent report, Glick et al. (1984) indicate that there may be two subgroups of chronic patients: schizophrenic patients with good prehospital functioning and a fulminant episode with major psychosocial disruption; and patients with affective disorders, who need to be hospitalized for longer periods. These authors advocate a treatment strategy based on rapid assessment of clinical diagnosis, psychodynamic and psychosocial functioning, effective crisis resolution, and symptomatic relief. The milieu functions as a facilitator, providing guidance and structure for the necessary activities. The primary goals defined for the short-term unit described by Glick et al. are crisis intervention and discharge planning, with a focus on family interventions. In such a setting, patients are able to organize quickly and rapidly resume functioning outside the hospital. These authors support the belief that a multimodal approach, aimed at symptom relief, psychological understanding, psychosocial rehabilitation, and education about the illness, provides the optimum method of treatment for acutely psychotic schizophrenic patients.

The treatment we will describe employs techniques developed in connection with psychodynamic milieus as well as with inpatient units that are primarily psychosocial rehabilitation oriented. Additionally, the treatment has a strong medical emphasis, with careful physical evaluation and medication management. We do not feel that our current state of knowledge is adequate to determine with any certainty the clear superiority of one model over another. We recognize that aspects of each model, if applied rigidly or in an inappropriately timed or mechanical manner, can have deleterious effects.

Hospitalization itself, in addition to the well-documented destructive effects of chronic institutionalization, can have a deleterious effect even with brief patient stays. Psychodynamically intensive milieus, if not adapted to the care of acutely psychotic schizophrenic patients, can be overstimulating, contribute to further regression, alienate patients from family and other support systems, interfere with ongoing outpatient treatment relationships, and otherwise negatively influence long-range outcome (Drake and Sederer 1986). Likewise, rehabilitation models, unless sensitively and flexibly applied, may miss opportunities for personal growth, misjudge the patient's psychological strengths, and ignore very problematic interpersonal problems in families that interfere with optimal recovery.

The degree to which different models can be profitably blended is unknown. We have found that the multivalent approach described below works effectively provided doctrinaire attitudes regarding the superiority of particular elements are carefully avoided. This requires strong, involved leadership and an open attitude on the unit that encourages lively but respectful discussion of the unit's function and areas of disagreement. The unit staff, though mostly psychodynamic in orientation, are often directive and forceful in assessing and providing for the ambulatory needs of the patient. Containment and support functions, however, cannot be carried out mechanically and unilaterally or they will result in the patient feeling abandoned, punished, and misunderstood. By providing a stable structure via such means as regularly scheduled meeting times and regulation of eating, sleeping, and recreational activities, the staff helps the patient's day become predictable. However, it must be remembered that adhering too rigidly to a schedule can also be harmful. It may be too stimulating and therefore counterproductive for some acutely psychotic patients to attend large group meetings even though the philosophy of the unit emphasizes maximum participation of patients in ward activities. The ward structure must be implemented with an understanding of how this structure affects each patient's perceptions, anxiety level, sense of interpersonal engagement, and need for privacy. Staff should seek to understand the particular requirements as well as limitations of each patient. Enforcing the general ward structure with understanding and flexibility conveys a message of empathy, caring, and interest.

Psychological Engagement

The psychological work with every patient is important both for understanding that particular patient's behavior and for helping him or her achieve a sense of mastery over life and its problems, including having a serious, possibly chronic illness. The schizophrenic patient is greatly aided in efforts toward greater self-awareness and better self-management by working on problems over a prolonged period of time. In a short-term unit, emphasis is on the beginning of such a process. Indeed, an essential purpose of hospitalization is to aid the patient in establishing a trusting treatment alliance that, because of destructive or disorganized behavior, could not develop or continue outside the boundaries of a hospital. This alliance develops best when the patient is able to work with a few others who have had a chance to get to know him or her well, and with whom the patient feels comfortable, safe, and trusting. Such "others" include a well-led, specially trained, multidisciplinary team (with a flat hierarchy assuming maximal autonomy at the patient/staff level) and some of the patient's peers. Caretakers should be essentially constant and reliable, responsive to the patient's affects and needs, and accepting of his or her temporarily dependent position, judging it with empathic concern.

Therapeutic work involves making mental phenomena and their behavioral manifestations as observable and as transparent as possible. The patient must be encouraged to understand and integrate these phenomena, with the goal of gaining mastery over the troublesome impulses, affects, and behaviors that are part of his or her illness. During brief hospitalization, attention should be directed toward helping the patient begin to look at his or her current problems as a particular part of his or her whole psychological experience, rather than as an alien, intrusive event to be denied, repressed, or otherwise rejected. In addition, problems arising out of the patient's disability, such as difficulties in his or her living situation, disordered social skills, changes in functional level in terms of work, leisure activities, and ability to manage finances, need to be assessed and initial plans made to address these issues. These plans may include beginning vocational training programs, attending multifunctional groups to improve social and self-care skills, and making necessary changes in current living arrangements.

Recovery Styles

Recovery from severely traumatic emotional experiences requiring hospitalization can be described in different ways. We have found it useful to conceptualize recovery in terms of "integration" and "sealing over" (Levy et al. 1975; McGlashan et al. 1977). These two styles of recovery are at opposite ends of a descriptive and dynamic continuum. In a short-term treatment setting, most psychotic patients use a mixture of both styles of recovery in the process of overcoming their difficulties.

Integration describes a process by which a continuity is established between thoughts and feelings experienced during psychotic periods and premorbid as well as posthospitalization life. During an integrative recovery, patients struggle with the conflicts expressed by their psychosis, are curious about and feel responsible for these conflicts, and try to redefine them in new psychological ways so that their experiences can be used as new information about themselves for use in modifying their methods of coping and functioning. To a large degree, this style reflects aspects of the patient's relatedness to the treatment itself and to the treatment staff. There is detectable interpersonal involvement, therapeutic engagement, and empathic interchange.

In the process of sealing over, psychotic experiences and symptoms are isolated from nonpsychotic mental life and made unavailable by defensive operations such as repression, denial, and projection. Intense resistances develop to any kind of intervention or influence. Patients who seal over are reluctant to discuss their disturbing thoughts and experiences and fail to place them into meaningful perspective with their problems prior to and after their acute illness. These patients tend to view their psychosis as an encapsulated, isolated event totally alien to their usual mental life. They rarely view anything about their psychosis as a source of new information about themselves or as a learning experience. Rather, patients who have sealed over tend to return to unchanged premorbid patterns of functioning and behavior. Treatment team members may come to view psychotic illnesses in a similar manner. Treatment units and therapists who view psychotic experiences only as mental aberrations are inclined to use strategies that emphasize controlling symptoms, with social recovery as the ultimate goal. This approach facilitates a tendency toward sealing over.

Treatment units and therapists interested in exploration—those who view the psychotic experience as an integral part of the patient's mental life, reflecting its struggles, strengths, and deeply felt affects—are curious about the patient and engage him or her in meaningful exploration of psychotic experiences with the aim of understanding and learning. Doing so does not imply failing to recognize that such experiences are part of a serious, recurrent illness. In the exploratory approach the patient feels more participant in the treatment process. It is our belief that an optimum recovery, in which the patient experiences some degree of satisfaction and mastery over himself or herself and his or her environment, can only occur through some process of integration. Nevertheless, for whatever reasons, many patients, despite efforts on the milieu aimed at integration, do seal over. We recognize that the time limitation of the short-term treatment unit places integrative work at a disadvantage. Despite this disadvantage, an effort to begin the integrative process should be attempted with all patients.

During short-term hospitalization, the milieu helps the patient begin to be curious about himself or herself and his or her illness. Although removal of distressing and dangerous symptoms is a desirable goal as well, it should always be tempered with attempts at understanding. Paying attention to target symptoms does not preclude being curious about them. For example, a patient may receive a phone call from a spouse, following which he or she gets agitated and perhaps even assaultive. Containment measures, including medication and restraints, may be indicated. The unit should also try to examine and make connections between the behavior and the phone call in all its meanings to the patient, no matter how distorted by psychotic thought processes these connections are. Having said this, it needs to be clarified that integration remains only one of the unit's efforts. Other objectives are aimed at helping patients become as functional as possible (in the sense of making social, occupational, personal, and recreational adjustments that are clearly necessary in order to enhance the quality of the patients' lives), as well as helping them to achieve some mastery over their environment and to participate in some pleasurable activities.

Most patients seal over some areas of difficulty while integrating others. As noted, the forces within short-term units such as we are describing tend to direct the treatment process toward sealing over. The reasons for this are many and include staff anxiety over their own unconscious conflicts. The staff need to experience a sense of satisfaction in their short-term work with patients. Success is most easily recognized in terms of symptom reduction and the ability to quickly discharge patients back to the community. External, administrative, and economic demands for control, symptom reduction, behavior stabilization, and cost containment contribute to collusion by the staff toward sealing over despite an avowed focus on understanding and exploration. It remains less anxiety-provoking to overtly or covertly encourage patients to seal over. Sealing over avoids uncomfortable affects and narcissistic injury in the face of the great difficulties encountered in trying to understand severely disorganized thinking, feeling, and behavior.

THE TREATMENT UNIT

Unit Size

The treatment unit should be small enough to allow personal interactions to take place and to allow meetings to be held in which all members of the milieu can participate. Treatment teams, involving 8–12 patients each, should be established. Each team should have a multidisciplinary staff. The staff/patient ratio generally should approach 1:1. Each team is headed by a psychiatrist or, in training settings, by an advanced psychiatric resident with a faculty supervisor. An experienced nurse should co-lead each team. The nurse (preferably a psychiatric clinical nurse specialist) should also function as coordinator for the team, particularly if the psychiatrist is a resident whose participation on the team is time-limited. A psychologist on the team should provide special diagnostic assessment as well as therapeutic and conceptualizing skills. The team should also include a social worker who deals with linkages between the patient and outside agencies and groups such as family and other needed resources. The social worker should be in contact with the family as soon as the patient is admitted, for purposes of information gathering and dissemination among patient, team, and family members. The social worker should also provide therapeutic guidance and education for the family (see Chapter 8). An activity therapist (occupational or recreational) assesses the needs for essential daily activities that are useful in helping the patient reorganize after a psychotic experience. Such activities are also useful in assessing the patient's skills and vulnerabilities with regard to posthospital activities. The nursing staff attend to the patient's personal and medical needs, as well as pay attention to interpersonal coping skills manifested on the treatment unit.

Boundaries

Preferably the treatment unit should be a regulated, open system. The unit director should control admissions with an eye toward continuity and stability. At times it may be necessary for the unit to function as a closed unit (for example, when a distraught patient threatens to run off or when unwanted substances or other items are being brought into the unit by visitors or patients). Both staff and patients are responsible for preserving the boundaries of the treatment setting. Once a treatment unit becomes a closed unit, there is danger of the staff becoming increasingly authoritarian and unilaterally assuming what ought to be the patients' share of the responsibilities for maintaining the boundaries of the milieu. The treatment team should consider commitment to psychiatric treatment a rudimentary milieu boundary. Often, however, the most seriously ill and disorganized patients are incapable of maintaining this very rudimentary boundary. Struggles around this issue (legal commitment) are a regular function of the milieu, and understanding should replace coercion and rebellion as ways of resolving such struggles.

Although it may appear from the outside somewhat rigid and preoccupied with impersonal procedures, the milieu should strive to convey to new participants its dynamic focus and egalitarian spirit. Most acutely psychotic schizophrenic patients, who are usually overburdened with primitive aggressive thoughts, feelings, and fantasies as a result of severe ego impairments in reality testing, impulse control, anxiety tolerance, and synthetic functioning, are greatly reassured by a stable and resilient milieu structure with clear-cut boundaries and procedures. At times it is necessary to use controlling measures and activities such as quiet rooms, restraints, and one-to-one nursing techniques. These powerful and clearly control-oriented activities reinforce boundaries and provide necessary reassurance to extremely disturbed patients and to the staff responsible for their care. It is important that these procedures, determined by a need for temporary control, do not become punitive, although they are often temporarily seen as such by the acutely disturbed patient. Such a punitive view of controlling activities may exist simultaneously with more difficult to detect feelings of relief in the face of anxiety about dyscontrol. Ultimately, the danger of being viewed as the psychotic person's keeper rather than enabler must be overcome by an exploration of the patients' experience of control procedures at a later time when patients are better able to understand why such procedures were needed and when they can explore in a less anxiety-filled situation their own responses.

It is crucial that the milieu regularly assess its boundary functions and understand the varied reasons for whatever actions are necessary in order to maintain boundaries. The therapeutic community meeting is a useful tool for such exploration. Some units tend to be too laissez-faire with regard to boundary functions. A casual rather than thoughtful attitude is rationalized in many different ways, and decisions are made without anticipating their consequences. If a unit lacks sufficient control over its own boundaries, it runs the risk of becoming flooded with external problems. This interferes with the implementation of the essential treatment plan, often leading to antitherapeutic effects. Enforcement of boundaries must always be tempered with a sense of understanding and empathy.

The stability of the unit and the continuity of its treatment philosophy are essential for the unit to maintain its therapeutic effectiveness. Admissions, discharges, and major decision-making should be carefully planned and regulated. Ideally, new arrivals and departures of staff and of patients should be anticipated events that are matters for community discussion. The unit should have information regarding new arrivals. Assessment should regularly be made regarding the suitability of that particular unit for the patient who is being considered for admission. Discharges should be carefully planned so as not to overwhelm the unit's capacity for termination. Even on a short-term (4 week) acute care unit, admission and discharge planning can be accomplished in a way that maintains the unit's boundaries intact.

Staff recruitment as well as staff departures should be carefully regulated. Staff members leave milieu treatment units for many reasons. Seldom is it solely for a better paying job, although this is the most commonly stated reason. Work on an acute care unit is often frustrating and at times even demoralizing. Staff may periodically feel unappreciated both by patients and peers. Work may no longer seem rewarding, particularly because therapeutic efforts with severely disturbed patients often result in apparent failures. Such issues need to be a constant focus of the milieu's exploratory efforts. During recruitment, a detailed discussion of expectations, a comprehensive job description, and a careful assessment of personal and professional attributes and vulnerabilities (e.g., special interpersonal skills, job dedication, motivation, psychological mindedness) should be made. Once a new member is recruited and accepted, a period of nurturing and training by the rest of the treatment team is necessary. When carefully planned as a learning experience, this adjustment period will improve the quality of the new recruit's performance.

Decision-Making and Leadership

Decision-making procedures on the milieu need to be carefully thought through. Many decisions need to be made spontaneously by online staff. The team leader should delegate variously defined tasks to those team members with the most expertise. Role definition of team members should be emphasized. The aim is not to create unnecessary differences or hierarchies but rather to take advantage of different skills and expertises as well as to foster interdependence among team members. The process of decision-making requires that the team look at psychological issues in the patient, reactions of staff members, and group dynamic phenomena that may be involved.

Major decision-making is a collaborative effort that team members share with the team leader, who functions as a central organizer. The necessary information must be gathered to enable the team as a whole to understand decisions from a centralized perspective and to outline, delegate, and sanction plans with a common purpose. This process represents what is often termed "participatory management" (as opposed to "decisions by consensus"), by which those who are affected by decisions have a voice but not necessarily a vote. This process clearly keeps responsibility and accountability with the team leader, who retains veto power and who specifically delegates authority on the basis of staff skill and patient need. Role definition as a boundary is important and is maintained with such a structure. Blurring of roles and ambiguity about responsibility causes confusion and insecurity among patients and staff members.

Acute care milieu units attempting to function as open systems must continuously monitor the inherent tendency to drift toward closure of information exchange processes and psychological exploration. This closure regularly occurs when, for a variety of reasons, the milieu becomes engaged in achieving goals other than that of resolving the problems of its charge patients. Such other goals reflect hospital, community, and family demands, as well as other outside pressures familiar to mental health systems. Likewise, closure may occur when staff on the unit feel overwhelmed in dealing with an unusually large number of severely regressed, demanding psychotic patients. When this occurs, a newly arriving psychotic patient may be mechanically processed rather than carefully piloted, encouraged, reassured, and made welcome. Careful attention to the unit's boundary functions is essential in maintaining the unit's open, exploratory, and humane treatment approach.

Structure

The structure of a milieu unit both defines the nature of that unit and determines its mode of treatment (Gunderson 1978a, 1978b). The unit's structure needs to be planned with clear ideas about the nature of the pathology of patients to be admitted to the unit, and equally clear and realistic expectations about what can be done that will be helpful in the period of time allotted. One form of the unit's structure is the assignment of time and space in a patient's daily routine in a manner that is predictable, organized, and at least potentially understandable even for a disorganized and psychotic patient. A well-structured day makes life predictable for patients as well as for staff. Such predictability reduces anxiety and need not be viewed merely as rigid, unalterable, and unnecessarily controlling.

On our unit the day customarily begins with a group exercise program following the morning meal. All patients who are judged able to participate attend this program for 30–45 minutes. The focus of this activity is on physical fitness of patients confined to a limited space. Our unit has found this activity stimulating and helpful in many ways. It is useful in assessing a patient's capacity for following directions and for participating in nonemotionally threatening group activities. The exercise program often serves as a way for new patients to meet other patients and staff in a pleasurable and nonemotionally taxing activity. This program can also be used to assess a patient's capacity to function outside the hospital.

Ward rounds follow, attended by all of the available staff. Rounds last between 1 and 1½ hours, during which staff present information pertinent to the care of established as well as new patients. A review of patients' activities and status during the previous 24 hours is presented by the nursing staff for general discussion. Each staff member is responsible for providing information pertinent to treatment decisions. After rounds, each treatment team meets to discuss treatment issues in greater depth. This daily treatment team meeting provides an opportunity to teach trainees and new staff members.

Community meetings, like treatment team meetings, are generally held after ward rounds. In the early literature about milieu treatment, an emphasis was placed on daily community meetings as useful and productive for patients and staff. Growing experience in dealing with acutely psychotic patients on a short-term milieu unit has indicated that such meetings may be too stimulating and anxiety-producing, particularly for patients newly admitted to the unit. Such patients feel frightened and anxious. Our unit has found that two community meetings of 45–60 minutes per week is optimal for a population of primarily acutely psychotic schizophrenic patients.

Exploring issues relevant to the functioning of the community and providing patients with an opportunity to develop social skills in step with other psychological work are the major purposes of community meetings. Various models for conducting these meetings have been proposed and described in the literature. The participants in the community meeting have different levels of skill and authority, as well as varying interpersonal styles and different purposes for participating. Care must be taken that the meeting maintain a focus on its multiple purposes and avoid various ways in which it can function nontherapeutically.

The community meeting examines how the community is functioning on behalf of patient improvement. Consequently, the meeting should address primarily here-and-now issues of daily living and plan for necessary posthospital functioning. It is assumed that all events and activities occurring within the milieu are open for scrutiny. Thus, challenging questions will be raised at such meetings, stimulating mixed feelings among those who are affected by the issues raised. Often, interdisciplinary or other forms of staff conflict, either latent or overt, will become the focus of the community's discussion. These forms of conflict are easily confused and intermingled with problems posed by the patients' severe psychopathology. Care must be taken to separate staff conflict from problems posed by patients and their difficulties. Whereas some staff conflicts may be clarified in such meetings, many such issues are more appropriately dealt with at other times.

It is best to maintain in clear focus the goal of understanding patients' modes of interaction as they contribute to the day-to-day successes and failures of community living on the unit. No matter how clearly defined, this task can easily become obscured and misunderstood. Large meetings such as the community meeting often provoke regression as a result of the severity of psychopathology and the inherent problems in communication arising from such problems. This is particularly true as the group gets larger and as the number of disorganized patients increases. In such settings, deep interpretations or the examination of highly charged intrapsychic phenomena can be extremely antitherapeutic. The leader of the community meeting must have clear goals and objectives in mind and must be skilled and experienced in confronting the inevitable problems that arise when these goals and objectives for the meeting are replaced by antitherapeutic trends. Whenever the meeting becomes embroiled for extended periods of time in the discussion of obscure, philosophical, or personally sensitive material rather than in working on practical day-to-day issues concerning all members of the community, the leader needs to intervene in order to return the group to the main work task.

Group Therapy Program

Much of the psychological and rehabilitative work with patients on the milieu occurs in group meetings, while in the larger community meetings, day-to-day ward functioning issues are addressed. Because acutely psychotic patients in different phases of the recovery process will vary in their capacity to participate in and benefit from group treatment activities, the group program should include different kinds of group experiences through which a recovering patient can progress in stages. One kind of group, which we refer to as a focus group, is a theme-oriented group experience that is highly structured. The focus group meets four times per week for one-half hour. This group is usually the first group experience in the group therapy program that the acutely psychotic patient participates in. Discussions within this group center on daily ward activities, the nature of the hospital's treatment programs, and issues related to the fact of being mentally ill.

The next level of group experience we refer to as the socialization group. This group, which meets daily for 1 hour, is primarily supportive in nature. The group's goals are developing communication skills, examining issues related to self-esteem, tolerance for conflict and temporary debilitation resulting from mental illness, and focusing on respect and understanding of others in a community setting. To be admitted to the socialization group, the patient must have the capacity to remain in a group setting with activity limited to verbal exchange for 1 hour.

The most intensive group experience is referred to as the psychotherapy group. This group meets four times per week for 1 hour. Criteria for admission to the psychotherapy group include the ability to discuss emotionally charged issues, some capacity for insight into the nature and effects of mental illness, and some motivation to examine and change behavior. The format for the psychotherapy group is interactional, and the focus remains on current problems, particularly as they are manifest within the milieu structure. Far-reaching, historically-based interpretations are avoided because they are invariably based upon distorted information and are often of little use to the recovering psychotic patient except in avoiding work on current and pressing problems.

In addition to these group activities, there is a weekly psychoeducational group in which patients and staff discuss the nature of mental illness; the purposes and details of medication, including dosage, scheduling, and side effects; and other related phenomena. Symptoms and their management are discussed, and other issues related to patient education, including informed consent, participation in follow-up care, family issues, and ward research activities, are explored. In addition to the psychoeducational group, a weekly 1-hour discharge planning group ensures smooth transition from inpatient to outpatient follow-up care. Many other group activities take place within the milieu. Already mentioned is a daily morning exercise group. Many activities that are part of the Occupational Therapy Program take place in groups, as do various activities often occurring during the evening hours and focusing, for example, on leisure skills, art, music, and literature.

Staff members from many different disciplines are expected to participate in the various group activities. Group leaders should be chosen based upon leadership skills, training in group therapy, experience, and motivation. Decisions about which group activities patients are to participate in require free and open communication among staff members. The group treatment program complements many other therapeutic activities taking place within the milieu. It is not meant to either replace or compete with individual psychotherapy, which we believe should continue to have an important place in the care of the acutely psychotic schizophrenic patient (see Chapter 6).

Conclusions

We have discussed issues regarding the structure of a milieu unit specifically designed for the short-term treatment of the acutely psychotic patient. Such units need to take each individual patient's particular needs into account. These include psychosocial rehabilitation and psychological understanding. Therefore, the milieu unit needs to be flexible and empathic while, at the same time, being rigorously goal-oriented and intensive. The essence of the therapeutic structure described is the maintenance of an attitude of exploration and understanding of the unique set of circumstances and events that led to each patient's pain and suffering in order to plan for a better adjusted posthospital course. The maintenance of such an attitude is essential if the patient is to recognize the intense interest and involvement of the treatment staff that will eventually lead to engagement, trust, and hopefully, recovery.

Many of the therapeutic activities described were developed

on long-term therapeutic milieus in which milieu treatment was the primary therapeutic activity. Principles developed in such settings have been adapted to the short-term treatment model in which milieu activities are part of a more diverse therapeutic effort including individual psychotherapy, rigorous psychopharmacological interventions, and intensive family treatment and psychosocial education and training. It is uncertain at this point in the development of our knowledge about treatment of acutely psychotic patients on a short-term unit how to optimally synchronize these various treatment modalities, many of which were developed independently of each other. It is unclear how many treatment modalities staff and patients can tolerate at one time! There are vocal proponents of and compelling arguments for all of the treatment approaches described. An atmosphere of respect, tolerance, and scientific inquiry is necessary in order to ultimately arrive at an optimal treatment approach. Differences in interest, aptitude, and treatment philosophy must be accommodated by the entire milieu staff. Leadership must come from skilled and experienced clinicians who maintain open minds and encourage a sense of enthusiasm and commitment among staff, tempered by thoughtful scientific attitudes toward learning about what is most helpful in the treatment of very disturbed patients.

Inpatient Psychosocial Treatment Guidelines

The acutely psychotic patient comes into the hospital with dysfunction in many areas, including behavior dysfunction, loss of self-esteem related to loss of control, breakdown of family, community, and financial support systems, as well as diminishing ability to care for the self (personal care and self-survival skills). Hospitalization is beneficial in that it protects the patient from his or her own disruptive impulses, helps to contain these impulses, provides a structure during this breakdown of internal systems, and provides safe, caring, empathic supportive systems in which the patient can gain essential empathy, understanding, and support. Hospitalization also provides an atmosphere in which the patient can, with the help of staff, begin to explore reasons for his or her breakdown. On the other hand, hospitalization can be a negative influence. It can be overshadowing and contribute to further decompensation and regression, increase loss of already diminished self-esteem, and further alienate the patient from family, community, and other support systems. Thus, ideally, a psychosocial treatment modality should formulate goals to minimize these negative effects and maximize the optimal functioning level for the patient during a short stay.

With these concerns in mind, we would like to propose the following guidelines for a psychosocial model of treatment:

1. Dyscontrol and disruptive behavior need to be managed by medications and other restraining measures such as seclusion rooms. Acute patients tend to get worse when placed in an atmosphere that is too stimulating. Allowing the patient quiet time by himself or herself is therapeutic. Other containment, supportive, and structural measures as outlined by Gunderson and described in this chapter are intensely beneficial. Use of adequate and ample medications while exploring and empathically dealing with the patient provides relief to him or her, as well as a sense that the treatment team is in control even though the patient feels out of control.
2. The ward community should actively try to engage the patient in its activities. Consequently, the patient should take active involvement in the day-to-day running of the ward. He or she should be helped in self-care skills. There should be gentle and empathic exploration into the patient's current difficulties. Effort should be made to help the patient gain some insight into and understanding of how his or her emotional conflicts have some relationship to the current disruption in his or her life. Apart from the structured activities, the patient should be encouraged to interact actively with staff and other patients to develop a sense of understanding, as well as a sense of "I am not alone." This atmosphere of gentle exploration, in which the patient is able to try out without recrimination for failure and assume responsibility for his or her own actions, will enhance self-esteem and encourage attempts at understanding and gaining more control.

   The occupational and recreational activities on the ward should be geared toward increasing self-esteem, assessing the current level of functioning, and helping patients improve that level of functioning, as well as helping them learn some new skills. These activities help patients to better organize and structure themselves. Most of these patients are unable to carry out day-to-day activities for survival, such as cleaning, self-care, dietary needs, attention to medical needs, to mention a few. The occupational therapy and recreational therapy group activities should focus on these skills, and the information gathered should be assessed regularly by the treatment team.

In addition, there should be specific groups and discussions geared toward aftercare. These groups would focus on issues related to illness and diagnosis, medications and their complications, and the importance of posthospital and outpatient care. Adequate education must be provided on the ward in all these areas.

3. The treatment team should meet with the faculty or the supportive groups at least one to two times a week. These meetings could take place with the patient present. Issues related to his or her breakdown should be discussed, and here psychoeducation of the support becomes crucial. The psychoeducation should be geared toward understanding the illness, the use of medications, the complications of these medications, and the need for aftercare. These meetings should assess living conditions, housing, financial needs, medical needs, etc. Most families go through tremendous trauma when a member is hospitalized; they are confused and upset, and may be unaware of needs and available resources. It is the responsibility of the treatment team to assess the needs of the patient and family and provide appropriate education. In addition, direct contact with resource agencies may be necessary.

All of the above-mentioned activities are of little use unless adequate discharge planning is carried out. The milieu should actively discuss discharge, issues of termination, and impact of reentry to the outside world. Outpatient care should be well planned. It is preferable if the outpatient care provider can meet the patient on the ward. But definite outpatient contact and an appointment must be available before discharge.

Globally, while discussing the issues of illness, the milieu should focus on enhancing strategies to increase coping skills as well as pay attention to remedial problems in living.

REFERENCES

Abroms EM: Defining milieu therapy. Arch Gen Psychiatry 21:553–560, 1969

Caudill W: Social structure and interactional process on psychiatric ward. Am J Orthopsychiatry 22:314–324, 1952

Cumming J, Cumming E: Ego and the Milieu. New York, Atherton Press, 1962

Drake RE, Sederer LI: Inpatient psychosocial treatment of chronic schizophrenia: negative effects and current guidelines. Hosp Community Psychiatry 37:897–901, 1986

Glick I, Hargreaves W, Goldfield M: Short vs. long term hospitalization. Arch Gen Psychiatry 30:363–369, 1974

Glick I, Howard M, David L: Guidelines for hospitalization of chronic psychiatric patients. Hosp Community Psychiatry 35:934–936, 1984

Gunderson J: Defining therapeutic processes in psychiatric milieus. Psychiatry 41:327–335, 1978a

Gunderson J: Overview of modern milieu therapy. Psychiatry 41:1–13, 1978b

Jones M: Therapeutic community practice. Am J Psychiatry 122:1275–1279, 1966

Levy ST, McGlashan TH, Carpenter WT: Integration and sealing-over as recovery styles from acute psychosis: metapsychological and dynamic concepts. J Nerv Ment Dis 161:307–312, 1975

Main TF: The hospital as a therapeutic institution. Bull Menninger Clinic 19:66–70, 1946

McGlashan TH, Levy ST, Carpenter WT: Integration and sealing over. Arch Gen Psychiatry 32:1269–1272, 1975

McGlashan TH, Wadeson ATR, Carpenter WT, et al: Art and recovery style from psychosis. J Nerv Ment Dis 165:182–190, 1977

Sullivan H: Social psychiatric research: its implications for schizophrenic problems and for mental hygiene. Am J Psychiatry 10:977–991, 1931

Tucker GJ, Maxmen JS: The practice of hospital psychiatry: a formulation. Am J Psychiatry 130:887–891, 1973

Wilmer HA: Toward a definition of the therapeutic community. Am J Psychiatry 114:824–833, 1958

Chapter 8

FAMILY MANAGEMENT

Rosalind Mance, M.B.B.S.

SCHIZOPHRENIA, A CHRONIC ILLNESS with a fluctuating course and uncertain outcome, has a major impact on the family of the ill individual, especially at times of acute psychotic relapse. Before the era of deinstitutionalization, the burden of care for chronically ill patients fell on state hospitals. Now it is family members who are likely to be in the caretaker role. As the number of beds available in state hospitals has diminished, pressure has increased on the remaining number of public sector beds to provide adequate care for acutely ill patients. Often families are forced into the position of being caretakers for relatives incompletely recovered from an acute psychotic episode. This occurs despite the time of greatest risk for rehospitalization of acutely ill schizophrenic patients being the first 6 weeks postdischarge. Additionally, there has been growing recognition of the effects that the environment has on the course of schizophrenia. All these factors have led to an increased interest in psychosocial and family interventions that help caretakers in their difficult role and contribute to better outcome for the schizophrenic individual.

Impact on the Family

Emotional Turmoil

The emotional turmoil experienced by families of schizophrenic persons was described by Creer (1978). She detailed the family distress caused by the schizophrenic member's symptomatic and socially impaired behavior. Some of this family turmoil stems directly from the disruptive effects of the schizophrenic relative's behavior during times of relapse. Rapid and inappropriate changes of mood leave family members exhausted by their attempts to relate to their ill relative. Also, the unpredictability of these changes makes family members anxious and unable to relax. Relaxation or even sleep time that family members continue to have is often disrupted by the patient's altered sleep and activity patterns. Their ill relative is often intensely demanding or suspicious. Even if the schizophrenic member withdraws, avoiding intimate interaction with anyone, the very strangeness of the patient's behavior demands attention and concern. Anxiety, fear, and anger are often felt as a confusing turmoil.

Family Burden

The disruption of a family's everyday functioning is not related solely to emotional turmoil. Grad and Sainsbury (1963) first described the concept of increased family burden. Family members tend to adapt their roles and routines to provide supervision and care for the ill member. Coping skills may be stretched past their limit. In a survey of 89 members of a self-help group, families reported disruption of sleep and eating patterns, deterioration of marital relationships, feelings of neglect of their other children, and interference with roles and relationships outside the family (Hatfield 1978). Reiss (1975), using a controlled experimental design, showed that parents of schizophrenic persons had difficulty in problem solving; this was found to be true as well of parents of character-disordered patients. Such difficulties are likely to be present in families dealing with the devastating effects of many chronic illnesses. They may lead to unhappiness, an increase in physical complaints, and economic difficulties.

Stigma

Studies of the impact of schizophrenia on the family have looked specifically at the issue of stigma (Rabkin 1974). Researchers have measured the changes in family behavior related to society's disapproval of deviant behavior (Yarrow et al. 1955). Many families show a tendency to be secretive about their ill relative, and withdraw rather than lean more heavily on their regular supports during times of stress. It is interesting that only a fraction of the families who show secretive behavior spontaneously report feelings of embarrassment or shame (McFarlane and Beels 1984). In part, this may be due to the tendency of family members to under-report negative feelings about their family or its members (Kreisman and Joy 1974). In addition, there is some indication that different socioeconomic and cultural groups vary in their responses to the effects of stigma. Some black cultural groups and lower socioeconomic groups may show more anger, resentment, and guilt when confronted with a relative's socially inappropriate behavior (Kreisman et al. 1979). However, clinical experience indicates that at other times, the less structured family life in these groups may lead to greater tolerance or even seeming indifference toward the ill member's unusual behavior. If such behavior includes threatening or physically violent actions, feelings of shame or guilt may make these families less able to reach out for help, particularly to mental health professionals.

Families also report experiencing stigma in their contacts with mental health systems. In a study by Hatfield (1981), families from a survey of self-help group members, primarily white and middle class, described feelings of rejection and hostility in connection with encounters with mental health professionals. Such families also reported feeling angry about the lack of adequate resources in many acute treatment settings. Private settings are often seen as hostile to the family, whereas public settings are viewed as simply overburdened. Families who initially seek care in the private sector may eventually turn to the public sector for treatment when their own resources are depleted and insurance benefits are used up. Despite increasing awareness of the issue of stigma, its social effects have not yet been fully addressed. Rabkin, in a 1974 review of studies of stigma, concluded that only slight progress had been made in reducing people's negative attitudes toward the mentally ill. Some additional gains have been made since then.

Reduction of stigma, and education of the public about mental illness, are currently the number one priorities of the National Alliance for the Mentally Ill (NAMI). This organization of families of mentally ill individuals has become a powerful advocate for schizophrenic persons, on both local and national levels. Nevertheless, it has been argued that the effects of stigma are so far-reaching that these family advocacy groups are in danger of losing their effectiveness. Family members, in their eagerness to be accepted after being stigmatized for so long, get distracted in their varied contacts with mental professionals from a single-minded insistence that their own and their relative's needs be met.

All families with a schizophrenic member must deal with some aspects of stigma. Mental health professionals working with schizophrenic patients are becoming increasingly responsive to the effects of this negative social pressure. The fact remains that a large proportion of mental health professionals choose not to work with schizophrenic patients. Many see the treatment of these patients as frustrating and unrewarding, and devalue the attempts of others who think differently. Even within the mental health professions, stigma is still an active force.

Restriction of Social Network

The social withdrawal and isolation found in many schizophrenic individuals and their families leads to a restriction of social supports and coping mechanisms. Tolsdorf (1976) found that schizophrenic individuals and their families have smaller and more family-based social networks than medical patients. Garrison's work (1978) with Puerto Rican women in New York City showed that such constriction of social networks and isolation become intensified after subsequent schizophrenic episodes.

WHAT FAMILIES NEED

The growing self-help movement among families of schizophrenic persons has contributed valuable insights into what these family members want from mental health professionals. Hatfield (1983) surveyed 400 families belonging to self-help organizations in nine states. Goals most frequently identified by families during their most recent use of these organizations were reduction of anxiety about their relative, understanding of the illness, development of appropriate expectations, acquisition of skill in managing their relative's unmotivated behavior, and receiving of assistance at times of crisis. Families were also asked to rate the degree to which their objectives had been met. In none of the 21 goal categories was any significant relationship found between goals identified by families and goals seen as having been accomplished. It is imperative that mental health professionals take into account the disruption to family life that schizophrenia can produce, as well as the preferred goals of families seeking services, when planning effective strategies for family management in schizophrenia.

Influence of Early Family Theorists

Families dealing with schizophrenia face many obstacles. Misuse of early theories of a family etiology of schizophrenia has in the past added to the family burden of guilt, while contributing little toward practical help in addressing the immediate situation. The first major family theorists in the 1950s were Bateson, Jackson, Haley, and Weakland. They described a certain type of family interaction pattern they called the "double bind," which they theorized might lead to schizophrenic thinking and behavior in children (Bateson et al. 1956). One message is expressed simultaneously with a quite contradictory message communicated on a different logical level or by different means. Action is often called for, but whatever action is taken is bound to have negative consequences. Bateson et al. hypothesized that these patterns of metacommunication lead to problems in the development of normal conceptual thinking in children raised in such an environment, leading to subsequent schizophrenic breakdown. Lidz (1958) studied 16 families and described problems in the marital relationship that he felt were related to the development of schizophrenia in the children. He described these relationships as skewed and schizmatic marriages in which there was either inequality of power or intense conflict between the marital partners, as well as profoundly distorted communication. Bowen (1960) described the concept of excessive emotional distance or "divorce" between spouses. He hypothesized that offspring of such marriages might have similar marital problems, leading in turn to the appearance of schizophrenia in the third generation. Wynne et al. (1958) used the terms "pseudomutuality," "pseudohostility," and "rubber fence" to describe a certain type of family social organization with rigid role structure and emotional enmeshment that they felt led to schizophrenia in the offspring. Wynne and Singer (1963) used projective tests to study the degree of thought disorganization and communication deviance in nonschizophrenic members of such families, and to predict the degree and type of thought disorder seen in the schizophrenic relative.

These researchers described important and valuable concepts relating to the family system. However, taken as a single hypothesis explaining why schizophrenia develops in any given individual, these theories are not persuasive. There is limited evidence that types of family interaction such as double bind and emotional divorce are specific to schizophrenia, although they clearly appear in many dysfunctional families (Bowen 1965). Furthermore, replication of this early work has not been successful. The work itself is based largely on case descriptions. These were carried out on families whose relative had already developed schizophrenia, and may bear little relevance to family interaction patterns during that relative's childhood. Case descriptions can provide important understanding of what goes on in families living with a schizophrenic member. Alone, these cases do not provide adequate support for an etiological formulation of the disorder. In addition, such family interaction patterns have been shown to exist in families with no schizophrenic relative. Many families have experienced being ignored or blamed by mental health professionals for actively contributing to their relative's disorder. Growing acceptance of a multifactorial etiology for schizophrenia, including genetic, traumatic, viral, and constitutional factors, has eclipsed family etiologies for the disorder and encouraged new approaches to families as collaborators in the treatment of their ill relative.

INFLUENCE OF FAMILY LIFE ON THE COURSE OF SCHIZOPHRENIA

Interest in the environment as an important influence on schizophrenia antedated the deinstitutionalization movement and was not lost when family etiology theories fell into disrepute. In the nineteenth century, hospitals such as the Bethlem Royal in England were opened to provide a humanitarian and structured environment from which mentally ill patients might benefit. Structured living can also erode autonomy, especially in the chronically mentally ill. Even prior to the advent of chlorpromazine and other antipsychotic medications in the 1950s, awareness of the negative effects of institutional living had led to interest in moving patients out of hospitals and into the community.

Since the deinstitutionalization movement, interest in the influence of the environment on schizophrenia has shifted toward exploring the effects of family life on the *course* of schizophrenia. Brown and Birley (1968) described a significant increase in stressful life events in the 3 weeks prior to psychotic relapse. Such life events include births, deaths, marriages, and changes in jobs, living accommodations, or relationships. Correction was made for those life events that might have resulted from incipient psychotic behavior. A clear correlation was shown between an increased number of life events and subsequent psychotic relapse. The same group of workers went on to observe that discharged schizophrenic patients returning to a boarding home tended to be readmitted less frequently than those returning to family living. This finding led Vaughn and Leff (1976) to identify measurable styles of family interaction at the time of admission that could be used to predict posthospital course. The critical factors, which were termed "expressed emotion," consisted of measures of criticism, hostility, and overinvolvement. High levels of these interaction styles during the standardized Camberwell family interview predicted earlier relapse for the schizophrenic relative.

As with the early studies exploring possible etiological factors in family communication styles, these studies do not provide evidence that such interactions predate the schizophrenic relapse. The interactions may be responses to the stressful situation in which families with a schizophrenic member find themselves. On the contrary, Goldstein and Doane (1982) argue that a distinction between family factors relating to onset and those relating to course of illness is not valid. In later prospective studies, a simpler measure of parental affective style was developed and shown to have cross validity to high expressed emotion. This measure, when combined with high measures of family communication deviance, predicted the development of schizophrenia spectrum disorder in high-risk adolescents (Doane et al. 1981). Other studies are ongoing to examine, prospectively, interaction patterns in families of children at risk for schizophrenia (Wynne 1984). Such studies are needed to examine further the effects of different aspects of family environment, both those shared by siblings and those specific to individual children, on the development of subsequent psychopathology in high-risk children.

There are other criticisms of these approaches to identifying family interaction patterns related to higher rates of relapse. The assumption that these approaches are specific to schizophrenia is in doubt since recent studies have shown that high expressed emotion also influences the course of affective disorder (Vaughn and Leff 1976). Additionally, the deleterious effects of emotionally charged or intense interpersonal relationships are not restricted to interactions among family members; there is evidence that active psychosocial training by mental health professionals can be toxic for patients under their care (Liberman 1982). The danger also exists that labeling families as having "high" or "low" expressed emotion can lead to families feeling that once again they are being blamed for contributing to their relative's problem.

Nevertheless, these new ways of conceptualizing the interaction between family and schizophrenia have led to important therapeutic findings. Studies of family management intervention during and following an acute schizophrenic episode indicate that relapse rate can be significantly reduced during the 6- to 12-month posthospital period (Falloon et al. 1982; Goldstein et al. 1978; Hogarty et al. 1986; Leff et al. 1982). Longer-term follow-up studies of such interventions are currently in progress. These family management programs rely on the understanding of schizophrenia as a condition giving its sufferers a "core psychological deficit" (Anderson et al. 1981). This deficit is thought to be stably present and increases the schizophrenic patient's vulnerability to external and internal stimuli. Complicated or emotionally charged communications could thus accelerate relapse in such vulnerable individuals, and the effects of such a disrupting influence on the family may in turn produce further stimulating responses from family members. The use of neuroleptic medication reduces a patient's vulnerability to stimulation. Additionally, new lower-dose and targeted strategies for maintenance neuroleptic treatment have more likelihood of success if family members are prepared for ongoing involvement in recognizing early relapse and potential stressors. Encouraging families to participate in programs that provide emotional support, educate about the illness and the benefits of medication, and help develop specific communication and problem-solving skills is clearly effective in reducing short-term relapse. Studies looking at other outcome measures, such as reduced symptomatology and social disability, are needed.

Modern management strategies for working with families coping with acute schizophrenia must address the devastating effects schizophrenia can have on the family, the influence the environment has on the course of schizophrenia, and the needs that family members have for knowledge, skills, and support in helping in the care of their ill relative. In the past, many clinical settings encouraged separating schizophrenic individuals from their families. For many schizophrenic persons, family ties have already been broken as a result of intolerable stresses on family members and of the difficulties schizophrenic patients have in maintaining social relationships. For the next generation of schizophrenic persons and their families, utilization of our growing understanding of psychosocial aspects of schizophrenia has led to collaborative family management approaches that address family needs, support family ties, and improve clinical outcome for the patient.

NEW APPROACHES TO THE FAMILY MANAGEMENT OF SCHIZOPHRENIA

Family Intervention Early in Treatment

Engaging a family with a schizophrenic member requires the clinician to be both active and flexible. After the initial crisis caused by the acute psychosis, relatively few families press forward for continuing involvement in the treatment process. The rapid growth of the family movement, as evidenced by the dramatic swell in the NAMI's membership, may change this reluctance. Currently, clinicians who wish to become involved with the families of acutely psychotic patients must be prepared to reach out with an array of strategies that will enable this family involvement to occur. Different approaches may be needed with a single family at various times during the course of the illness. When families are mobilizing themselves for a crisis, as at a time of acute schizophrenic relapse, they may be eager to involve themselves with the treatment team. The clinician's ability to deal effectively with family members' primary concerns at this time will be an important factor in developing a good alliance for continued collaboration during the recovery period. The burden experienced by families in crisis may make it difficult for them to negotiate time and energy for family meetings or conferences. The clinician who takes these factors into consideration is likely to find family members most responsive to involvement when they first seek services for their relative's acute psychotic relapse.

Engaging the Family

When a family member has become acutely psychotic, almost inevitably the family feels a sense of failure and dissatisfaction with recent family events and interactions. While not minimizing the importance of these interactions, the clinician can relieve distress by helping legitimize such feelings as natural responses to a difficult situation. When a family is despairing or frustrated about repeated relapses or rehospitalizations, the clinician must be able to empathize while conveying a sense of hope.

Families dealing with a first psychotic episode may find it hard to accept the diagnosis of a chronic illness and thus may fail to see the relevance of family involvement in treatment. Their distress is focused primarily on the current situation. Giving the family a chance to talk about the distress they are experiencing brings some relief and optimism about the possibility of further help, and supports the family in confronting the longer-term consequences of their relative's illness.

To focus explicitly on family needs and anxieties in a crisis situation is difficult. Often, there is urgency on the part of mental health professionals to gather information from family members about the development of the illness. This may result in spending early discussions with relatives asking questions rather than offering support. Inadvertently, this questioning may augment feelings of guilt the family may have about how they could have handled things differently. Many families are accustomed to feeling blamed for their relative's condition. Mental health workers increasingly are becoming aware of how their actions can either confirm or counteract these feelings. Exploration of relatives' responses to previous treatment experiences is important in assessing the family's present readiness to be involved.

When the ill relative presents for treatment, immediate contact with the family is essential to convey that the clinician is interested in, and expects, family involvement. The ideal situation is for the family to be interviewed by the family clinician when they first bring their relative for treatment. When the ill family member is being hospitalized, this interview provides a forum in which the clinician can offer help with both practicalities and emotional distress relating to their relative's hospitalization. In many settings, it is not feasible for the family clinician to be involved in this way. Often, admission is handled predominantly by emergency clinic staff. In these circumstances, a request for the family to return later to meet with the inpatient clinician can communicate the same expectation of involvement. If the family does not accompany the patient to the clinic or hospital, but can be contacted within the next 24 hours, a definitive appointment can be made for a face-to-face meeting.

Anderson (1977) suggests that on an inpatient unit, the early identification of a family representative is helpful in the process of engaging the family. This counterbalances the natural tendency of staff to identify with the patient, often to the exclusion of the family, and allows the designated family representative to concentrate on engaging the family through focusing explicitly on their needs.

These strategies must all address the emotional turmoil and stigma that arise in families with an acutely psychotic member. The initial phase of engaging the family also requires paying attention to the family's social network. It is important to identify those members who have authority in the family system as well as those who assume most responsibility for the ill relatives. Attempts to arrange a family meeting should not necessarily be restricted to contact with one family member who is expected to pass the message on to everyone else. The clinician may ask the most available family member whether a direct call to other family members would be viewed as helpful or intrusive. Goldstein and Dyche (1983) stress the importance of respecting different cultural attitudes and family structures by avoiding covert criticism of family members who are not accustomed to a more involved role in their relative's treatment. A letter or phone call to inform an important but absent member about a missed session can help to enlist his or her future support in the treatment effort. Contact with relatives outside the immediate circle who have particular involvements or influence with the ill family member may be helpful. Such relatives may be contacted individually, and the clinician can communicate personally how important their participation in the treatment is for their ill relative and for the whole family.

Disengaged families. In some cases, schizophrenia results in the isolation of the patient from his or her whole family. Often the patient has been living in a boarding home or a single room occupancy hotel or hostel, and the family has withdrawn after a series of frustrating encounters with both the patient and the mental health system. This withdrawal can be seen as an attempt by the family to deal with overwhelming burden and protect themselves from further pressures. Such families may feel impotent and guilty. To the clinician, the job of engaging them in the treatment process may seem overwhelming. Initial attempts to contact such family members must be persistent and supportive. Suggesting simple ways the family can be of help, such as bringing items to the hospital or even providing accurate information about the patient, can be a useful strategy. Offering understanding of the family's dilemma and explanation of the patient's behavior and illness through telephone or home visit contacts can provide a supportive ambience that will enable family members to overcome their reluctance to be involved. The clinician should identify ways in which even such a disengaged family has been supportive of the patient in the past so that credit can be given and mutual respect established. In the face of severe family resistance, sometimes the clinician must make it clear that successful treatment cannot be accomplished unless family participation occurs.

In engaging the family, the clinician must recognize and respond to the degree of family burden or chaos. The family may be exhausted and disorganized, with few resources available for rearranging schedules or finding transportation for hospital or clinic visits. Initially, the clinician may need to offer an evening appointment, make a home visit, or establish extensive telephone contact until an actual meeting can be arranged. Being available in a way that is responsive and practical for the family at this difficult time lays a solid foundation for future trust and collaboration. In some families, there may be a significant degree of family stress or disorganization unrelated to the patient's current psychosis. Schizophrenia may come low on the family's list of priorities. Helping such a family get the electricity turned on or arranging treatment for the drug abuse of another family member may be more important initially than exploring the feelings of distress about the quiet psychosis of a schizophrenic family member. These active and varied treatment interventions may be difficult for family therapists trained in more conventional family therapy. Nevertheless, the effects of schizophrenia on a family system can be so powerful that without such an approach, the therapist may find it impossible to make meaningful contact with the system at all.

Family assessment. Much of what is learned during this early phase of getting the family involved in the treatment will comprise the working material of later sessions. Falloon et al. (1984) describe a more formal family "functional assessment" as part of their Behavioral Family Therapy. This approach can be helpful in looking at specific examples of what family members do and say to help each other or themselves. Detailed assessment of factors such as expressed emotion, parental affective style, and communication deviance is realistic only in a research setting. In clinical settings, observation of family interactions, however, makes it evident that some families deal with difficult situations and problems more easily and effectively than others. Assessment of how and whether family members are able to successfully solve problems and cope with stressful situations is helpful in planning further interventions to suit each particular family's needs. In addition, these early contacts can assess whether there is evidence of other disturbances of family functioning or interaction. There may be evidence that the psychotic family member is being scapegoated for other problems in the family. For another family the gains from keeping the patient dependent may seem to outweigh the advantages of letting him or her improve; parents may have given up control of the family to a son or daughter with schizophrenia or they may have given up the effort to support each other as they put all their energy into coping with a schizophrenic son or daughter.

Negotiation of goals. Finally, the process of engaging the family needs to include explicit negotiating of goals. The therapist must describe the treatment to be offered and the possible outcomes of family involvement in the treatment process. Open discussion of therapist and family expectations is a prerequisite for negotiating specific goals important to both family and therapist. Often these goals include reducing the number of hospitalizations, easing family stress, and improving the patient's compliance with treatment. Falloon et al. (1984) stress the importance of setting individual goals for family members other than the patient. When setting such goals, they emphasize that it is important to be specific so that family and therapist can assess future progress.

Crisis Intervention

The process of engaging the family of an acutely ill schizophrenic patient often involves active crisis intervention. Maladaptive coping strategies may have developed in a family in the face of a seemingly impossible situation; or there may be maladaptive patterns of family interaction that antedate the onset of the illness and negatively influence its course. The therapist must be ready to intervene actively, either to empower a flagging family executive, to clarify unclear communications between stressed family members, or to take responsibility for dealing with part of the situation. For example, the parents of a son acutely ill with schizophrenia who wants to return home from the hospital prematurely, may need to be given explicit authority and support by the therapist in persuading the patient to stay. Other families in an outpatient setting may be helped by the therapist's offer to share the often conflict-ridden responsibility of getting an unwilling family member in for treatment. This may be the promise that draws such a family to participate.

Initial interventions may need to focus on issues that interfere with the family's capacity either to be involved in treatment or to offer support for their ill relative. At other times, crisis intervention is necessary to help the family cope with simple survival issues. Support may need to be mobilized so that, for example, the husband of a woman needing hospitalization can find day care for their children, which will enable him to return to work. The clinician needs to be adept at identifying strengths in the family and utilizing them to restore better immediate functioning.

Identifying stressors that may have precipitated the current psychotic episode is an integral part of a crisis intervention approach. Parental or sibling discord that seems to be implicated in the onset of decompensation may need attention if the ill person is to remain at home or return there shortly. The therapist may not be able to reduce the discord, but he or she may help arrange temporary alternative accommodations for the patient with another relative.

It may also be necessary to address stressors that continue to be hazardous for the patient. An extreme example is the father who insisted on visiting his hospitalized son to help him by praying over him in a loud voice, thereby stimulating further the son's religious delusional system. Moving to an educational stance might produce change in a father's behavior, but finding a relative or religious counselor who could share the father's prayers off the ward might provide more supportive crisis intervention. An emphasis on looking for strengths in the family rather than focusing solely on problems has advantages for both family and therapist. In crisis intervention, as in engaging the family, the therapist's stance must continue to be an active and flexible one.

Family Education

Goldstein et al. (1978) describe the goals of a family crisis intervention approach to be the family's recognition and acceptance that a psychotic episode has occurred, the identification of possible precipitating and future stressors, and the carrying out of anticipatory planning. While engaging the family and offering crisis intervention, the therapist must form not only a collaborative relationship with the family but also one in which information about schizophrenia can be usefully and practically exchanged. Additionally, much of the fear, uncertainty, confusion, and guilt that families experience can be helped by a straightforward discussion of our current knowledge about the nature, causation, and outcome of the disorder. Also, the therapist's open and professional approach to discussing frightening or seemingly inexplicable symptoms and behavior, and to addressing the issues of social unacceptability and stigma, can serve as a model for families who feel ashamed or rejected because of their schizophrenic relative. Information about the high prevalence of schizophrenia and the growing effort to research and understand it helps families feel less isolated in struggling with schizophrenia in their personal lives. Many families feel so defeated by previous attempts to help their ill family member that the suggestion of a new direction brings hope and encouragement. Educating families about schizophrenia, about the influence of the environment on its course, and about the potential in the family for improving things can motivate families to try different behaviors or be involved in treatment.

Formats for family education. Family education about schizophrenia is aimed at addressing family members' feelings and attitudes, sharing information with the family, and helping family members, where necessary, to change their behavior. These three goals relate to the three domains of learning discussed in the educational literature: the affective or attitudinal, the cognitive, and the behavioral. Different techniques and processes are effective in addressing these three different areas of learning. Discussion of feelings and beliefs is helpful in the affective domain. Sharing new information in a more didactic mode addresses the cognitive domain. The use of demonstration and role play, with rehearsal and feedback, is effective in changing family behaviors. As in structural and strategic family therapy, the emphasis is on the here and now; intrapsychic and family history issues are secondary. The role of the therapist using a psychoeducational approach is expressly that of an educator and collaborator.

Formats for family education can be varied. After the initial phase of engaging the family and crisis intervention, an agreement can be made with the family to use the next few meetings to talk specifically about schizophrenia. On an inpatient unit, an economical and effective format is an ongoing relatives group or seminar. Relatives of patients with schizophrenia are invited to meet with professional staff to discuss specified topics at a regularly scheduled meeting time. These meetings are geared to be especially helpful and supportive to families. The meetings can function as a continuous open group or can be a repeated series of more didactic presentations with time for discussion. The multifamily group format has the additional benefits of providing families an opportunity for sharing experiences and giving mutual support, and of enlarging their often restricted social networks. Such groups can also be offered in an outpatient setting, in which case the ill relative is more likely to be well enough to participate.

The concept of the psychoeducational workshop, based on Hogarty and Anderson's Survival Skills Workshop (Anderson et al. 1986), has been developed in several treatment centers. A meeting takes place, usually lasting several hours or even all day, in which up to 20 families with schizophrenic members meet together with several professionals for didactic presentations, exchange of information, discussion, and sharing of feelings. Refreshments are offered to enhance a sociable and informal atmosphere. Such workshops are usually offered to families early in the treatment of the current episode or exacerbation, and can be used as a prelude to future family involvement in either group or individual family format. Whether or not the ill member is included in family education meetings is best decided based on that individual's ability to tolerate such a group setting, as well as on the other family members' needs to have time to focus precisely on their requirements and feelings as caregivers and relatives. Preparation of printed materials, slides, or even videotapes can enhance the educational experience as well as give families tangible evidence of the therapist's wish to share information and collaborate with them in the treatment effort. Family education should be a part of every encounter between clinical staff and family, whether it be in an office setting, emergency room, inpatient ward, or home. Patient and family education in all branches of medicine is often sorely neglected. In the treatment of schizophrenia, as of other chronic illnesses, there is growing interest in these strategies as their potential benefits become clearer.

Therapist attitude and knowledge. The way a therapist talks about schizophrenia will inevitably reflect his or her beliefs and understanding of the illness. Thus it is important for therapists to have a clear idea of what they really do know and believe, of how to express their understanding, and of how to introduce different concepts to the family at appropriate times. This process can be facilitated by the availability of up-to-date training about schizophrenia for the clinical team, and by opportunities for discussion among treatment team members of their understanding of the illness and its relationship to the family. The therapist must be able to convey to the family a genuine appreciation of the difficulties the family has been experiencing. The therapist must be prepared to enter into a collaborative relationship with the family. This includes a readiness to answer questions in an open and direct manner, including expressing ignorance if this is the case, along with a willingness to find out.

Family attitude and experience. A collaborative approach naturally will include discussion of the family's own views of what is happening to their ill relative. It is important to gauge and understand the family's current beliefs about their relative's behavior and its origins. In this way, a process of negotiation can begin about terms and definitions used. The therapist can usefully refer to specific examples from the family's own experience to illustrate general points made in more didactic parts of the educational process. For example, the family's description of a particular behavior shown by their ill relative can be related to a particular type of symptom or side effect described in more clinical terms by the therapist. This reframing and negotiation of viewpoints can also lead to a clearer definition of the goals that both family and therapist are trying to achieve.

Content of family education. Family education about schizophrenia should cover not only up-to-date information about the illness but also knowledge about the interactions between schizophrenia and the family environment, including the potentially positive role the family may have. Phenomenology, psychobiology, etiological theories, the role of environmental stressors, early signs of illness, and current treatment and medication issues, including side effects, are important areas of interest to most families. Description of possible resources for treatment, support, and rehabilitation is useful and enlightening to many families. Often such information is essential if families are to negotiate the intricacies of the public mental health system, get help in a crisis, or find suitable day treatment or vocational rehabilitation opportunities for their ill relative. Recognition of early signs of illness, potential stressors, and side effects of medication can be presented as practical contributions the family can make toward improving outcome for their relative. The importance of recognition of early signs for management of future symptomatic episodes has been stressed by Herz (1985). Trouble sleeping, difficulty concentrating, social withdrawal, poor personal hygiene, restlessness, and depression are among such nonpsychotic early signs. Families can often identify additional characteristic behaviors they have noted in their relative just prior to the onset of the psychotic episode, which may help them in recognizing future episodes at an earlier and more manageable stage.

Family Communication

It is in the family that individuals are likely to experience their most intense emotional relationships. Different styles of family communication about feelings correlate with outcome for the schizophrenic relative. Information offered during educational sessions regarding the difficulties shown by schizophrenic individuals in processing information and handling emotional intensity can help family members accept a rationale for changing family communication styles that does not leave them feeling blamed for worsening their relative's condition. Many families are dismayed as to how best to respond to disorganized or irrational speech, and welcome discussion of how to react most effectively.

The therapist's assessment of the particular problems in communication within a family can be used to tailor the focus of work with that family. Another approach is to address a range of communication issues likely to be important to many families with a schizophrenic member. Anderson et al. (1981) suggest four issues that should be addressed consistently: keeping discussions clear and specific, differentiating between what happened and one's feelings about what happened, making statements about one's own responses rather than about the other's behavior or motives, and expressing positive and supportive messages. Similar goals are addressed by Falloon's skills of active listening, expression of positive and negative feelings, and positive requests (Falloon et al. 1984). It is important that the therapist is able to demonstrate, in interaction with the family, those skills that are to be learned. That certain skills may be helpful is presented in a way that suggests a collaborative approach toward making things better, rather than a critical appraisal of currently inadequate family communication. Here again, the therapist models the emphasis on positive messages and supportive comments.

Attention is paid to clarifying and facilitating communication in every meeting with a family. Sessions that focus specifically on communication change usually should not occur until the immediate crisis of the acute episode is resolving. The ill family member may then be able to participate more fully in family meetings. For new skills acquisition, a focus on the here and now in the family meeting is particularly important. Family members can be asked to rephrase or curtail digressive or abstract discussion or to reword a comment about someone's behavior, and thus be given a chance to rehearse new strategies and see the effects. Actual role playing situations can be set up, with the therapist describing the task to be achieved and helping the family to recall real situations from their everyday life for use in role play during the session. Initial resistance to such exercises usually is overcome if the therapist is persistent, low key, and supportive. Children sometimes help by adding a game-like quality to the process. Feedback should focus on the positive, with opportunity for the family to comment first on their own performance. All family members are encouraged to join in the evaluation process.

A balance must be kept between general endorsement of a collaborative family effort and microcounseling on specific skills acquired. Such communication skills training is best carried out in the single family group. In multifamily group contexts, rehearsal and feedback are difficult, and the therapist must rely on more didactic techniques for helping families develop better communication patterns. However, families have more opportunity in the multifamily group to learn from each other through discussion, observation, and group pressure. Measured psychophysiological responses suggest that relatives of patients from families with low expressed emotion seem to exert a calming effect on patients (Tarrier et al. 1979). It is also possible that in a multifamily group setting, other participating families may learn from soothing strategies used by the families with low expressed emotion.

Problem Solving

In the early stages of intervention with a family coping with a relative's acute schizophrenic relapse, the therapist takes an active crisis intervention approach. Problems are identified and strategies planned to address them with active intervention by the therapist. Encouraging families to recognize potential stressors and set limits helps in preparation for future problems. Enhancing communication skills may enable the family to achieve more effective problem solving. As a patient is nearing discharge from the hospital or as the crisis is being resolved, specific sessions may be set aside to work on family problem solving.

Falloon's method (Falloon et al. 1984) includes a structured approach to teaching problem solving. The family is taught to identify problems clearly, to contribute a range of possible solutions, to outline likely outcomes of each of these, and finally, to select one solution, carry it out, and assess its outcome. As in communication skills training, rehearsal of new skills by the family at home between meetings is important if the training is to be effective. In a multifamily group setting, family members can learn from each other different strategies they have found effective in talking about their problems.

Summary

Despite the overwhelming difficulties experienced by many families with a schizophrenic member, there is increasing optimism that families and clinicians can address together some of the aftereffects of deinstitutionalization and schizophrenia on the family and work together to improve treatment outcome for schizophrenic patients. Programs attempting to do this have been set up in clinical as well as research settings. Important components of such psychosocial programs are crisis intervention, family education, communication, stress management, and problem-solving training. These types of family intervention must be integrated with psychotherapeutic and pharmacological treatment of the patient rather than be seen as alternative treatment strategies. These interventions can contribute to the most effective use of somatic therapies as well as facilitate the use of lower-dose and intermittent medication strategies that may reduce side effects. Together with psychotherapeutic and pharmacological strategies, family intervention strategies aim at providing optimal recovery from the acute episode, additional protection from relapse, and improvement in social functioning for patient and family. Several studies have shown that family intervention during an acute episode significantly reduces the risk of relapse during the first year after hospital discharge. Efforts to assess effects on the longer-term social functioning and relapse rates are underway. Family interventions have been shown to reduce emotional intensity in the home. More studies are needed to measure further the benefits of family involvement in psychoeducational treatment.

The growth of family intervention programs along side the growing family advocacy movement is reducing the isolation felt by families with a schizophrenic member. Such families have been isolated from other afflicted families as well as from the professional staff who treat their ill relatives. The wider application of family management principles may ultimately reduce the number of isolated young schizophrenic men and women who have lost contact with their families of origin and who lead marginal lives in inner cities and halfway houses. Research efforts continue to explore the relationships of constitutional and environmental factors in the pathogenesis of schizophrenia. In the meantime, psychoeducational family management is taking its place as an important everyday clinical strategy in the treatment of those suffering from schizophrenia.

REFERENCES

Anderson CM: Family intervention with severely disturbed patients. Arch Gen Psychiatry 34:697–702, 1977

Anderson CM, Reiss DJ, Hogarty GE: Schizophrenia and the Family. New York, Guilford Press, 1986

Anderson CM, Hogarty J, Reiss DJ: The psychoeducational family treatment of schizophrenia, in New Developments in Interventions with Families of Schizophrenia. Edited by Goldstein MJ. San Francisco, Jossey-Bass, 1981

Bateson G, Jackson DD, Haley J, Weakland J: Toward a theory of schizophrenia. Behav Sci 1:251–264, 1956

Bowen M: A family concept of schizophrenia, in The Etiology of Schizophrenia. Edited by Jackson D. New York, Basic Books, 1960, pp 346–372

Bowen M: Family psychotherapy with schizophrenia in the hospital and in private practice, in Intensive Family Therapy. Edited by Boszormenyi-Nagy I, Framo J. New York, Harper and Row, 1965, pp 213–243

Brown GW, Birley JLT: Crises and life changes and the onset of schizophrenia. J Health Soc Behav 9:203–214, 1968

Creer C: Social work with patients and their families, in Schizophrenia: Towards a New Synthesis. Edited by Wing JK. London, Academic Press, 1978, pp 233–251

Doane JA, West KL, Goldstein MJ, et al: Parental communication deviance and affective style: predictors of subsequent schizophrenia spectrum disorders in vulnerable adolescents. Arch Gen Psychiatry 38:679–685, 1981

Falloon IRH, Boyd JL, McGill CW, et al: Family management in the prevention of exacerbations of schizophrenia. N Engl J Med 306:1437–1440, 1982

Falloon IRH, Boyd JL, McGill CW: Family Care of Schizophrenia: A Problem-Solving Approach to the Treatment of Mental Illness. New York, Guilford Press, 1984

Garrison V: Support systems of schizophrenic and nonschizophrenic Puerto Rican women in New York City. Schizophr Bull 4:561–596, 1978

Goldstein MJ, Doane JA: Family factors in the onset, course and treatment of schizophrenic spectrum disorders. An update on current research. J Nerv Ment Dis 170:692–700, 1982

Goldstein MJ, Rodnick EH, Evans JR, et al: Drug and family therapy in the aftercare of acute schizophrenics. Arch Gen Psychiatry 35:1169–1177, 1978

Goldstein SJ, Dyche L: Family therapy of the schizophrenic poor, in Family Therapy in Schizophrenia. Edited by McFarlane WR. New York, Guilford Press, 1983, pp 289–307

Grad J, Sainsbury P: Mental illness and the family. Lancet 1:533–547, 1963

Hatfield A: Psychological costs of schizophrenia to the family. Soc Work 23:355–359, 1978

Hatfield A: Coping effectiveness in families of the mentally ill: an exploratory study. J Psychiatr Treat Eval 3:11–19, 1981

Hatfield A: What families want of family therapists, in Family

Therapy in Schizophrenia. Edited by McFarlane WR. New York, Guilford Press, 1983, pp 41–65

Herz M: Prodromal symptoms and prevention of relapse in schizophrenia. J Clin Psychiatry Vol 46, No 11 (sec 2), 1985, pp 22–25

Hogarty GE, Anderson CM, Reiss DJ, et al: Family psychoeducation, social skills training and maintenance chemotherapy in the aftercare treatment of schizophrenia. Arch Gen Psychiatry 43:633–642, 1986

Kreisman D, Joy V: Family response to the illness of a relative: a review of the literature. Schizophr Bull, No 10, Fall 1974, pp 34–57

Kreisman D, Simmons S, Joy V: Deinstitutionalization and the Family's Well Being. New York, New York State Psychiatric Institute, 1979

Leff J, Kuipers L, Berkowitz R, et al: A controlled trial of social intervention in the families of schizophrenic patients. Br J Psychiatry 141:121–134, 1982

Liberman RP: Social factors in the etiology of the schizophrenic disorders, in Psychiatry 1982: The American Psychiatric Association Annual Review, Vol 1. Edited by Grinspoon L. Washington, DC, American Psychiatric Press, 1982, pp 97–112

Lidz T: Schizophrenia and the family. Psychiatry 21:21–27, 1958

McFarlane WR, Beels CC: Family research in schizophrenia, in Family Therapy in Schizophrenia. Edited by McFarlane WR. New York, Guilford Press, 1984, pp 311–323

Rabkin J: Public attitudes towards mental illness: a review of the literature. Schizophr Bull 10:9–33, 1974

Reiss D: Individual thinking and family interaction, in Family Processes and Schizophrenia. Edited by Mishler EG, Waxler NE. Northvale, NJ, Jason Aronson, 1975

Tarrier N, Vaughn C, Lader M, et al: Bodily reaction to people and events in schizophrenia. Arch Gen Psychiatry 36:311–315, 1979

Tolsdorf CC: Social networks, support, and coping: an explanatory study. Fam Process 15:407–417, 1976

Vaughn CE, Leff JP: The influence of family and social factors on the course of psychiatric illness. Br J Psychiatry 129:125–137, 1976

Wynne LC: The University of Rochester Child and Family Study: overview of the research plan, in Children at Risk for Schizophrenia. Edited by Watt NF, Anthony EJ, Wynne LC, et al. New York, Cambridge University Press, 1984, pp 335–347

Wynne LC, Singer M: Thought disorder and family relations of schizophrenics. I. Research strategies. Arch Gen Psychiatry 9:191–198, 1963

Wynne LC, Ryckoff I, Day J, et al: Pseudomutuality in the family relations of schizophrenics. Psychiatry 21:205–220, 1958

Yarrow M, Clausen J, Robbins P: The social meaning of mental illness. J Social Issues 11:33–48, 1955

Chapter 9

CURRENT RESEARCH AND CONCLUSIONS

Philip T. Ninan, M.D.
Elias Shaya, M.D.

BETWEEN 1 AND 2% OF THE POPULATION will develop an episode of schizophrenia in their lifetime (Robins et al. 1984). The cost of schizophrenia is staggering both in emotional and in financial terms. Overall annual spending for the care of schizophrenia is estimated to be about $25 billion. Because the illness tends to strike individuals early in their lives, the cost of lost productivity when added to treatment is calculated to be a staggering $48 billion annually. Even a minor advance in the treatment of schizophrenia will have a major impact on the costs associated with the illness.

The increasing national awareness of the tragedy of schizophrenia, spearheaded by the growing organization of families of mentally ill patients and highlighted by publicity about the homeless mentally ill, has encouraged more research funding for schizophrenia. There has been a gradual shift away from treatment modalities that are primarily theoretically driven to those that are based on systematically collected data. The stage is set for a concerted attempt to break new ground in the search for better understanding and treatment of this complex and puzzling illness.

This work was supported in part by NIMH Grant Nos. MH-40597 and MH-42298 (PTN).

At a time when a revolution is occurring in the neurosciences, there is only subdued excitement in the field of schizophrenia research. Although there have been advances in the basic sciences relevant to schizophrenia, the problems at a clinical level still loom enormous. The inherent heterogeneity of the illness, the methodological problems in scientific inquiry resulting from the nature of the illness, the ethical problems associated with withholding neuroleptics for periods of time, and other hurdles, have slowed scientific advances. In addition, young researchers have been attracted to other areas that progress at a faster pace and are less complex.

Heterogeneity of Schizophrenia

Major advances in delineating the phenomenology of schizophrenia have taken place, including the division of schizophrenic symptomatology into "positive" and "negative" symptoms. A descriptive approach has fostered reliability in diagnosis, which has in turn aided research and helped in the collection of epidemiological data about the illness.

The inherent heterogeneity of schizophrenia and the inability to classify the illness into relevant subgroups have made studying schizophrenia difficult. The lack of homogeneity of variables in groups of schizophrenic patients results in a tremendous variance in the data collected. To be successful in advancing knowledge in the presence of such variability requires that large numbers of patients be studied—a daunting task. This also means that if a subgroup of patients had a common parameter, it would easily be missed because of the noise resulting from patients not belonging to that subgroup. Previous efforts at classification have focused on the symptomatology and the course of illness. Because both these parameters are multidetermined, such classifications are analogous to attempts at classifying pneumonias based on symptomatology and outcome prior to the discovery of infectious organisms or antibiotics.

Neuroleptics and Schizophrenia

The first half of this century was an era of astute clinical observation of schizophrenia. With the fortuitous discovery of neuroleptics, the treatment of schizophrenia underwent a revolution. The results were a large-scale discharging of schizophrenic patients from state hospitals and the development of the community mental health movement.

The neurobiological research approach to schizophrenia is based on the assumption that biological deviation underlies the core of the illness. Though the evidence for this is indirect—we still lack a diagnostic test for schizophrenia—this assumption has been driven by the discovery that neuroleptic agents significantly ameliorate many of the symptoms of schizophrenia. Pharmacological data have shown that the average therapeutic dose of neuroleptic required for its clinical antipsychotic effect is highly correlated to the capacity of the neuroleptic to block dopamine (type 2) receptors. This would strongly suggest that dopamine is a neurotransmittor involved in schizophrenia.

Though neuroleptics are a major advance in the treatment of psychoses, they are a mixed blessing. Neuroleptics are not helpful in about 20% of patients with schizophrenia and are only partially effective in an even larger group of patients. Neuroleptic medications are symptomatic rather than curative treatments, leaving patients prisoners to chronic treatment with these medications. The natural fluctuations and variability inherent in the illness make it impossible to develop strict guidelines in terms of dose, length of treatment, etc. There are complex side effects associated with neuroleptics that were slow to be recognized, including tardive dyskinesia and apathy, resulting in further social impairment.

Clinicians have been hesitant to discontinue neuroleptics in patients who do not respond to these medications and have significant side effects. The partial benefit provided by the neuroleptics also limited the search for novel pharmacological agents in the treatment of schizophrenia because pharmaceutical companies limited their efforts to developing "me too" compounds. Thus if a novel compound lacked dopamine-blocking properties, it was not considered a likely antipsychotic agent. From an ethical standpoint, the advent of the neuroleptic era made it more difficult to observe the patient's illness for significant periods of time prior to pharmacological intervention. This complicated the interpretation of biological measures—were findings related to the natural course of the illness or to the neuroleptic treatment?

The group of schizophrenic patients who do not respond to neuroleptics are a challenge and a burden. Various strategies have attempted to control the psychotic symptomatology in this group. These strategies include use of high doses of neuroleptics and augmentation of neuroleptics with lithium, benzodiazepines, carbamazepine, and ECT. Success with these strategies has been reported in individual patients, although the general outlook is still gloomy. Recent reports in some well-characterized patients suggest that

ECT might be an attractive treatment option for schizophrenic patients who do not respond to neuroleptics (Friedel 1986).

NEUROBIOLOGY OF SCHIZOPHRENIA

Attempts to find biological markers that are traits or vulnerability factors for schizophrenia have produced mixed results. Platelet monoamine oxidase (MAO) activity, which presumably reflects central neuronal MAO activity, was thought to be reduced in schizophrenia. However, this finding is probably the result of treatment rather than being a vulnerability marker. Poor eye tracking as a vulnerability marker is currently generating considerable interest (Holzman 1985). Though present to a significantly greater degree among families of schizophrenic patients than among controls, poor eye tracking is present in only 65% of patients with schizophrenia and is not specific to this illness. Recently, there has been a resurgence of interest in homovanillic acid (HVA), a metabolite of dopamine. Whether low HVA levels in the plasma and CSF can be considered a trait vulnerability for the development of schizophrenia needs to be further evaluated.

Attempts have been made to define biological variables (e.g., brain atrophy) that would adequately divide schizophrenia into relevant subgroups. Morphological abnormalities recognized using CT scans have been correlated with poor premorbid functioning, specific symptomatology (negative symptoms), cognitive impairment, impaired smooth pursuit eye tracking, and poor response to treatment (Maser and Keith 1983). However, the replicability of these findings has been less than ideal. Conflicting findings can result from sampling differences (e.g., chronic state-hospital schizophrenic patients versus younger, more acute and ambulatory schizophrenic patients), from differences in measurement techniques, or from the limited statistical power of the majority of negative studies. In classification attempts, biological variables are often assumed to be independent rather than dependent ones. However, biological factors can also be epiphenomena as much as psychosocial factors.

The preponderance of data suggests that schizophrenia is etiologically multifactorial. There are vulnerability factors that aggregate in families, are genetically transmitted, or are environmentally induced. Vulnerability may be conceptualized not only as a static but also as a dynamic process. For example, random fluctuation in the norepinephrine system might result in a biological state that "permits" a psychotic relapse. Triggers that could express underlying vulnerability may include developmental stages (e.g., the frontal cortex coming "on line" in late adolescence/early adulthood) (Weinberger 1987).

Undoubtedly the new technologies of neuroscience are going to revolutionize our understanding of schizophrenia. Regional blood flow studies allow us to look at dynamic processes inside the functioning brain. Xenon 133 inhalation studies have shown that schizophrenic patients lack a capacity to activate the dorsolateral prefrontal cortex when assigned a task that involves abstract reasoning and problem-solving (Weinberger et al. 1986). With appropriate ligands, specific neurotransmitter systems can be studied using PET scanning. Preliminary data in schizophrenic patients suggest that there is increased D-2 receptor binding in the caudate nucleus (Wong et al. 1986).

The Dopamine Hypothesis Revisited

A unifying hypothesis that would explain the disparate elements of schizophrenia may be slowly developing (Bannon and Roth 1983). The original dopamine hypothesis stated that schizophrenia was the result of increased dopaminergic activity. This hypothesis was based on indirect evidence: dopamine agonists like amphetamine could induce a condition that was clinically indistinguishable from schizophrenia, and dopamine antagonists (neuroleptics) were effective in controlling the symptoms of schizophrenia.

Some aspects of the negative symptoms can be conceptualized as the trait vulnerability for schizophrenia. These symptoms can be the result of prefrontal cortical atrophy, which would make them relatively nonresponsive to neuroleptics. Positive symptoms, on the other hand, may be the result of subcortical dopamine overactivity. They can be conceived as the state components of the illness, and are more responsive to neuroleptic agents. Lesion studies in rats have explored the relationship of cortical dopamine systems and subcortical ones (Pycock et al. 1980). Destruction of the cortical dopamine projections results in a disinhibitory upregulation of subcortical dopamine systems. Such a condition could theoretically explain a number of the clinical and neurobiological phenomena seen in schizophrenia (Weinberger 1987).

Crow (1985) has attempted to tie clinical symptomatology, morphological and biochemical abnormalities, and treatment response into an elegant typology of schizophrenia, which is open for scientific testing. Whether or not the data will agree with the ideas, a testable hypothesis has been proposed, which in itself is an advance.

GENETICS OF SCHIZOPHRENIA

Familial aggregation of the illness has been well documented. However, 90% of patients do not have a first-degree relative with schizophrenia, suggesting that a significant number of patients have a sporadic (in contrast to the familial) version of the illness. Twin and adoption studies suggest that there is genetic transmission of a significant vulnerability factor to acquiring the illness (Gottesman and Shields 1982). The type of transmission is in question—classic dominant or recessive patterns of inheritance along Mendelian lines do not fit the data. Various groups have put forth hypotheses, some suggesting a single gene locus, others multiple genetic causes.

Recent advances in molecular genetics raise the intriguing possibility that markers close to the gene(s) responsible for possibly a subgroup schizophrenia will be identified in the near future.

PSYCHOSOCIAL RESEARCH IN SCHIZOPHRENIA

Psychosocial research in schizophrenia has moved from etiology to factors that have a major impact on the course of the illness. Concepts like the "schizophrenogenic mother" have lost emphasis to factors like communication deviance (Doane et al. 1981), which defines a pattern of communication that is more specific for families with a schizophrenic member or a schizophrenia-spectrum disorder member. The communication pattern in these families is characterized by odd, ambiguous, tangential messages and modes of interaction. The etiological significance of this kind of communication is still open to question—does it represent a subclinical version of schizophrenia present in family members, a manifestation of social isolation associated with the stigma of having a mentally ill relative, or an environmental inducer of schizophrenia (i.e., a vulnerability or a causative factor)?

Highly critical and overinvolved attitudes toward schizophrenic patients by family members have been termed "expressed emotion." Behaviors that reflect high levels of expressed emotion include intrusive behaviors, distressful responses to the patient, viewpoints of the patient as not having a legitimate illness, and lack of tolerance for the disturbances in behavior and long-term social impairments. Expressed emotion among family members has been shown to be an important predictor of short-term (9–12 months) relapse in schizophrenic patients (Brown and Wing 1972). Family intervention in families with high expressed emotion had a dramatic effect in reducing short-term relapses (Falloon et al. 1982). Whether such family interventions will have a more long-term effect on the course of the illness is as yet uncertain.

Conclusions

Schizophrenia is an illness the understanding of which would allow us a better vision into the world of the human psyche. It is not without reason that this illness has confused many of the best minds in a number of different specialties for a considerable period of time. We are now at least in a better position to ask more appropriate questions, though how enlightening the answers will be remains to be seen. In the meantime, the management of patients with schizophrenia, especially during acute episodes, should be based on both data-driven studies and accumulated clinical expertise. This book has been an attempt to provide an overview of the complex and multidisciplinary approach that is crucial in the management of schizophrenic patients today.

References

Bannon MJ, Roth RH: Pharmacology of mesocortical dopamine neurons. Pharmacol Rev 35:53–68, 1983

Brown JLT, Wing JK: Influence of family life on the course of schizophrenic disorders: a replication. Br J Psychiatry 121:241–258, 1972

Crow TJ: The two syndrome concept: origins and current status. Schizophr Bull 9:471–486, 1985

Doane J, West KL, Goldstein MJ, et al: Parental communication deviance and affective style. Arch Gen Psychiatry 38:679–685, 1981

Falloon IRH, Boyd JL, McGill CW, et al: Family management in the prevention of exacerbation of schizophrenia. N Engl J Med 306:1437–1440, 1982

Friedel RO: The combined use of neuroleptics and ECT in drug resistant schizophrenic patients. Psychopharmacol Bull 22:928–930, 1986

Gottesman II, Shields J: Schizophrenia: The Epigenetic Puzzle. New York, Cambridge University Press, 1982

Holzman PS: Eye movement dysfunction and psychosis. Int Rev Neurobiol 27:179–205, 1985

Maser JD, Keith SJ: CT scans and schizophrenia–report on a workshop. Schizophr Bull 9:265–283, 1983

Pycock CJ, Kerwin RW, Carter CJ: Effect of lesion of cortical dopamine terminals on subcortical dopamine receptors in rats. Nature 286:74–76, 1980

Robins LN, Helzer JE, Weissman MM, et al: Lifetime prevalence of specific psychiatric disorders in three sites. Arch Gen Psychiatry 41:949–958, 1984

Weinberger DR: Implications of normal brain development for the pathogenesis of schizophrenia. Arch Gen Psychiatry 44:660–669, 1987

Weinberger DR, Berman KF, Zec RF: Physiological dysfunction of the dorsolateral prefrontal cortex in schizophrenia. Arch Gen Psychiatry 43:114–124, 1986

Wong DF, Wagner HN, Tune LE, et al: Positron emission tomography reveals elevated D2 dopamine receptors in drug-naive schizophrenics. Science 234:1558–1563, 1986

INDEX